Literary Research and British Postmodernism

Literary Research: Strategies and Sources

Series Editors: Peggy Keeran & Jennifer Bowers

Every literary age presents scholars with both predictable and unique research challenges. This series fills a gap in the field of reference literature by featuring research strategies and by recommending the best tools for conducting specialized period and national literary research. Emphasizing research methodology, each series volume takes into account the unique challenges inherent in conducting research of that specific literary period and outlines the best practices for researching within it. Volumes place the research process within the period's historical context and use a narrative structure to analyze and compare print and electronic reference sources. Following an introduction to online searching, chapters will typically cover these types of resources: general literary reference materials; library catalogs; print and online bibliographies, indexes, and annual reviews; scholarly journals; contemporary reviews; period journals and newspapers; microform and digital collections; manuscripts and archives; and Web resources. Additional or alternative chapters might be included to highlight a particular research problem or to examine other pertinent period or national literary resources.

1. *Literary Research and the British Romantic Era* by Peggy Keeran and Jennifer Bowers, 2005.
2. *Literary Research and the Era of American Nationalism and Romanticism* by Angela Courtney, 2008.
3. *Literary Research and American Modernism Era* by Robert N. Matuozzi and Elizabeth B. Lindsay, 2008.
4. *Literary Research and the American Realism and Naturalism Period* by Linda L. Stein and Peter J. Lehu, 2009.
5. *Literary Research and Irish Literature* by J. Greg Matthews, 2009.
6. *Literary Research and the Literatures of Australia and New Zealand* by H. Faye Christenberry and Angela Courtney, 2011.
7. *Literary Research and British Modernism* by Alison M. Lewis, 2010.
8. *Literary Research and the British Renaissance and Early Modern Period* by Jennifer Bowers and Peggy Keeran, 2010.
9. *Literary Research and the Victorian and Edwardian Ages, 1830–1910* by Melissa S. Van Vuuren, 2011.
10. *Literary Research and Canadian Literature* by Gabriella Natasha Reznowski, 2011.
11. *Literary Research and Postcolonial Literatures in English* by H. Faye Christenberry, Angela Courtney, Liorah Golomb, and Melissa S. Van Vuuren, 2012.
12. *Literary Research and the British Eighteenth Century* by Peggy Keeran and Jennifer Bowers, 2013.

Literary Research and British Postmodernism

Strategies and Sources

Literary Research:
Strategies and Sources, No. 13

Arianne Hartsell-Gundy
Bridgit McCafferty

ROWMAN & LITTLEFIELD
Lanham • Boulder • New York • London

Published by Rowman & Littlefield
A wholly owned subsidiary of The Rowman & Littlefield Publishing Group, Inc.
4501 Forbes Boulevard, Suite 200, Lanham, Maryland 20706
www.rowman.com

Unit A, Whitacre Mews, 26-34 Stannary Street, London SE11 4AB

British Library Cataloguing in Publication Information Available

Library of Congress Cataloging-in-Publication Data

McCafferty, Bridgit, 1984– author.
 Literary research and British postmodernism : strategies and sources / Bridgit
McCafferty and Arianne Hartsell-Gundy.
     pages cm. — (Literary research: strategies and sources ; 13)
 Includes bibliographical references and indexes.
 ISBN 978-1-4422-5415-2 (hardcover : alk. paper) — ISBN 978-1-4422-5416-9
(pbk. : alk. paper) — ISBN 978-1-4422-5417-6 (ebook)
 1. English literature—20th century—Research—Methodology. 2. Postmodernism
(Literature)—Great Britain. 3. Literature—Archival resources. I. Hartsell-Gundy,
Arianne, author. II. Title.
 PR56.M43 2015
 820.72—dc23
                                                                2015016261

Printed in the United States of America

Contents

Introduction

Defining any moment in literary history within the artificial parameters of an artistic age is difficult, perhaps futile. Literary eras blend into one another like colors in a Tiffany window—the edges are not always very clear, though the larger patterns are easily discernable. For postmodernism, this task seems particularly impossible, fraught with the complexities that come from an age predicated on the decentralization of knowing itself. True to its intellectual roots, postmodernism resists, in many meaningful ways, any attempt to be firmly "known." The era is a chameleon: when you have finally got it into your line of sight, it has slipped off again, to become something else entirely.

Still, some definition of postmodernism must be identified, if only to set the boundaries of what we will cover throughout this work. We propose to take the approach of Andreas Huyssen in his excellent essay "Mapping the Postmodern."[1] We will resist defining "what postmodernism *is*," recognizing that the term *postmodernism* is truly only "relational," positing a reaction to or continuity with modernism. In this framework, we understand postmodernism in its relationship with modernism. This allows us to identify the historical "breaks" that led to postmodern art and literature.[2]

Attempts to define postmodernism often identify varying dates for its start. Some look to the end of World War II, and especially the atomic bombing of Nagasaki. That event was a significant "break" between the modern and postmodern mind, they argue, because the bomb first introduced the notion that humanity could be wiped out entirely by modern technology. This realization is believed to have generated misgivings about the rise of technology and led to the questioning of social structures, dichotomies, and other cultural forces that is the hallmark of postmodernism.

Though it is clear that postmodernism's reaction to western modernist thought entwined with and in some cases preceded World War II, starting as early as the 1930s with Horkheimer, Adorno, and the Frankfurt School, placing the beginning of postmodernism at the end of World War II seems a little premature for us, particularly for Great Britain, which was still in the last years of high modernism in 1945. Film, literature, art, and music were celebrating the end of the war and nostalgically looking back to the period of the British Empire as India, and then a host of other colonies, broke away. We view the immediate reaction to World War II not as the great "break" from modernism, or at least the rarefied elitism of high modernism, but rather one last attempt to reestablish British culture as it had been before the war, in a remembered "golden age."

As a result, we will place the beginning of British postmodernism ten years after Nagasaki, in 1956, with the debut of John Osborne's *Look Back in Anger*; the very earliest films in Karel Reisz's Free Cinema movement, which later became British New Wave cinema; the beginning of British rock and roll, including the Skiffle craze of the mid-1950s; and the appearance of writers like Doris Lessing and Anthony Burgess. In a myriad of forms, these artistic developments were the true beginning of postmodernism in Britain. They were a reaction to the elite modernism of T. S. Eliot, Ford Madox Ford, Virginia Woolf, and others, as well as to the colonial mindset. This critique of modernism hit its stride in the 1960s and 1970s, and finally led to the acceptance of new modes of literature, art, and culture in the 1980s, 1990s, and the new millennium.

As to what postmodern literature actually encompasses, we will take a holistic approach that recognizes the ways digital media, film, critical theory, popular music, and more traditional print sources are inextricably linked. Through this approach, we will present a broad examination of "postmodernism" that contains a large variety of British authors writing in the last half of the twentieth century. Our working definition of *postmodern* will comprise works that engage issues central to cultural theory, including the social construction of gender, sexuality, and power; the subjectivity of truth; technology as a social force; intertextuality; metafiction; postcolonial narrative; and fantasy. Geographically, we will cover sources concerned primarily with the United Kingdom and Ireland, though former British colonies of significance to postcolonial studies, such as Australia, India, South Africa, and Canada, are also incorporated. We recognize that the diversity of perspectives celebrated in postmodern literature requires a wide view of what might be important to researchers working in this era.

Our focus will be on the unique challenges faced by scholars of postmodern literature. Because of the complexity of the movement and because most of the authors associated with it are still alive, many researchers find that there is not a huge body of scholarship. For this reason, doing research in the time period requires flexibility and determination. Throughout the chapters of this book, we will address these issues to help make them less of a deterrent to research in this period.

The first four chapters cover basic search techniques and resources. In chapter 1, we begin with tips for conducting inquiries online by providing examples using British postmodern authors to model advanced methods for optimizing information retrieval. The chapter contains sections on creating a topic, choosing keywords and search strategies, and using databases. Chapter 2 describes general literary reference sources (research guides, encyclopedias, biographies) to aid in understanding basic, overarching concepts about a complex moment in our cultural history. Both chapters 3 and 4 elucidate how to search basic research tools. Chapter 3 discusses how to search library catalogs. The importance of library catalogs will be explained, coupled with strategies that maximize the use of local and national and union catalogs. We also address the changing nature of catalogs in order to ensure the best results. Chapter 4 expands on the search strategies of earlier chapters to illustrate how to utilize print and electronic bibliographies, indexes, and annual reviews, highlighting general and specific bibliographies and giving tips on how to find information in important indexes.

After covering some of these basics, this book begins to delve into more specialized sources. A variety of scholarly journals are considered in chapter 5, including those specifically dealing with the twentieth century and postmodernism, as well as those that are more general. Postmodernism is a relatively recent literary moment, so a scholar might discover that contemporary reviews are more valuable than scholarly articles. Chapter 6 will clarify the importance of these reviews and suggest helpful places to look for them. Newspapers and other periodical sources often carry stories about contemporary artistic works, authors, and movements, so in chapter 7 we discuss general periodicals, as well as literary magazines and "zines" that are important to British postmodernism. Since archival collections that are related to prominent postmodern authors can be difficult to locate, in chapter 8 we expound upon how to identify these collections, along with tips about doing archival research, attaining documents in archives, and scheduling time at archives. Additionally, this chapter covers special considerations when archival material is a film, a computer hard drive, or an audio recording, rather than a document.

The last four chapters investigate issues that are more specific to working with postmodernism. Though discovering multimedia and performance art is important for this research, the tools for completing this task are not well known by many literary scholars, since they are more closely related to art, communications, and film studies. As a result, chapter 9 incorporates information about film resources, as well as recorded interviews and other multimedia material related to artists and authors. Since critical theory is foundational to much of postmodern literature, chapter 10 sheds light on how to identify, understand, and research it. Because many postmodern authors and critics are writing in the digital age, chapter 11 addresses web resources. Scholarly gateways; electronic text archives; author, fan, and promotional websites; cultural and historical web resources; and social media are covered. In addition to these resources, the chapter explains how to evaluate and search for them. The final chapter walks the reader through researching a particularly thorny topic by using Neil Gaiman's novel *The Ocean at the End of the Lane* as an example. Many of the major problems scholars might face will be present when trying to research this new text. We offer methods for finding different source types, and we discuss ways of recognizing subject headings and Library of Congress (LC) call number ranges that are appropriate to Gaiman. We also provide more unique methods for locating resources with living authors and new texts, such as contacting publishers, blogs, and fan organizations.

An appendix is included, which is an annotated bibliography of research tools (such as dictionaries, encyclopedias, and handbooks) from many different disciplines like art, history, music, philosophy, religion, science, social sciences, and theater.

Literary Research and British Postmodernism will help scholars navigate the complex relationships between print and multimedia, technological advancements, and the influence of critical theory that converge in postwar British literature beginning in the 1950s. This era is unique because, unlike other literary eras, strict boundaries between fiction, nonfiction, multimedia, and print are not useful. Since postmodern literature is defined by the breaking down of boundaries as a reaction to modernism, it requires an innovative, multifaceted approach to research. In this guide we explore these complex relationships and offer strategies for working with contemporary literature.

NOTES

1. Andreas Huyssen, "Mapping the Postmodern," in *A Postmodern Reader*, ed. Joseph Natoli and Linda Hutcheon (Albany, NY: SUNY Press, 1993), 105–56.
2. Huyssen, "Mapping the Postmodern," 110–11.

Chapter One

Basics of Online Searching

Successful research has always required thoughtful inquiry on the part of the scholar, but a good search strategy is even more important today because of the increased reliance on digital tools. As a result of the wealth of information now available, doing research is both easier and harder. Planning your search strategy in advance will encourage you to clarify your ideas and to find more valuable resources throughout the research process. This chapter will discuss the various steps that will lead to fruitful results. Some brief explanations for how online search tools function will also be provided in order to help you understand how to formulate successful queries. Many of the concepts introduced in this chapter will be explored with more depth in later chapters.

STEP ONE: RESEARCH QUESTION/TOPIC SENTENCE

A good way to begin the process is to turn your research question into a concise topic sentence, and then narrow it down to the major concepts that need to be queried. For example, if you want to understand Doris Lessing's connection to Africa, your topic sentence might be "I want to explore how Doris Lessing's childhood in Southern Rhodesia influenced her later novels," and the main concepts might be *Doris Lessing*, *Southern Rhodesia*, and *novels*. Another example would be to explore how scholars have reacted to postmodern literature. Your topic sentence could then be "I want to learn how literary scholars have responded to postmodern literature," with the main concepts being *postmodernism*, *literary criticism*, and *literary scholars*. Of course, sometimes it will be necessary to revise your research question as you learn more about a topic, so be adaptable when thinking about your subject and the relevant concepts. Since research is often a reiterative process, do not become discouraged if you need to revisit Step One.

STEP TWO: BRAINSTORM KEYWORDS

Your main concepts will become your basic keywords, but a successful search will require flexibility with terminology. For instance, Southern Rhodesia is now known as Zimbabwe, so only using the name *Southern Rhodesia* might not retrieve all the possible results. Broadening the query to include the entire region of southern Africa might also retrieve helpful items. Instead of the term *novel*, also try *fiction* or *science fiction*. On the other hand, narrowing down to a specific title instead of all of Doris Lessing's novels could be effective. Brainstorming multiple options before searching will make you more flexible if your initial attempt does not give the best list of resources. Additionally, you will have options for doing some of the more advanced search strategies explored later in this chapter.

Consider creating a table of possible keywords to begin brainstorming terms and as a way to organize your options. It is good practice to make connections between terms since they will help develop pertinent strategies. Table 1.1 is an example of how seeing various words in different columns can aid reflection about how they might be related. If you are a visual person, think about creating a concept map to make connections between different keywords by either drawing the concept map by hand or using an online program like FreeMind (freemind.sourceforge.net/wiki/index.php/Main_Page) or Bubbl.us (bubbl.us). Figure 1.1 illustrates how a concept map can aid in creating different relationships between keywords. As in figure 1.1, start with Doris Lessing's name, and then draw concepts, places, and genres that were important to her as a writer. You can then easily change the connections made by creating different paths between these concepts.

STEP THREE: ELECTRONIC RECORDS

Before discussing different kinds of search strategies, it is beneficial to understand the structure of a MARC (machine-readable cataloging) record.

Table 1.1.

Concept #1	Concept #2	Concept #3
Doris Lessing	Southern Rhodesia	Novels
Lessing	Zimbabwe	Fiction
	Southern Africa	Science Fiction

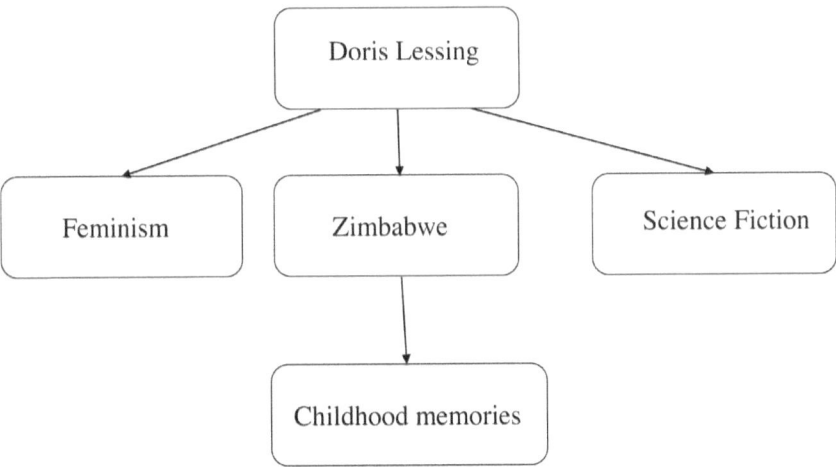

Figure 1.1.   Concept Map about Doris Lessing.
Bubbl.us.

MARC records are created by librarians as proxies for the items they represent. While the MARC record is not used by all database providers, it is the standard for library and union catalogs, and most other records have a similar structure. The MARC format is the standard for the Library of Congress. Think of these records as the description of a book, journal, or other resource. Librarians generate them by examining the physical or digital item, and then writing a detailed description using the rules set by the MARC format. These kinds of descriptions are sometimes referred to as metadata (data about data). Metadata gives descriptive information that can include the purpose of the information, how it was created, who created it, and its location.

You do not need to be an expert on MARC records since library catalogs generally do not show the MARC tags in the public display. Still, a basic understanding of the structure of MARC will aid with the research process because it will provide insight into the information contained in the entries of many databases, regardless of what format is employed. The goal of the carefully created structure of these records is to allow a user to produce an effective search. When you enter terms into a database, you are not only telling the system the word for which you want to look, but also where to find it in a record. If you know the title of a book or the name of the author, you can tell the database to look in only those specific fields. Fields in this case refer to the basic units of information (title, author, subjects) that create a record, making it possible to search just one part of the entry. By understanding and using fields to create complex searches, you can take advantage of these structured entries.

We will look at both book records and periodical records because they are slightly different. The MARC record's structure is a series of tagged fields and subfields, with each field representing a specific piece of descriptive information about the item. This structure allows separate parts of the record to be searched, such as author, title, or series. When you choose to conduct a search for any of these, the databases will query the exact index for that field (author, subject, title, etc.). An index in this context is a list of the keywords found in each record, which has been especially created to make it easier for researchers to locate particular terms. Indexed words appear in what we have called "fields." These fields are populated with precisely delineated descriptive terms in a formalized language, or a "controlled vocabulary," which is a standardized set of words used in a catalog or database. This controlled vocabulary helps to organize and categorize the sources in the catalog or database. Since a controlled vocabulary is standardized, it can be a good tool for finding more relevant results.

Figure 1.2 represents a book, *The Counter-Memorial Impulse in Twentieth-Century English Fiction*, and although some fields have been removed for this example, the contents of the record provide a good idea of what can be found inside the resource. Information about the author is listed in the 100 field in many different records, including books, so if you know the name (or part of the name) of the author, you might limit the search to the 100 field. When you do this, the search engine that runs the database will only look at the 100 field for the terms you entered. The title is in the 245 field for books, and the 260 field holds the publication information (publisher, place, and date). An index is derived from the 520 field, or the "summary, Etc., field," where you can find natural language (instead of controlled vocabulary) information about the scope, which refers to the extent of the subject matter that is covered. In this example the 520 field has a publisher summary, although not every record will include this field. The 600s and 650s will contain subject headings, which are a controlled vocabulary assigned by library catalogers. The most common source of subject headings is the Library of Congress. The 600 field is for a personal name, and the 650 field is for a topical term. The 600, 650, and 520 fields will be important for keyword searching, which will be addressed later.

Figure 1.3 represents a periodical, *Room of One's Own*. This entry is similar to the book record above, but it does have some important differences. For instance, the 222 field is called the "Title Key," which is often the periodical name, though the 245 field can also hold this information. Knowing where a periodical's contents are indexed is frequently helpful so that an item is easier to locate. This information will be provided in the 510 field, the "Citation/References" note field. The 785 field will indicate if the

```
050  00  PR888.G67|bH46 2009
100  1   Henstra, Sarah,|d1972-
245  14  The counter-memorial impulse in twentieth-century English
         fiction /|cSarah Henstra
260      Basingstoke, UK ;|aNew York :|bPalgrave Macmillan,|c2009
300      ix, 182 p. ;|c23 cm
504      Includes bibliographical references and index
505  0   Introduction : literature beyond consolation --
         Melancholia, group psychology, irony : psychoanalytic
         foundations -- The end of empire : grieving, Englishness,
         and Ford Madox Ford's The good soldier -- Mourning the
         future : nuclear war, prophecy, and Doris Lessing's The
         golden notebook -- Embodied grief : the elegiac tradition
         and Jeannette Winterson's Written on the body --
         Conclusion : literature of hope : ethical mourning
520      "A wide-ranging study that examines the tendency in 20th-
         century English fiction to treat grief as an occasion for
         social critique, unconventional readings of works by Ford,
         Lessing, and Winterson demonstrate how narrative
         experimentation in this period responds to socio-historic
         conditions like post-imperial melancholy, nuclear fear and
         homophobia"--Provided by publisher
650  0   English fiction|y20th century|xHistory and criticism
650  0   Grief in literature
650  0   Grief|xPolitical aspects
650  0   Memorials in literature
650  0   Authors, English|y20th century|xPolitical and social views
650  0   Literature and society|zGreat Britain|xHistory|y20th
         century
```

Figure 1.2.   Modified MARC record for The Counter-Memorial Impulse in Twentieth-Century English Fiction with tags 100, 245, 260, 520, and 650 highlighted.
Miami University Libraries catalog.

publication has been continued under another name, in order to identify all the issues, regardless of title changes.

Of course, MARC records have even more parts than those shown above, but this introduction should provide the researcher with a better understanding of what he or she is seeing when looking at a result in a catalog. Ideally, having a familiarity with the structure behind the database should aid users in constructing better searches that will retrieve records more appropriate to their needs. Step Four will build upon this familiarity with an exploration of search strategies.

```
090     PR9194|b.R665
210 0   Room one's own
222   0 Room of one's own
245 00 Room of one's own
260     Vancouver,|bGrowing Room Collective
300     v.|bill.|c21 cm
362 0   v. 1- 29; spring 1975-2006
490 1   1984: Tessera;|v8, no. 4
500     A feminist journal of literature and criticism
500     Vol. 8, no. 4 (1984) issued in series: Tessera
530     Also available on microfiche from: Toronto : Micromedia
776 1   |tRoom of one's own (Vancouver, B.C.)|x0316-1609
785 00 |tRoom (Vancouver, B.C.)|w(OCoLC)121522882|w(DLC)
        2007256008
```

Figure 1.3. Modified record for Room of One's Own with tags 222, 245, and 785 highlighted.
Miami University Libraries catalog.

STEP FOUR: SEARCH STRATEGIES

People who are new to research will often type an entire sentence in the first search box they see, or try to string together random keywords that they think have relevance. This approach can result in either too many or too few results. To maximize searches, there are several strategies that will result in more precise retrieval, or in some cases, expand the number of resources discovered, typically by using the "Advanced Search" screen available in most catalogs and databases. Many search tools will default to a basic search that contains one box where keywords can be entered, but the advanced search screen will show more choices, which is why many of the search strategies outlined in this step require using the advanced option.

Field Searching

One simple way to narrow your results is to do a field search instead of just a keyword search. With a field search, you are querying an individual field instead of the entire record. Recall that these are the basic parts that make up an entry (such as author, title, or subject), which means a researcher can target just the information that is needed by searching them. Bibliographic records, like the MARC records described earlier, have many searchable fields, each of which is used to create a specific index of searchable terms within the database. The database that is designed to utilize MARC records will scan any index of a field that a user indicates, and it can combine several searches at one time. Usually you can indicate a specific field using a drop-down menu provided in the search box. For example, a library catalog can be searched for *Doris Lessing* in the author field by finding the author option in a drop-down menu, which would give results for the books Lessing wrote. If you were interested in her science fiction work, you could search for records with *Doris Lessing* in the author field and *science fiction* in the subject field. Searching these two fields will result in more precise retrieval because Doris Lessing is only targeted in the author field, not subject or title. The retrieval of irrelevant records is further prevented by adding a qualifier to the search, such as *science fiction* as a subject. There is always the possibility, though, that a scholar will create a search so narrow that it will not return enough records to answer the research question.

Since field searching can be rigid, many prefer keyword searching, at least in the beginning of the process. Keyword searching will query a variety of fields, depending on the database, including author, title, subject, and source. This can be a valuable way to discover important terms and appropriate fields in order to develop a more specific strategy.

Boolean Searching

Most online databases use Boolean logic. Even the Google search engine uses Boolean logic behind the scenes. George Boole, a nineteenth-century British mathematician and philosopher, created this system of thought to establish relationships between sets of ideas. Boolean searching employs the operational terms *and*, *or*, and *not* to connect search terms. Taking advantage of the Boolean options available in online databases will allow for specific results without becoming too restrictive. Step Two touched on how to use keywords to broaden and narrow your results. Now we will examine how to combine these keywords using Boolean operators.

Boolean And *Searching*

Use *and* to narrow results. If you utilize *and*, all of the keywords must appear in the record in order for it to be retrieved. For instance, combining the terms from table 1.1 in Step Two to make it a Boolean *and* search might look like this:

Doris Lessing **AND** *Zimbabwe* **AND** *novels*

Figure 1.4 illustrates this combination.

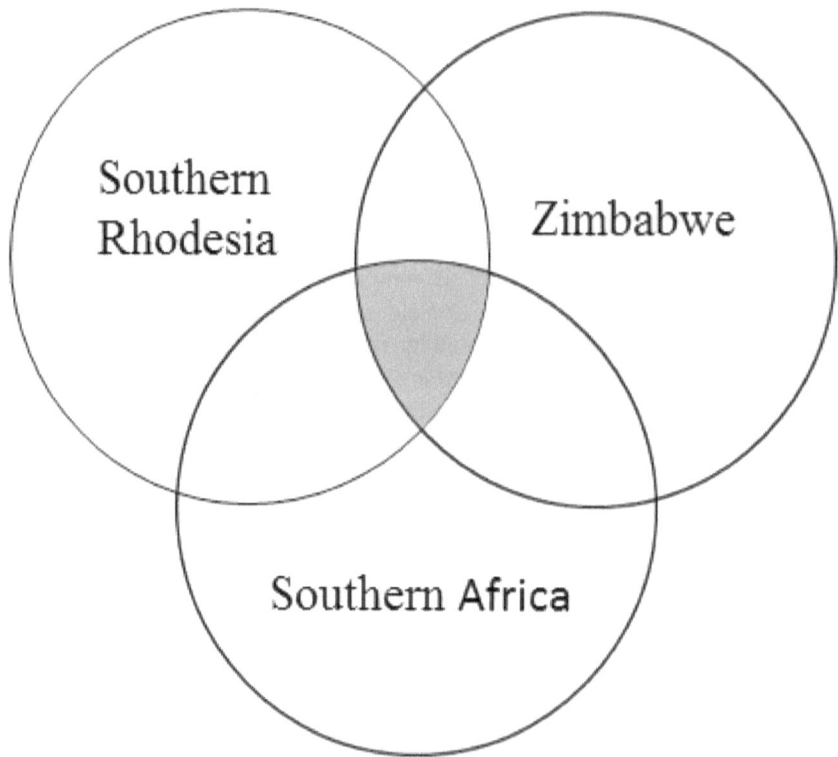

Figure 1.4.   Boolean "And" Search

If you were to do this search in a literature-related database like the *Modern Language Association International Bibliography* (*MLAIB*), the results would be similar to the record shown in figure 1.5, with the three terms in bold. Notice how all three appear in the record, though they are in different fields.

Boolean Or *Searching*

Use *or* to broaden results. You can search for any of your keywords at the same time using this operator, which is especially important when looking for synonyms or related terms. For instance, the following illustrates a search for concept two in table 1.1:

Southern Rhodesia **OR** *Zimbabwe* **OR** *Southern Africa*

Figure 1.6 illustrates this combination.

White Postcolonial Guilt in **Doris Lessing**'s The Grass Is Singing
Authors: Wang, Joy
Source: *Research in African Literatures* (RAL) 2009 Fall; 40 (3): 37-
47.   General Subject Areas:

      Subject Literature: English literature
      Period: 1900-1999
      Primary Subject Author: **Lessing, Doris** (1919-)
      Primary Subject Work: The Grass Is Singing (1950)
      Genre: **novel**

Subject Terms: by white women novelists ; treatment of colonial society ; in **Zimbabwe** ; interracial friendship
; relationship to guilt ; apartheid

Figure 1.5. Modified record retrieved from MLAIB using Boolean AND to narrow results.
MLAIB, via EBSCOhost.

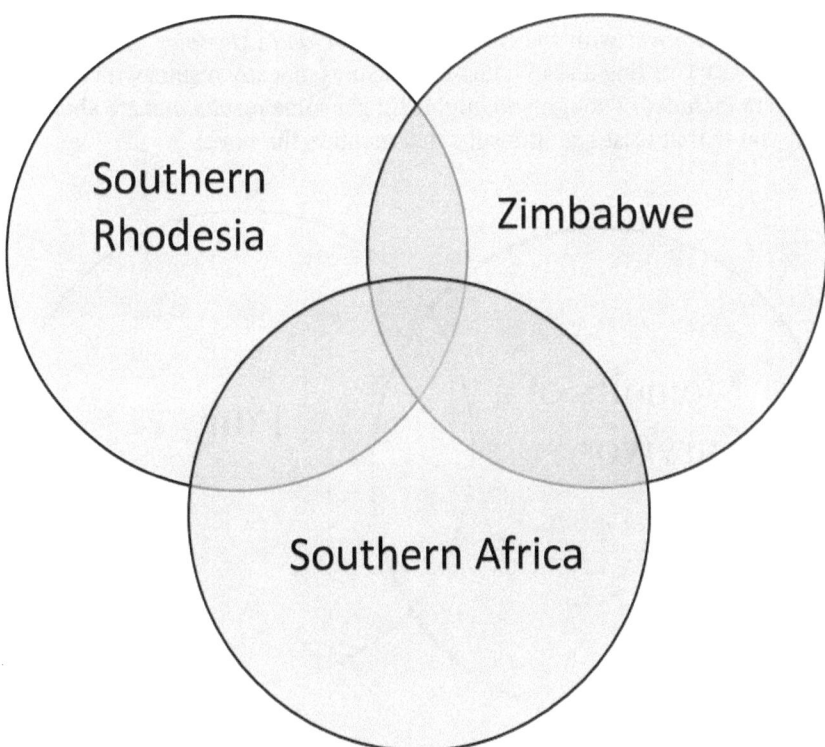

Figure 1.6. Boolean "Or" Search

A database that employs Boolean searching will show records with any of these words. When just one of these appears in a record, it is retrieved, which is why the *or* operator is utilized to broaden your search.

Boolean "NOT" Searching

You use *not* to exclude any terms that are inappropriate. For instance, if you wanted to research Doris Lessing's novel *Memoirs of a Survivor*, sometimes you will retrieve articles about the film adaptation in addition to the novel. Avoid articles about the film by using *not*:

   Memoirs of a Survivor **NOT** *film*

This search will eliminate results that are about the film adaptation, though sometimes searching like this might be limiting by removing articles that mention the film in passing but are not specifically about it, which might still be of interest to you. If you are not getting enough results, consider approaching the search in a different way. Instead of performing a *not* query, add the term *novel* with the Boolean operator *and* (*Memoirs of a Survivor* **AND** *novel*). Crafting a search this way ensures that any results with the term *novel* are included. Though you might still get some results that are about the film, you will at least get all results that mention the novel.

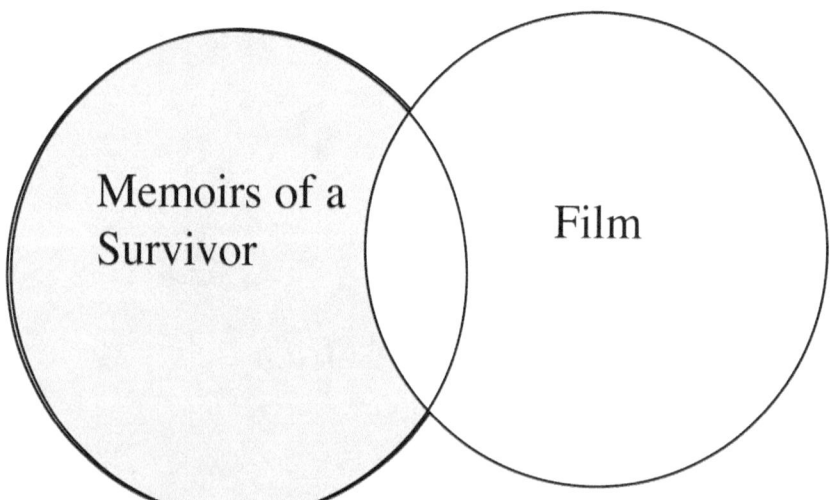

Figure 1.7.   Boolean "Not" Search

Command Search

Many databases provide field search options (described earlier) through drop-down menus listing all the fields. If a database does not list certain fields in the drop-down menu, it is possible to do a "command search" with abbreviations for each field, which will allow you to take advantage of those fields. A command search will usually consist of a large search box where you can type in the field abbreviations along with the keyword, for example, in the *MLAIB* you could type this: *Doris Lessing in au AND The Grass Is Singing in ti AND Crowell in pb AND 1950 in py* (*au* is the abbreviation for author, *ti* is for title, *pb* is for publisher, and *py* is publication year). This search would ensure that the exact publication is found instead of a different edition of the novel. Utilize the "Help" menu of the database or examine MARC records to learn other relevant field abbreviations. Not every database will offer a command search option, so first check to see if it is a possibility.

Truncation

Sometimes you will want results that give all the variations of a word. Truncation can help avoid multiple searches or typing a long list of words linked with the Boolean operator *or*. For example, *modern** will retrieve *moderns*, *modernism*, *modernity*, *modernists*, and so on, and *south** will retrieve both *south* and *southern*. Be careful not to truncate too much. Using *mode** would retrieve *modern*, but it might also retrieve *modes*, *model*, and *modem*. Some systems will automatically look for singular and plural forms but will not find the adjective form. Others allow for different "wild card" symbols to indicate the replacement of one or more than one letter. In some cases, a different symbol is employed for the replacement of a letter within a word or at the end of the stem. Often a question mark will replace one letter within a word. For example, *wom?n* will retrieve both *woman* and *women*. The help screens in each database will explain which symbols are used, if any.

Nesting

Nesting creates a complex search that combines some of the searching strategies outlined above. For example, if you want to research how Doris Lessing portrayed Southern Rhodesia in her novels, try the following searches:

Doris Lessing **AND** *novels* **AND** *Southern Rhodesia*
Doris Lessing **AND** *novels* **AND** *Zimbabwe*
Doris Lessing **AND** *novels* **AND** *Southern Africa*

All three of these searches would find everything connected to Southern Rhodesia (and the related terms for that geographic area), but you could save time by nesting the search. When conducting a nested search, place one Boolean search inside a larger Boolean search. Parentheses show where the smaller Boolean search is separate from the larger one, and as a result, everything inside the parentheses will be queried together as one concept. The sets of terms in the parentheses are connected to the other elements of the search with Boolean operators:

Doris Lessing **AND** *novels* **AND** (*Southern Rhodesia* **OR** *Zimbabwe* **OR** *Southern Africa*)

You are able to incorporate a variety of synonyms for more than one word in one simple search. Be careful to nest the right terms together, or errors might cause no results to be returned. Imagining it to be like a math problem (where the nesting can affect the order of operations) can be helpful. If you decide not to do nesting and instead run each search separately, the combined records will have many duplicates. This duplication will create more work since you will need to eliminate extraneous results.

Phrase Searching and Proximity Operators

So far this chapter has focused on developing searches based on individual terms that can be combined to form a larger concept. An effective researcher will find that it is sometimes necessary to use a whole phrase together instead of individual terms to yield the best results, which is called phrase searching. Sometimes proximity operators can be utilized to establish how closely different keywords should appear near each other. Often a close proximity is preferred because it shows that these terms have some relationship to each other. For example, if the words *science* and *fiction* appear in the same article, but they do not appear anywhere near each other, it is very possible that the article has nothing to do with science fiction. Using phrase searching and proximity operators ensures that the resource is about science fiction. Though phrase searching and proximity operators are often beneficial, they might also complicate your query. A sample search for information on *Doris Lessing* will illustrate the variations in results, depending on the techniques used.

Database search tips in the "Help" menu are important because databases can differ in what kinds of symbols are needed to perform a phrase search. WorldCat, powered by a search engine called FirstSearch, allows a phrase to be enclosed inside quotation marks or by using proximity operators. Quotation marks are a very common way to signal a phrase search.

A search for *"Doris Lessing"* in WorldCat retrieves a list of records that contain the specific phrase somewhere in the bibliographic information, but does not retrieve records that list those words in a different order. For example, *Lessing, Doris* might not be in the results. Since they give flexibility, using proximity operators will provide a more thorough search (see table 1.2). WorldCat allows specific operators, such as the ones described below:

w (with): When this operator is placed between terms, WorldCat will search for records containing both the terms next to each other in the order that they are written. To find the words close to each other, type *w* and a number between one and twenty-five to indicate how close you want the terms to appear to each other, in the order that you entered them. Just remember, a larger number can result in more words in between the terms than is necessary. Here is an example of what this search might look like: *Doris w2 Lessing*. We will look at the results of this search a little later.

n (near): When this operator is placed between two terms, WorldCat will search for records containing both of the terms next to each other in any order. To find the words close to each other, type *n* and a number between one and twenty-five to indicate how close you want the terms to appear to each other, in any order. Here is an example of what this search might look like: *Doris n2 Lessing*. We will also examine the results of this search.

Table 1.2 shows the results that the FirstSearch search engine retrieves from WorldCat when using the different search strategies explained earlier.

Table 1.2.

Search Strategy	Retrieves	Number of Results
"Doris Lessing"	Doris Lessing	7924
Doris w2 Lessing	Doris Lessing	7951
	Doris May Lessing	
Doris n2 Lessing	Doris Lessing	9464
	Doris May Lessing	
	Lessing, Doris May	
Doris Lessing	Doris and Lessing	9519

As you can see from table 1.2

• The first search, for *"Doris Lessing,"* returned the smallest number of results because it limits the search engine to records in which the names occur right next to each other, in that order. Since Doris Lessing is the most common version of her name, the number of results is not as small as it would be if this version were less common. This search is good for narrowing results when your author is also known by nicknames, or when she has a name that can be spelled differently.

- The second search, for *Doris w2 Lessing*, allows the search engine to retrieve records that have both *Doris Lessing* and *Doris May Lessing*, but it would not contain those where the author's last name comes before other parts of the name. Records with only the Library of Congress subject heading *Lessing, Doris May, 1919* are not included.

- The third search, for *Doris n2 Lessing*, is more flexible because the search engine retrieves records in which the author's first and last name can occur in any order. Also, the middle name might or might not appear. While "false drops" (records where both terms appear but they do not refer to Doris Lessing) are possible when using this search strategy, it creates a flexible but fairly specific query.

- The last search, for *Doris Lessing*, yields the largest number of results because the search engine queries the terms separately in the database. This strategy can often result in "false drop" records.

None of the searches shown in table 1.2 is conclusively better than the others. Even the broadest search could yield potentially valuable results that the other searches would miss. To be thorough, a scholar will usually try several different techniques.

Keyword vs. Subject Searching

A bibliographic record will contain a section for subject headings or descriptors. These headings contain words and phrases from a controlled vocabulary (described in Step Three) from which catalogers select words that accurately describe the item. These descriptive terms can be very precise or very general. The most common controlled vocabulary is called the Library of Congress Subject Heading (LCSH). These subject headings can be found online at the Library of Congress website (id.loc.gov/authorities/subjects.html). Fortunately, many databases provide a field for these subject headings, so you will not usually need to consult an outside source. Since many databases favor keyword searching, you will frequently be able to determine the best controlled vocabulary terms by examining the fields in records retrieved through keyword searches.

For example, if you do a keyword search to find resources about women's roles in postmodern British literature, using *women* and *postmodernism* and *British* as the search terms, one of the titles retrieved is *Feminism and the Postmodern Impulse: Post–World War II Fiction*, displayed in figure 1.8. The

```
Author  Michael, Magali Cornier
Title   Feminism and the postmodern impulse : post-World War II fiction /
Magali Cornier Michael
Imprint Albany : State University of New York Press, c1996
Descript. x, 275 p. ; 24 cm
Note     Includes bibliographical references and index
Subject English fiction -- Women authors -- History and criticism
        Feminism and literature -- Great Britain -- History -- 20th century
        American fiction -- Women authors -- History and criticism
        American fiction -- 20th century -- History and criticism
        English fiction -- 20th century -- History and criticism
        Postmodernism (Literature)
        Feminism and literature
        Women and literature
        Lessing, Doris May, 1919- Golden notebook
        Piercy, Marge. Woman on the edge of time
        Atwood, Margaret, 1939- Handmaid's tale
        Carter, Angela, 1940-1992. Nights at the circus
Call #  PR888.I45 M53 1996
```

Figure 1.8. Modified record illustrating LCSH for Feminism and the Postmodern Impulse: Post-World War II Fiction.
Miami University Libraries catalog.

shaded areas in the figure are an example of the LCSH terms listed above. Some of these terms are likely to be valuable for incorporating into a search on this topic. "English fiction--Women authors--History and criticism" might broaden the results to a variety of female authors writing English fiction, while "Feminism and literature--Great Britain--History--20th century" might narrow down to specific research on feminism and literature in Great Britain. "History and criticism," which was shown in an earlier example, is a good subject heading for finding criticism written about a literary work, providing results that cover the history, literary criticism, and analysis of a topic. Another helpful subject heading is "Criticism and interpretation," which will deliver results that are critical analyses of an author's work, but it generally excludes biographical information.

These subject headings often assist in creating more precise searches, but clearly are not structured in the same way that people normally speak and think. Fortunately, since practically every library catalog is now online, the subject headings are often hyperlinks, so you can quickly follow a relevant subject heading by clicking on it in the record. Remember, though, that some subject headings will remove you from the original search. For instance, if you were to click on "Postmodernism (Literature)," you would no longer be searching for records related to women or Britain. When you find a record for an item that exactly matches your research needs, it is good practice to make note of the subject headings provided, for often those same headings will be used in other catalogs and databases. Once a good list of subject headings has been generated, add different terms to the subject heading searches. For instance, much of postmodern literature was written in the twentieth century, so add "20th century" to other subject headings, such as "Women authors," which might create this search: "Women authors--20th century." We have mostly focused on subject headings developed by the Library of Congress, but be aware that controlled vocabulary can vary in different databases.

The decision to perform a keyword search or do a subject heading search depends on how precise you need the results to be. Sometimes when you are less sure of what you are looking for, the large results of a keyword search can enable browsing through many records, which can help with understanding your research needs as you shift through the information, deciding what is and is not important. Other times very specific results are needed in order to find a particular kind of resource, and a subject heading search is appropriate in this case. Still, a combination of keyword searching and subject searching is often most effective because by starting with a keyword query, you can examine the subject headings listed in the records that are the most applicable to the research and refocus your efforts in new directions.

Relevancy Searching

Have you wondered how databases present your results, or why the results are shown in a particular order? Many databases will default to relevancy order, which means they will show the results that are considered the most helpful based on certain criteria and algorithms used by that resource. The most relevant results will appear first in the list. Google results are famous for this kind of relevancy ranking. Criteria can be different for each database, but common criteria includes a match (or partial match) of words in the subject field, a match in the title, frequency of the occurrence of the terms in the record, or proximity of keywords to each other. Knowing the criteria behind the relevancy ranking can help with understanding why the search has retrieved certain results.

One particularly important concept you should understand is that the relevancy ranking implies a value for the first results that might not really be there. A helpful result does not always depend on whether a searched term appears multiple times in the abstract, but whether or not the result best matches the idea a researcher is trying to study. If the results are not as relevant as you hoped, sometimes you need to redo your query or try changing the way they appear to make it easier to sort through them.

Many databases allow relevancy order ranking to be turned off, and a different order for the results selected. One useful order ranking is by date. If you want the latest research on a topic, change the order to show the more recent articles first. If you want to see the original primary sources for a topic, change the order to list the oldest resources first. In many databases, the ability to change relevancy ranking to results organized by date or in alphabetical order is provided by a drop-down menu.

Limiting/Modifying

Once you have a list of results, it might be necessary to narrow down your query even more to make the number of sources more manageable. Your original search can be changed using several different strategies. Most databases allow switching from the results list back to the initial search to revise it. Sometimes the initial search can be found under the search history. You can then modify it by adding new search terms (or in some cases removing them). For instance, if the original query was a search for *Doris Lessing*, the results were possibly much larger than expected. Go back to the original search and add the phrase *science fiction* to create more precise results.

Limiting, a way to narrow your search to specific fields or document types, is also available in many databases and can be set before you even start, or after performing the search. This technique can eliminate a type of resource from the results, limit the search to a specific publication date range, find only texts written in English, or target peer-reviewed journal articles. When setting limits, you can narrow down results to the kinds of resources needed for your research. For example, if you are finding too many mainstream book reviews for Doris Lessing's novels in popular publications, try limiting the search to just peer-reviewed articles before you begin.

In many catalogs and databases you can opt to limit the search after the search is performed by taking advantage of *faceted searching*. Think of facets as filters that help narrow the results by selecting different criteria. Facets can often be found on the left or right side of the results list and usually involve checking a box near them or clicking a hyperlink. When you select these facets, organized by fields and document types, they are applied to the results. For instance, at the beginning stages of your research, you might want to find reference works to provide background information about an author. With faceted tools, you could do a keyword search for *Doris Lessing* and then, if it was an option, select the reference section in your library as the location. See figure 1.9 for an example of what a faceted search might look like.

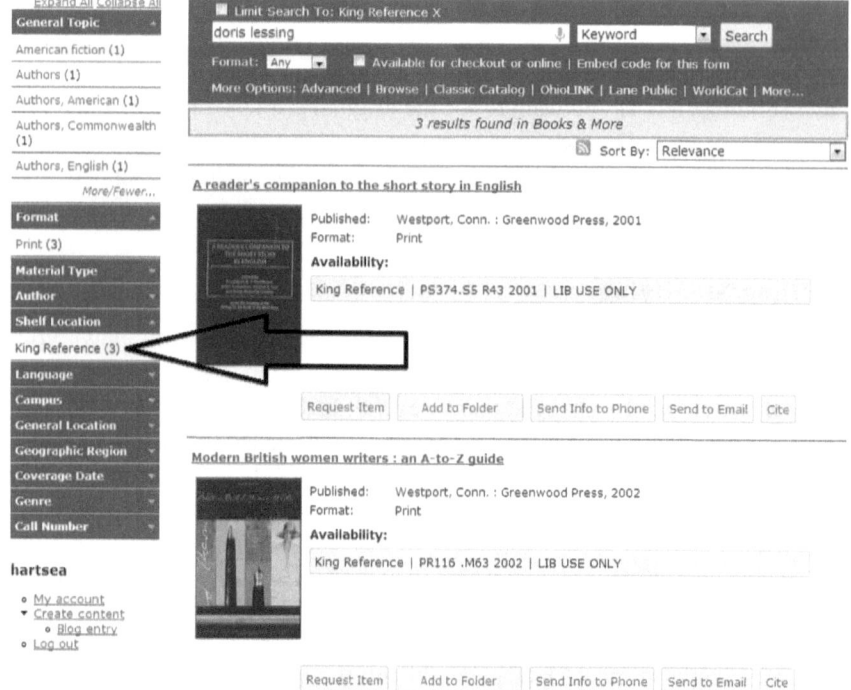

Figure 1.9. Example of the results of a faceted search in a library catalog.
Miami University Libraries catalog.

STEP FIVE: CHOOSING A DATABASE

After you have created a strong search, start deciding which tools to select. Several search tools will be necessary to find various kinds of sources and to answer different aspects of the research question. In turn, each of these tools will require unique strategies. For example, if you want to find books, you will most likely need to use a library catalog. Library catalogs are further explored in chapter 3, but sometimes it is beneficial to employ subject headings instead of Boolean searches because subject headings can give more precise results.

For articles, think about how you can utilize targeted search strategies in subject-specific databases. A database is a searchable catalog or index (usually online) that contains metadata about various resources. Many of these resources will be provided by publishers and other vendors. A database will often contain items that are either united by subject (like literature) or united by type of item (such as newspapers). Look closely at the descriptions of individual databases and at the kinds of resources listed to see if a particular resource will aid your research. Sometimes databases will give the full text of the article, but they also might include only bibliographic information needed to find the full text in a different place. Explore the search interfaces of the selected database to find out what options are available. For example, several different companies offer access to the Modern Language Association International Bibliography, a standard academic literature-related database. Search strategies will need to be adjusted sometimes, depending on whether the library subscribes to *MLAIB* through EBSCO, Gale, Chadwick-Healey, or another vendor.

A good way to find out what kinds of search options are available in a given database is to look for links to "Help," "Search Tips," or "Frequently Asked Questions." Talking to a reference librarian might also be fruitful. Here are a few questions to consider to make searching more efficient:

- Does the database recognize or require Boolean operators? Do you have to manually enter them, or is there a drop-down menu?
- Is truncation an option? If so, what symbols are recognized by the database?
- Does the database recognize quotation marks for phrase searching?
- Does the database allow you to limit by date, language, or type of source?
- How are results displayed? Can you display results by date, title, author, or relevancy?

Vendors frequently update their search interfaces, so look out for changes because you might need to alter search strategies, depending on the kinds of changes made.

In addition to subject-specific databases and catalogs, many libraries now have discovery tools that link their resources together. A discovery tool presents search results from multiple resources in one place. They often have one search box and rely on features like facets (filters to narrow down results) to help researchers find specific results. The advantage of a discovery tool is the ease with which you can search many resources all at once instead of each one individually, saving valuable time. Many of the techniques outlined in Steps Four and Five will work with these new tools, though variations in the search options given between discovery tools and different databases can be challenging. At times you will want to switch back to an individual database to take advantage of a specific feature, such as date limits and special advanced search options. For instance, many databases have a thesaurus for identifying controlled vocabulary specific to that discipline. *MLAIB* includes the *MLA Directory of Periodicals*, a good resource for identifying significant journals.

STEP SIX: WEB SEARCHING

Web search engines such as Google and Bing can be effective when exploring topics in the initial stages and to find different sources, such as archives, special collections, digital content from these types of repositories, images, public domain texts, and more. If you are unfamiliar with a topic, looking for information with a web search engine can help you gather background information. When doing an image search, remember to check carefully to see if the images are in the public domain or are free to use through Creative Commons, which is a copyright license that creators can opt to apply to give others permission to share or use the work created, as long as it falls into the conditions that are set.

These web search engines share some similarities with the subscription-based databases described earlier, mainly in terms of the retrieval options that are possible, but they differ in some major ways. Web resources are usually free to use, and they search the entire visible web. The "invisible web," which search engines will usually not query, can include subscription-based databases, resources that update in real time, and information walled off by companies and institutions (like an intranet). Since almost anyone can create a website, the quality of the information that is provided can vary greatly. Even if the information is accurate, in many cases it will not be as in-depth as what can be found in a scholarly source. Most websites have descriptions, general definitions, and basic biographical information, but they do not give the kind of analysis and criticism that researchers in literature need.

The fact that search engines yield many results can be both promising and overwhelming. Take advantage of many of the strategies described above to limit results. As with databases, look at the "Help" pages to find out what kinds of options are available. Remember that "Advanced Search" options can focus retrieval lists. Often even web search engines let you target an exact word or phrase, allow certain words to be restricted, or give options to limit results by language, region, site, domain, file type, or usage right.

Searching Google Scholar will help direct results to just scholarly resources, though sometimes you will find that while searching for literature-related topics it is essential to sort through a lot of digitized books to find literary criticism. Always be aware that many of the resources that appear in Google Scholar, including scholarly articles, are behind a pay wall. They might be available instead through a subscription database in your library. Google Scholar can be used to find citations, but unless you are on campus or logged into your library's proxy services, full-text articles will usually not be available. If you find appropriate resources online for your research, check to see if the library can provide access, or if interlibrary loan is an option. In addition to searching for resources, Google Scholar can find out how frequently a journal article or book has been cited.

Understanding both the strengths and weaknesses of an online search engine is important when deciding on a strategy to guide your research. Generally, the most effective queries will be a combination of tools that could include search engines.

CONCLUSION

Hopefully, this chapter has increased your understanding of some of the basics of literary research. The theories behind many of the techniques outlined here will transfer between different databases and search engines, even if some of the particular steps differ. Referring back to this first chapter while reading through the rest of the book and doing the research might prove helpful. Though the strategies mentioned here are general tips, many of them can be employed to navigate the resources mentioned throughout this book. The following chapters will discuss more specific kinds of resources and search strategies that will build on what you have already learned. Remember, it is often advantageous to plan out research questions and to brainstorm keywords before beginning the research. Good planning can save a researcher work later. If you want to be thorough, try to combine a variety of the search strategies outlined in this chapter instead of just relying on one or two tricks. Remember that different catalogs and databases can have different rules and will require more than one technique. Finally, do not forget to consult the help pages of these resources, and ask a reference librarian for further guidance as appropriate.

Chapter Two

General Literary Reference Sources

Literature reference sources, such as research guides, companions, handbooks, dictionaries, and encyclopedias, are good places to begin researching authors, works, and subjects related to British postmodern literature. In addition to listing and describing information essential for exploring a topic, they record significant primary and secondary sources and give helpful background information and factual details, as well as overviews. Many of the print and online publications described in this chapter cover such broad categories as postmodern theory or English literary studies. Though these sources might seem too general for understanding British postmodern literature, they often contain sections that will focus more specifically on the topic and might provide contextual insight for literature from that period. For all of the works mentioned in chapter 2, pay close attention to the notes and bibliographies because they can open further avenues to pursue.

Consider carefully the research questions you want answered when deciding which reference works to utilize. A general dictionary or encyclopedia will give a short overview or a quick definition, while a specialized reference work might offer more in-depth background about the topic. If you are not sure about the best way to identify appropriate reference works, you might want to start by consulting your librarian. Usually, reference works can be searched in a library catalog or found among the online resources on a library's website. Pairing words like *encyclopedia*, *companion*, or *dictionary* with your author or topic will often yield relevant results. If you find a pertinent resource in your library catalog, you might want to look at the subject headings ("Literature, modern--20th century--Bio-bibliography--Dictionaries") listed for other search ideas, a strategy covered more thoroughly in chapter 3. Be aware that subject headings for reference works can be too broad or too narrow, so it might be best to experiment with different search terms. Some of the books described in the following sections are also available in an ebook format, so when you do a search at your library, check to see what is offered.

RESEARCH GUIDES

Bracken, James K. *Reference Works in British and American Literature*. 2nd edition. Englewood, CO: Libraries Unlimited, 1998.

Harner, James L. *Literary Research Guide: An Annotated Listing of Reference Sources in English Literary Studies*. 5th edition. New York: Modern Language Association of America, 2008.

———. *Literary Research Guide*. 6th edition. New York: Modern Language Association of America, 2014–. www.mlalrg.org.

Marcuse, Michael J. *A Reference Guide for English Studies*. Berkeley: University of California Press, 1990.

James Bracken's **Reference Works in British and American Literature** describes more than 1,500 reference works and focuses on sources about individual authors, listing bibliographies, dictionaries, encyclopedias, handbooks, indexes, concordances, and journals, when possible. The attention to individual authors makes this resource especially helpful because it can track down reference works devoted to an author instead of general encyclopedias and dictionaries that cover many different authors in one publication. The lists of sources are not meant to be comprehensive, but instead they represent the most important and useful items available. Entries are arranged alphabetically by author, with British and American authors listed together. The descriptive annotations note specific features for resources, provide some evaluation, explain the scope, and give cross-references to other related entries. Many postmodern British authors, such as Anthony Burgess, John Fowles, Harold Pinter, and Jean Rhys, are included. The end of the book has a chronological and a nationality appendix, as well as an author/title index and a subject index.

Both James Harner's *Literary Research Guide: An Annotated Listing of Reference Sources in English Literary Studies* and Michael Marcuse's *A Reference Guide for English Studies* are widely used literary research guides that describe standard literary sources.

James Harner's **Literary Research Guide: An Annotated Listing of Reference Sources in English Literary Studies**, often referred to as just "Harner," is the primary handbook for literary studies in the United States because of its comprehensive scope and thorough organization. This guide is a great place to begin research and a good tool for identifying additional materials to investigate. Advanced undergraduates, graduate students, and scholars are the intended audience. More than 1,200 annotated entries evaluate selected print and online resources, giving both the strengths and weaknesses of each resource. Items are organized into sections by general resource type (such as reference books, library catalogs, manuscripts, dissertations, websites, etc.), genres, national literatures, other literatures in English, foreign-language literatures, comparative literature, and literature-related topics.

Entries, following a standard format, begin with a complete citation to the sources mentioned (often recording different editions), as well as Library of Congress and Dewey call numbers. The annotation covers the source's scope and arrangement, assesses its strengths and weaknesses as a research tool, compares it with similar works, and explains how the indexes work. Selected reviews are also listed. Entries finish with "see also" references to other sections and sources within the *Literary Research Guide*. Name, title, and subject indexes are provided. A regularly updated and revised online version of the *Literary Research Guide*, to which some libraries subscribe, allows the user to search within the source for authors and titles of specific reference works.

Though many of the sections in this guide might prove helpful, postmodern researchers should pay special attention to "Section M, English Literature," subsection "Twentieth-Century Literature," which contains "Guides to Primary Works" and "Guides to Scholarship and Criticism." "Section U, Literature-Related Topics and Sources" might also be fruitful since subjects like cultural studies, literary criticism and theory, and popular culture are discussed.

Michael Marcuse's *A Reference Guide for English Studies* evaluates English-language and literature reference works published through 1990. Entries are arranged into twenty-four sections, which are comprised of general works, libraries, serial publications, history and ancillae to historical study, archives and manuscripts, language, poetry and versification, the profession of English, and more. Marcuse recommends that people begin by consulting the subject index instead of the table of contents, as works applicable to their research might be listed in unexpected parts of the book.

Sections are usually comprised of annotated entries describing standard reference sources, while some scholarly journals and recommended works might be recorded without annotations. Comparable to Harner's guide, entries have citations and call numbers, and annotations outline a work's publication history (such as number of editions and previous titles), purpose, scope, organization, strengths, and weaknesses, and often have "see also" notes and cross-references to other sources.

Though there might be information related to British postmodern literature throughout the work, there are three main sections that will be useful. "Section M: English Literature" contains bibliographies, literary histories, hand-books, and guides to individual authors; some works discussed in this section are related to general studies, while others examine specific time periods and authors. "Section R: Literature of the Twentieth Century" covers topics like age of transition and has general bibliographies and guides on poetry, drama and theater, and prose and criticism. A helpful record of scholarly journals in "Modern Studies" and frequently recommended works on "Modern Litera-ture" are also included, which will aid researchers trying to map connections between postmodern and modern literature. The last section that is potentially relevant is "Section X: Theory, Rhetoric, and Composition," particularly "Literary Criticism and Literary Theory after ca. 1950." Sources for theories such as poststructuralism, deconstruction, and phenomenology are offered. Researchers should look up individual authors in the "Index of Subjects" and the "Authors-as-Subjects" index. As an example, William Golding is listed in a source that is described as R-55 in the "Literature of the Twentieth Century—part of the Prose Fiction section." The specific title for R-55 is *Bibliography of Modern British Novelists* by Robert Stanton.

Marcuse's work has some limitations, such as the fact that it only covers works published through 1990, but it also contains unique features that make it worth consulting. These features range from author-specific reference materials and citations to frequently recommended resources, which point a researcher to a great number of valuable sources. Utilizing both of these refer-ence works will aid a scholar in identifying appropriate sources.

POSTMODERN ENCYCLOPEDIAS AND COMPANIONS

Cambridge Collections Online. West Nyack, NY: Cambridge University Press, 2006–. universitypublishingonline.org/cambridge/companions/.
Connor, Steven, ed. *The Cambridge Companion to Postmodernism*. New York: Cambridge University Press, 2004.
Mason, Fran. *Historical Dictionary of Postmodernist Literature and Theater*. Lanham, MD: Scarecrow Press, 2007.
Sim, Stuart, ed. *The Routledge Companion to Postmodernism*. 3rd edition. New York: Routledge, 2011.
Taylor, Victor E., and Charles E. Winquist, eds. *The Encyclopedia of Post-modernism*. New York: Routledge, 2001.

Specialized encyclopedias and companions, such as those discussed in this section, can offer in-depth treatments of topics with broad applications or appeal to scholars. Though they are different in the ways that they cover an area of interest, they are both essential to scholarly research. Encyclopedias are more comprehensive than companions in scope because they attempt to examine all aspects of a subject in several volumes and often have signed articles of different lengths, while companions offer analytical overviews and generally provide an introduction to the critical discourse in an area of interest. Indexes and bibliographies are usually parts of both of these kinds of reference works. They might also contain definitions and chronologies. Some of the titles described here focus on postmodern theory and philosophy instead of literature, but of course this theory informs the literature. Postmodernism is a complex concept with many facets, so the background information found in these sources can be especially useful.

The Cambridge Companion to Postmodernism is a collection of essays written by scholars. Steven Connor, the editor of the book and professor of modern literature and theory in the School of English and Humanities at Birkbeck College, London, begins with an excellent introduction that outlines what he records are the four different stages in the development of postmodernism, which are accumulation, synthesis, autonomy, and dissipation. Examples of relevant chapters are "Postmodernism and Film" by Catherine Constable, "Postmodernism and Literature" by Steven Connor, and "Postmodernism and Performance" by Philip Auslander. The collection also features a chronology, from 1947 to 2001. Further readings appear at the end of the book, divided by individual chapters. Terry Eagleton, Fredric Jameson, Jean Baudrillard, Peter Brooker, and Jacques Derrida are some of the authors and thinkers listed for further study.

Cambridge Companions, such as *The Cambridge Companion to Postmodernism*, can be searched and read online through the *Cambridge Collections Online*, a subscription resource. You can either look at a specific companion or search the entire collection at once. For instance, a search through all the companions for *Salman Rushdie* results in eighty-four hits. He is mentioned in a variety of titles, including *The Cambridge Companion to Salman Rushdie*, *The Cambridge Companion to Modern British Culture*, *The Cambridge Companion to the Twentieth-Century English Novel*, and *The Cambridge Companion to Modern Indian Culture*. The results page provides a "View More" option where a researcher can see where the search term is mentioned in the companion. With the advanced search option, you can look through the full text of the volumes, or search by author, volume, title, year, subjects, or article types (critical essay, book review essay, interview, and more). Each chapter can be read as a PDF, and there is a "My Collections" feature, which allows you to create an account and then save queries, keep notes on chapters, or create shared-access workgroups.

The ***Historical Dictionary of Postmodernist Literature and Theater***, part of Scarecrow Press's Historical Dictionaries of Literature and the Arts series, has an alphabetical record of definitions for authors, texts, scholars, movements, writing forms, theories, and ideas. Individual definitions are fairly extensive and have bolded terms that can be looked up in the dictionary. The introduction explains the difficulties in defining postmodernism and discusses some context for the major issues involved, like the historical events influencing the thinkers and writers of the period. A chronology begins in 1939, with Arnold Toynbee using the phrase "the Post-Modern Age" to refer to the period after 1914, and covers the century until 2006. A concluding bibliography is divided into several sections, such as general works, postmodernist aesthetics, postmodernist literature (fiction, drama, and poetry), postmodernist literature (critical works), journals, and websites.

The Routledge Companion to Postmodernism begins with essays that are similar in scope to those found in *The Cambridge Companion to Postmodernism*, but it also contains an A-to-Z list of critical terms, bolded throughout the essays, for easy identification. The third edition also has new essays on topics including aesthetics, business, gender, and the performing arts. There is an extensive bibliography at the end that will help the researcher find other important sources to explore, and an index to key writers, thinkers, and concepts. Martin Amis, Roland Barthes, bricolage, hypertext, magic realism, posthumanism, post-postmodernism, Edward Said, and Jeanette Winterson are examples of the kinds of topics found in this companion.

The Encyclopedia of Postmodernism is a single-volume work that covers academic disciplines, critical terms, and central figures of postmodern studies. The entries are written alphabetically and cross-referenced. There are disciplinary essays, critical terms, and biographies. Relevant entries address cultural studies, fiction, postmodernism, genre, literary theory, literature studies, and metaphor. Entries are short but deliver good information on necessary concepts, such as alterity, erasure, game theory, liminality, and semiosis. Many of the entries also have a "Further Reading" section. According to the introduction, the encyclopedia does not utilize a single definition of postmodernism but tries instead to document the use of the term across different disciplines, such as art, religion, and rhetoric. The index provides access to concepts and people.

LITERARY THEORY ENCYCLOPEDIAS AND DICTIONARIES

Groden, Michael, Martin Kreiswirth, and Imre Szeman, eds. *The Johns Hopkins Guide to Literary Theory & Criticism*. 2nd edition. Baltimore, MD: Johns Hopkins University Press, 2005.

————. *The Johns Hopkins Guide to Literary Theory & Criticism*, Baltimore, MD: Johns Hopkins University Press, 2012. litguide.press.jhu.edu.

Ryan, Michael, Gregory Castle, Robert Eaglestone, and M. K. Booker, eds. *The Encyclopedia of Literary and Cultural Theory*. 3 volumes. Malden, MA: Wiley-Blackwell, 2011.

Since literary theory informs much of postmodern fiction, it is important to have a strong understanding of the core concepts. Most of these encyclopedias and dictionaries will give information about the primary theoretical texts to be consulted, in addition to definitions of terms and summaries. Chapter 10 will provide more information about applying critical theory in literary research.

The print version of **The Johns Hopkins Guide to Literary Theory & Criticism** is a one-volume work with 241 entries arranged alphabetically that explore key theorists, critics, movements, schools of thought, modern literary theory, and older critical theories. Reading the relevant entries will give a researcher information about the origins of a theory, the people associated with it, and its significance. Each entry has cross-references and bibliographies of primary and secondary sources. The lists of primary sources are especially valuable when tracing a theory back to its origins to read foundational works. The entry for "postmodernism" includes primary-source titles such as *The Idea of the Postmodern: A History* by Hans Bertens, *The Illusions of Postmodernism* by Terry Eagleton, *Postmodernism, or The Cultural Logic of Late Capitalism* by Fredric Jameson, and *Postmodernist Fiction* by Brian McHale. Indexes of names and of topics conclude the volume. The topic index will point to the entries that contain references to postmodernism (e.g., Baudrillard; Feminist 5; Film I; Jameson; Lyotard).

The online subscription version of **The Johns Hopkins Guide to Literary Theory & Criticism** makes it even easier to find references to the term *postmodernism*. A basic keyword search for postmodernism returns forty-nine documents where the word appears, with the term postmodernism highlighted throughout each document. This highlighting will give the researcher an idea of how pertinent an individual entry is by showing the frequency with which a term appears and how it is used. Important terms in an entry are hyperlinked, so that a researcher can easily navigate these concepts. For instance, the entry for "postmodernism" has hyperlinks to Jacques Derrida, cultural studies, globalization, and Julia Kristeva. The online version is also updated with several new entries every year.

The Encyclopedia of Literary and Cultural Theory is a three-volume set from Wiley-Blackwell. The first volume covers literary theory from 1900 to 1966, the second volume examines literary theory from 1966 to the present, and the third volume discusses cultural theory. Taken together, they ground the reader in literary and cultural theory. There are entries for theorists, schools of thought, and concepts. Individual entries offer definitions and explanations of ideas, and they end with a "see also" section, references, and suggested readings. Relevant entries for understanding postmodernism include Judith Butler, modernity/postmodernity, new critical theory, self-referentiality, and social constructionism. The volume on cultural theory offers discussions on popular media and art, which is especially valuable for examining postmodernism and its tendency to blur the lines of literature and media. Each volume lists entries in alphabetical order, but there is a helpful index at the end of the third volume to locate specific concepts in the text.

GENERAL BRITISH AND IRISH LITERARY
ENCYCLOPEDIAS AND COMPANIONS

Foster, John W., ed. *The Cambridge Companion to the Irish Novel*. New York: Cambridge University Press, 2006.

Kastan, David S., ed. *The Oxford Encyclopedia of British Literature*. 5 volumes. New York: Oxford University Press, 2006.

Serafin, Steven, and Valerie G. Myer, eds. *The Continuum Encyclopedia of British Literature*. New York: Continuum, 2003.

John Wilson Foster's **The Cambridge Companion to the Irish Novel** explores the history of the Irish novel and provides a thorough examination of the relationship between Irish literature and British literature. Beginning with a chronology and an introduction by the editor, the volume also includes individual chapters on a variety of topics that will be of interest, though chapters on "Women Novelists, 1930s–1960s," "Two Post-Modern Novelists: Samuel Beckett and Flann O'Brien," and "Life Writing in the Twentieth Century" will be especially pertinent. Each chapter ends with notes and a guide to further reading. The index at the end of the book can be used to identify relevant subjects, particularly postmodernism, which is listed twelve times, and postcolonialism, which is recorded six times.

The Oxford Encyclopedia of British Literature, a five-volume set published by Oxford University Press, contains five hundred in-depth articles written by experts in the field. They cover the history of British literature in English and mostly focus on major authors, though there are entries for themes, movements, genres, and institutions. Not included are writers writing in English outside of Britain, such as those in America, Canada, or South Africa, while Welsh, Irish, and Scottish authors are present. Each entry has a bibliography and end references, and a table in the first volume lists in chronological order the items that appear in the volumes, while an index and a list of all contributors are a part of the fifth volume. Researchers on postmodernism will find entries about postmodern authors useful, as well as those that explore the background and context surrounding British literature. Scholars researching this time period might sometimes need to look back at authors and literary styles that predate the twentieth century to understand what postmodern writers were responding to culturally.

The Continuum Encyclopedia of British Literature functions as a survey of the development of British literature and comprises literatures written in English from Africa, Australia, Canada, the Caribbean, India, and New Zealand, as well as the British Isles. This massive volume is not as comprehensive as the previous Oxford encyclopedia, but it does provide relevant information. In addition to the alphabetical entries, there is a list of "Monarchs of Great Britain," a "Historical-Literary Timeline," a list of "Poets Laureate," and a list of "Literary Awards and Prizes." Applicable topical articles for research on postmodernism are detective fiction since 1945, drama since 1956, fiction since 1945, literary criticism since 1945, poetry since 1945, postmodernism, and satire.

CONTEMPORARY BRITISH LITERATURE ENCYCLOPEDIAS AND COMPANIONS

Aston, Elaine, and Janelle G. Reinelt, eds. *The Cambridge Companion to Modern British Women Playwrights*. New York: Cambridge University Press, 2000.

Brown, Ian, and Alan Riach. *The Edinburgh Companion to Twentieth-Century Scottish Literature*. Edinburgh: Edinburgh University Press, 2009.

Caserio, Robert L., ed. *The Cambridge Companion to the Twentieth-Century English Novel*. New York: Cambridge University Press, 2009.

Cockin, Katharine, and Jago Morrison, eds. *The Post-War British Literature Handbook*. New York: Continuum, 2010.

Di, Mauro L. *Modern British Literature*. 2nd edition. 3 volumes. Detroit: St. James Press, 2000.

Dowson, Jane, ed. *The Cambridge Companion to Twentieth-Century British and Irish Women's Poetry*. New York: Cambridge University Press, 2011.

Shaffer, Brian W., ed. *A Companion to the British and Irish Novel 1945–2000*. Malden, MA: Blackwell, 2005.

Stringer, Jenny, ed. *The Oxford Companion to Twentieth-Century Literature in English*. New York: Oxford University Press, 1996.

The Cambridge Companion to Modern British Women Playwrights examines the works of women playwrights in Britain, Wales, Scotland, and Northern Ireland in the twentieth century, providing historical, political, and theat-
rical contexts. The companion begins with a chronology and an introduction
that gives a historical overview. Four parts divide this work: "Retrospec-
tives," "National Tensions and Intersections," "The Question of the Canon,"
and "The Subject of Identity." Some chapters focus on a specific time period
or theme, while others target individual playwrights (Caryl Churchill, Tim-
berlake Wertenbaker, and more). The companion has photos from some productions and ends with an index of playwrights, plays, and topics.

To learn more about modern Scottish literature and its relationship to
British literature, consult ***The Edinburgh Companion to Twentieth-Century Scottish Literature***. This work begins with an introduction that outlines the trends in Scottish literature during the twentieth century, followed
by chapters on key authors, periods, and topics. Poetry, drama, and popular
fiction are covered, along with topics such as "Post-War Scottish Fiction"
and "Entering the Twenty-First Century." The book concludes with a further reading section and an index.

Though ***The Cambridge Companion to the Twentieth-Century English
Novel*** centers exclusively on the novel, it is a useful source because many
postmodern novelists are featured. The book's introduction explains that
the companion attempts to find continuities and connections between modernism and postmodernism. A comprehensive survey of the past century of
fiction and close readings of specific novels are at the core of this work,
which also contains discussions of more than a hundred major and minor
novelists, including a chapter about postmodern authors: "Postmodernisms
of English Fiction." This section is written by Adrzej Gasiorek, a reader
in twentieth-century literature at the University of Birmingham. Other
potential chapters of interest consider detective novels, multiculturalism,
transnationalism, and satire. There is a chronology that begins in 1900 and
ends in 2007, as well as further readings.

The Post-War British Literature Handbook provides a wealth of important information, starting with an introduction that touches on the concepts
of postwar, postcolonial, postmodern, postfeminist, posthuman, and post-
9/11 issues. A detailed timeline lists literary, cultural, and historical events.
The main part of the book has four sections: contexts, case studies, critical
approaches, and mapping the field. Part 1 covers historical, literary, and
cultural contexts. Part 2 consists of case studies on reading literary texts and
reading critical/theoretical texts. Part 3 describes key critics and theorists,
as well as essential concepts and topics. Part 4 discusses issues of gender
and sexuality, changes in the canon, and the current critical landscape. The

end of the book features an appendix of teaching plans, an annotated bibliography, and references. This handbook offers a reliable overview of the state of postwar British literature.

The second edition of *Modern British Literature*, a three-volume set published by St. James Press, is significantly expanded from the first edition and covers writers from England, Ireland, Scotland, and Wales. Organized in alphabetical order across the volumes, each entry consists of excerpts of reviews and criticism about the author and his or her works (along with brief citations), which offers a good sense of the reception the author has experienced over time. Since some modern authors might not have as much written about them compared to more established writers from earlier eras, this source can help researchers track down important, and sometimes scarce, resources relevant to their study. Since it was published in 2000, more recent criticism or reviews will not be covered, though chapter 6 of this book describes methods to find newer reviews for those who require these sources. Each entry finishes with a bibliography of the author's works along with the year it was published.

The Cambridge Companion to Twentieth-Century British and Irish Women's Poetry discusses both well-known and obscure poets, such as Sylvia Plath, Carol Ann Duffy, Anne Stevenson, and Edith Sitwell. The companion begins with a chronology and an introduction written by the editor and concludes with a selected reading list that includes poetry anthologies, critical works, and special magazine editions of women's poetry. Individual chapters cover a variety of topics: "Post/Modernist Rhythms and Voices," "Verbal and Visual Art in Twentieth-Century British Women's Poetry," and "The Irish History Wars and Irish Women's Poetry." Using the index will lead you to eight references for postmodernism.

A Companion to the British and Irish Novel 1945–2000, part of the Blackwell Companions to Literature and Culture series, is divided into two parts, with the first focusing on contexts (chapters on dystopian satire, the feminist novel, postcolonial novels, and postmodern fiction's relationship to critical theory) and the second part examining readings of individual texts and authors. Many of those featured are postmodernists, including William Golding, Iris Murdoch, Doris Lessing, John Fowles, Angela Carter, Julian Barnes, and more. The chapters in this book are good models of the kind of criticism and analysis written about British authors of this time period. Each article ends with references and further readings.

Entries in *The Oxford Companion to Twentieth-Century Literature in English* are short but numerous, covering all English-speaking countries and providing entries for novelists, dramatists, poets, critics, scholars, and journalists, as well as individual works, genres, critical concepts, literary groups, and movements. Examples of relevant entries are Martin Amis, cultural materialism, *The Golden Notebook*, Ted Hughes, popular culture, and postmodernism. Of special interest is the appendix at the end for literary prizes, which includes the Booker McConnell Prize for Fiction, Nobel Prize for Literature, and Pulitzer Prizes for fiction in book form, plays, and poetry, because these lists could help generate a reading list for someone interested in the noteworthy works of fiction of the twentieth century. Libraries with an online subscription to Oxford Reference Online might have access through this platform.

CHRONOLOGIES

Cahalan, James M. *Modern Irish Literature and Culture: A Chronology*. New
    York: G. K. Hall, 1993.
Cox, Michael. *The Oxford Chronology of English Literature*. 2 volumes. New
    York: Oxford University Press, 2002.

The main purpose of a chronology of literature is to help a researcher learn when a particular text was published and to put that work in context with others published at the same time, but it can also be utilized to get a sense of the kinds of publications to appear in a given year. In addition to books devoted to chronologies, you will also find chronologies in many reference works, such as the Cambridge Companions discussed in this chapter. If you are trying to find the dates for more recent publications, you might need to consult online resources. For instance, author and publisher websites can have relevant information, which are covered in chapter 11.

James M. Cahalan's ***Modern Irish Literature and Culture: A Chronology*** aims to relate literature to Irish history and society and can be used to gain a greater understanding of Irish fiction, nonfiction, and poetry from 1601 to 1992. The book is arranged by year, and entries are grouped under years by topics and genres. Drama, Irish language and literature, music, poetry, and prose nonfiction are examples of some of the subjects you will find. Information about various texts and authors are provided, along with details about important events. In addition to the chronology, there is a section in the beginning of the book called "Biographical Sketches of Recurrent Figures," which features famous authors like Samuel Beckett, James Joyce, and George Bernard Shaw. A section on secondary works cited and an index finish the work. Using the index reveals references to several postmodern Irish authors, such as John Banville, Neil Jordan, and Flann O'Brien.

One of the most valuable chronologies is *The Oxford Chronology of English Literature*, edited by Michael Cox. This chronology lists literary achievements from 1474 to 2000 and has entries for approximately thirty thousand texts, including fiction, poetry, dramatic works, biographies, criticism, historical and literary scholarship, and reference works. The main focus of the chronology is literature written in English by British authors, but some works from foreign-born authors who spent much of their career in Britain are present, along with those who lived in the British colonies during the colonial period. Entries in volume 1 are listed by year of publication and then alphabetically by the author's last name. If an author published more than one work in a year, the titles are itemized alphabetically. Most entries describe the author's date of birth, the title, title-page matter, imprint details, and notes about items, like serialization details, the illustrator, dates of other editions, contextual information, and cross-references. An abbreviation to the left of the entry will explain if the work is fiction, verse, drama, or another kind of resource (see the abbreviations guide for a complete list). Volume 2 contains the abbreviations guide, an author index, a title index, and an index of translated writers. Using the author index reveals that titles by postmodern British authors, such as Anthony Burgess, Zadie Smith, John Osborne, and Philip Larkin, are included.

BIOGRAPHICAL SOURCES

The Dictionary of Literary Biography. Detroit: Gale, 1978–.
Janik, Vicki K., Del I. Janik, and Emmanuel S. Nelson, eds. *Modern British Women Writers: An A-to-Z Guide*. Westport, CT: Greenwood Press, 2002.
Matthew, H. C. G., and Brian H. Harrison, eds. *Oxford Dictionary of National Biography: In Association with the British Academy: From the Earliest Times to the Year 2000*. Revised edition. 60 volumes. New York: Oxford University Press, 2004.
———. *Oxford Dictionary of National Biography*. Oxford: Oxford University Press, 2004. www.oxforddnb.com.
McCaffery, Larry, ed. *Postmodern Fiction: A Bio-Bibliographical Guide*. New York: Greenwood Press, 1986.

Biographical information about postmodernist authors might be limited since many are still alive. Still, when it is possible, learning more about an author's life will help a researcher gain a greater understanding of his or her literary inspirations. Other sources listed in this chapter might also have biographical information, but here the sources are exclusively concerned about the lives of the authors.

The Dictionary of Literary Biography (*DLB*), which began in 1978 and now comprises over 375 volumes, is an essential source for literary scholars, offering biographical and historical information about authors from many time periods, national literatures, and genres. Though the series covers some international writers, the focus tends to be on British and American authors.

Author entries consist of a detailed list of publications, separated into formats, including books, plays, or scripts, a biographical essay, bibliographical information, cross-references, and a "see also" section that will refer to other volumes where an author might appear. The biographical essay discusses the author's life and career, has critical appraisals of selected works, gives some assessment of his or her reputation and influence, and provides excellent illustrations and photographs. Some appendixes have further readings, critical reviews, interviews from newspapers and journals, and chronologies, which are very valuable for researchers. The newest volume of the *DLB* will always have the current cumulative index.

Researchers interested in British postmodern literature will find the following sampling of volumes useful: volume 310, *British and Irish Dramatists since World War II* (fourth series), examines playwrights like Caryl Churchill and Harold Pinter, while volume 326, *Booker Prize Novels 1969–2005*, discusses postmodern authors who have won the Booker Prize. For instance, the entry for *The Sea, the Sea* by Iris Murdoch focuses mainly on that novel, but also looks at her life and other works as they are related to the book.

The online edition of the *DLB* allows for searching by fields, such as author, title, subject, ethnicity, nationality, year of birth or death, and full text. The electronic version is regularly updated, though some versions of the online editions might not show every illustration found in the corresponding print volume. Access depends on a library subscription.

One example of a specialized biographical and critical reference source is *Modern British Women Writers: An A-to-Z Guide*, which discusses writers belonging to a specific social group and is centered on gender, sexuality, ethnicity, or other categories not always fully represented in reference sources. The fifty-eight women featured in this guide are either modernists or postmodernists. Those born in England are primarily represented, though it does have some women writers from the former colonies. Each entry starts with a brief biography and then proceeds to background, analysis, assessment, and bibliographies with both primary sources and secondary sources. The guide concludes with a selected bibliography that lists more general titles for a researcher to pursue.

The *Oxford Dictionary of National Biography* has over fifty thousand biographical entries about individuals connected to the history of the British Isles from the fourth century to the twentieth century, from a variety of professions, such as artists, scientists, writers, industrialists, performers, explorers, criminals, politicians, church leaders, soldiers, mariners, doctors, and lawyers. Entries are arranged alphabetically and give an overview of a person's "activities, character, and significance," as well as an assessment of the person's reputation since his or her death. Factual information listed in the entries are full birth name and any name changes; dates and places of birth, baptism, marriage(s), death, and burial; and information about family members, such a names, dates, and occupations for more well-known family members. Depending on the amount of information known, entries can vary from short snippets to full scholarly essays. Each is signed by the contributor and provides primary and secondary sources. When available, information about archives, artists, and galleries responsible for portraits of the individual will be cited. Only biographies of people who have been deceased since 2000 are eligible for inclusion, so there will be a limit to the number of postmodern authors available. Still, the *Oxford Dictionary of National Biography* is a definitive source and should be consulted when possible.

The online version of the *Oxford Dictionary of National Biography*, updated three times a year, has biographies of people who have been deceased since 2008, so it will be more relevant than the print version for research about postmodern authors, and the texts have hyperlinks to articles about people related to the person featured in the entry. External links to sources such as the National Portrait Gallery, National Registry of Archives, and Royal Historical Society Bibliography are another important feature. Strong search options are also a significant improvement over the print resource. While the default "quick search" will perform a standard keyword query, the "people" search option will enable you to look by fields of interest, sex, dates spanning the person's life, places, life events, religious denominations, and keywords appearing throughout the essay. These options allow you to compile lists of people who might have been linked to one another, like those with similar professions alive at the same time period. You can also browse by themes and groups, such as "Angry Young Men (act. 1956–1958)," "British New Wave (act. 1959–1963)," and "Theatre Workshop (act. 1945–1973)."

Postmodern Fiction: A Bio-Bibliographical Guide is somewhat dated, though it is still a reliable source about authors associated with postmodern fiction. The guide is part of Greenwood Press's Movements in the Arts series and consists of two sections. The first part has overview articles about topics related to postmodern fiction, including experimental realism and metafiction. Each of these articles ends with notes and a selected bibliography, which includes primary and secondary sources. The second part alphabetically item-izes authors and critics of postmodern fiction. Each author entry comprises a brief biography and analysis of the writer's work followed by a selected bibliography of primary and secondary sources. British authors (John Fowles, J. G. Ballard, and more) are part of this guide. A selected bibliography of postmodern criticism and an index round out the end of the book.

INDIVIDUAL AUTHOR SOURCES

Aubrey, James R. *John Fowles: A Reference Companion*. New York: Green-wood Press, 1991.
Begnal, Kate. *Iris Murdoch: A Reference Guide*. Boston: G. K. Hall, 1987.
Gifford, Terry, ed. *The Cambridge Companion to Ted Hughes*. New York: Cambridge University Press, 2011.

Finding reference sources for individual postmodern authors can be especially challenging since many of them are still alive and writing, and these types of reference works are not being published as frequently as they were in the past. Usually, these reference works are written about authors who are firmly established in the canon and have a broad critical following, and they can be very useful when they do exist because they identify scholarship that has been done about an individual author, as well as primary sources. Searching WorldCat for companions, bibliographies, and encyclopedias about an author is a good way to start. Your searches might be constructed like these: *Ian McEwan* AND *companion*, *Ian McEwan* AND *bibliography*, or *Ian McEwan* AND *guide*. The following three titles are just a sample of those available.

Books such as ***John Fowles: A Reference Companion*** often provide not just lists of resources but also background information, an overview of an author's life, and the reception of his or her work. This particular companion starts with the life of John Fowles, followed by information about both his nonfiction and fiction texts. The fiction section, in which individual creations are examined, offers information on how it was composed, a summary, in-terpretations, receptions, and adaptations. Next you will find discussions of the critical approaches to his fiction, and notes about the fiction itself, which gives page numbers and explanations about historical figures and works to which Fowles refers. An appendix, which contains a census of characters, and a bibliography finish the book.

Iris Murdoch: A Reference Guide, part of a series called A Reference Guide to Literature, is an annotated bibliography, with two parts: "Writings by Iris Murdoch" and "Writings about Iris Murdoch, 1953–1983." Of course, newer criticism is still being written about Murdoch, but this thorough book guides the reader through the foundational approaches taken in the criticism about her literary output. The primary writings section consists of her philosophy, fiction, drama, and verse, with dates of the first editions, but no archival information. The secondary works section is organized by years and has books, critical articles, dissertations, and reviews, and annotations are often brief, though they do give a clear idea of the concepts addressed.

A good example of the Cambridge Companion to Authors series, which is especially illuminating because of the focus on one author in each volume, is *The Cambridge Companion to Ted Hughes*. A chronology that spans from 1930 to 2011 opens the work, followed by chapters with biographical information and details about the critical debates surrounding Ted Hughes. Other chapters examine specific aspects of his writing, like "Hughes's Social Ecology" and "Hughes and His Critics." The book ends with a guide to further reading, which itemizes both primary materials (books, uncollected essays, and recordings) and secondary works (biographical titles, bibliographical works, websites, reviews of criticism, critical studies, collections of critical essays, articles, and essays and chapters in books).

CONCLUSION

The resources listed in this chapter are meant to be basic tools to aid you in planning your research or confirming factual information. Many of these will offer in-depth information and context, but they will not have all the information you might need. Consulting more than one source in order to obtain a thorough overview of the topic is often wise. You might want to double-check a fact or a date in multiple sources, or you might want to consult several different points of view to help form your own arguments. Both older and newer reference works can be beneficial since more recent sources will often deliver the most current information, while longer-standing works might cover older historical periods that are still relevant. Throughout this book you will discover other print and electronic resources that will expand your research, and you will learn about search strategies to uncover reference titles that are not covered here. The sources discussed in this chapter will act as your starting point and should help you understand what to expect when you pick up or log in to a reference work.

Chapter Three

Library Catalogs

Library catalogs, a vital tool for research in the humanities, contain information about all of the items available to a scholar at his or her local library, in the same region, or across a nation. When thinking of catalogs, there is a natural tendency to consider only print materials physically located in the library building, but increasingly, they contain access to electronic resources and even information available freely on the web. As resources continue their transition to electronic media, the nature of the catalog will become more fluid, allowing users to explore seamlessly across databases and print holdings. Some universities already offer this capability through high-powered discovery tools that combine all of the library's search platforms into one interface.

These advances are important as we discuss the function of the library catalog. Though discovery tools have only existed for a few years, they are rapidly growing in popularity and are likely to become the primary method of accessing a library's collection over the next decade. A discovery tool is a system that allows searching through indexed content housed on many different platforms, both local and remote. This means that a user can type terms in a single box on a library homepage to retrieve items from the local collection, research databases, digital archives, and other designated targets. There are many different types of discovery tools. Common ones are Summon, EBSCO Discovery, and Primo. Though it is easy to focus on the differences between them, and the changes that they bring for those accustomed to traditional catalogs, remember that most library resources are based on the same fundamental building block, discussed in chapter 1: item records indexed with controlled vocabulary. Catalog records are fully searchable using a discovery tool, as are indexed articles and other resources. These records will come from a central database provided by the publisher. The tool might also contain records from major literary indexes to which your library has access, such as with EBSCO Discovery. These indexes are discussed further in chapter 4. The strength of these tools is that they retrieve a diverse array of resources. With a well-crafted and precise query so that good results do not get buried under bad ones, this powerful means of retrieval can be harnessed to ensure more comprehensive results.

Another advance to keep in mind as we discuss library catalogs is the rise of the ebook. Most libraries now have ebook content searchable in the catalog or through a discovery tool. As a result, when looking at a catalog record, you will need to pay extra attention to how the resource is made available. Additionally, there are many advanced options for finding ebooks in databases of origin, such as EBSCO eBook and ebrary. By querying the full text of the library's ebook databases, smaller sections not searchable in catalogs can be identified, which is particularly helpful for rare material that might be difficult to find otherwise. For instance, searching for *Roald Dahl* in ebrary will retrieve hundreds of results. Though some of them will only mention the author once, some will have several paragraphs of information not noted in a catalog record. Significantly, discovery tools often search the full text of ebooks available through the library, which is another way they can save time compared to the more traditional catalog.

In a decade or two, advances in discovery systems and the availability of online content might make more traditional library catalogs seem as out of date and archaic as card catalogs are today. However, there are some fundamental concepts that will probably continue to inform the way we think about catalog searches, which we will cover throughout this chapter. These concepts form the basis for cataloging in MARC (machine-readable cataloging record) and other metadata standards, which determine how users can search and what they are expected to retrieve. Though MARC (discussed in chapter 1) will likely adapt to new technological frameworks, the same principles should apply to the basic record at the core of any catalog. Even in discovery systems, MARC records, and other descriptive entries, are one of the primary access points to a library's holdings.

When an item is cataloged, the information is standardized with controlled vocabularies so that it is generally consistent with the data in all other records for the same item, author, subject, and so forth. As defined in chapter 1, a controlled vocabulary is a formalized glossary of terms authorized to define a concept or entity in a specified context. Controlled vocabularies exist across many types of resources, but, in catalogs, this term often refers to subject headings, which are assigned by catalogers. Studies of British postmodern literature could be represented by subject headings such as "English literature--20th century," "Postmodern," "Postmodernism (Literature)," and "Novelists, English-

-20th century." These headings are a type of authority record, the controlled vocabulary that defines the authorized format of a concept, event, person's name, title, or place name in cataloging. The authorized format is generally the most effective way to locate an item. Because these are predetermined category labels that identify the term the computer recognizes to represent that group of resources, researchers who use this language to search will be more successful. For example, most scholarship about cinema is categorized by the controlled vocabulary terms *motion pictures* and *films*. If you were to search for *motion pictures* or *films* instead of *movies*, you would have better luck retrieving resources, because cinema will be categorized using these terms.

When items are cataloged, they are also classified with a system of numbers and letters that allow users to find materials. Most academic institutions classify material using Library of Congress (LC) call numbers. The Dewey Decimal System is more common in school and public libraries. Familiarizing yourself with these classification systems will aid in research because they facilitate browsing. PR is the call number range specific to British literature. Within this range, PR6050–PR6076 and PR6100–PR6126 will be the most useful because they contain primary literature and author studies for 1961–2000 and 2001 forward, respectively. More general studies of literary periods can be found in PR471–PR479 for twentieth-century literature and PR481–PR488 for twenty-first-century literature. Usually, each author will have an exact range assigned to his or her work and related studies. Browsing these call numbers is an efficient way to identify materials linked to a topic that might not otherwise get consideration. Because books are grouped by subject, similar items should appear in close proximity to the resources identified through the catalog. Computerized queries are often just a starting place. The tried-and-true method of using the catalog as a beginning point and then browsing in the physical library remains an important research skill, though ebooks are beginning to change this since an ebook cannot be browsed in this way. Luckily, many library catalogs will now allow users to browse holdings by call number. This can be achieved through a browsing option in a catalog or a call number search option. One benefit of browsing items electronically is that ebooks, books that are checked out, books in restricted collections, and other special items not located near one another are represented.

When querying a library catalog, the information contained in records is the focus. This can encompass subjects, book summaries, tables of contents, and other pertinent facts, in addition to authors, titles, and dates. A basic search, the default in most catalogs, combs through predetermined fields in the record that the library has indicated should be queried; to review the concept of a field, look back to chapter 1. Often, these are the author, subject, title, and table of contents, though some scan the whole record rather than this subset.

Keyword searches are probably the most familiar. You likely practice this every day to retrieve items using Internet search engines. Because these are so familiar, many people believe that they are the easiest way to find information, but this type of query is not effective without the right terms, which are sometimes difficult to determine. Keyword searching is discussed in more depth in chapter 1, but a few recommendations can be made for library catalogs. Because catalogs contain primarily books and journals, not articles, starting with broader terms is useful. For instance, begin with *postmodern* or *postmodernism*, or use truncation to retrieve multiple variants of the word, *postmodern**. Truncation, discussed more in chapter 1, is particularly useful with words such as this, which can have multiple permutations. Add to these *Britain* or *British* with the Boolean operator AND. Keep in mind that *British* will retrieve more resources than *Britain*, because many books use *British* as a modifier in front of various types of writing, for instance, women's novels or war poetry. Add a word to the terms to narrow the focus. If works about postcolonialism are the aim, try *postmodern**, *British*, and *postcolonial**, again using truncation. For the most effective results, "mix and match" terms, testing out which searches are productive. When research is related to specific authors or titles, use quotation marks to keep the author's first and last name together or to keep the words in a title next to one another, such as *"Zadie Smith"* or *"On Beauty."*

Though many might not notice the default search a library is using, this detail will determine the accuracy of a query. Because researchers are more familiar with web browsers, where keywords govern what is returned no matter where a term is located in the document, *what* data you search is often overlooked. Web browsers search the Internet and give few advanced options. Catalogs, on the other hand, search highly structured data and easily query only specified categories. As a result, *what* you look for in a catalog is just as important as the words used, and this requires some attention before moving into author, subject, and title categories. Catalogs allow the creation of complex inquiries through field searching, which give an accurate definition of what gets included. Field searching is available through advanced options in most cases. With this type of query, separate filters are applicable to different terms. For instance, specifying that you want to search for the words *White Teeth* in the title field and *Zadie Smith* in the author field, as in figure 3.1. In this example, data in the title field of the record is surveyed for one set of keywords, and data in the author field for another, which will retrieve fewer, more accurate results.

Most catalogs also allow refining a request using other types of search limiters. As illustrated in figure 3.2, results can be restricted by publication year, format, library, or language. Specifying how results are sorted might also save researchers time sifting through pages of extraneous sources. Commonly, sorting options will consist of relevance, title, author, or publication date.

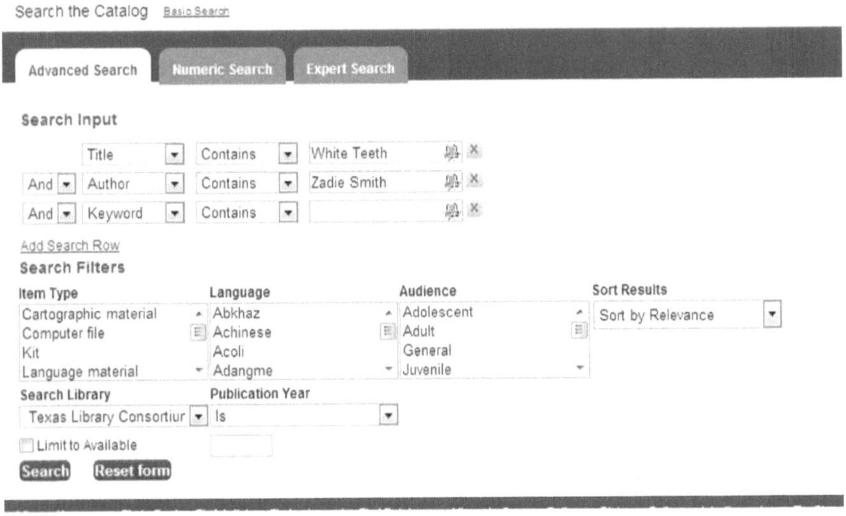

Figure 3.1. **Advanced Search by Title and Author for White Teeth by Zadie Smith.**
TAMUCT WarriorCat.

Once limiters and search categories are chosen, think about what terms will be beneficial. The most helpful inquiries in the humanities are often for authors, titles, or subjects. Each of these are complex, and understanding their nuances can aid humanities scholars immensely.

AUTHOR SEARCH

Author searches used to be more difficult than they are today. Contemporary researchers will find that library online catalogs have evolved significantly in their capabilities over the past few years. The syntax of the words is often no longer significant, while in the past, a last name followed by first name was

Figure 3.2. **Catalog Search Limiters.**
TAMUCT WarriorCat.

required. Still, spelling the author's name wrong or using a version of the last name not found in library records will lead to a browse screen created from the author index in older catalogs, which will be in alphabetical order by last name. As a result, last name first is still the best practice when looking for an author.

Author names that appear in library catalogs are defined by LC authority records. The authorized name for many postmodern authors is fairly intuitive, because they are still living. Since the authorized version of the name under which they write should be readily available from their publisher, this cuts down on variant spellings. As a result, simply putting the last and first name in an author field search is frequently enough to retrieve all of the library's holdings for a specified writer.

Works in anthologies might or might not be found by doing this simple search, so experimenting with the catalog to figure out if contributing authors are listed in records and can be retrieved through the author field will be beneficial. A keyword search is valuable because it will usually query the table of contents in addition to the author field. If you still do not discover works by the author, or you do not find everything you expect, also try searching for just the writer's last name. Although this works in cases where the name is relatively unique, for instance, Salman Rushdie, it will not work for authors with common last names, such as Zadie Smith.

For cases where the author has a common last name, look for a well-known book by that writer using a title search. Somewhere in the record for that book there should be a linked version of the authorized name for the writer, as seen in figure 3.3 for Anthony Burgess. By clicking on this link, most of the items in the library's catalog written primarily by this author will appear. If a catalog includes contributing author tags, or information in the catalog record about different individuals who have written parts of a larger book, anthological works are retrieved in addition to monographs. When these links are not available, at least the version of the name given in the catalog record is available for future queries, because this is the name all records for this author should have, with some notable exceptions; if an author has frequently written under a pseudonym that is shared with other writers, or has written anonymously, these records might not be retrieved.

Author search strategies become more complicated when pseudonymous names are a factor. For instance, Julian Barnes has penned many crime novels under the pseudonym Dan Kavanagh and wrote briefly under the name Edward Pygge in a literary review, a pseudonym famously shared with several of his literary contemporaries. This represents two problems one might face with postmodern author searches: a famous pen name and a shared one. A catalog will not generally provide a "see also" cross-reference for either of these pseudonyms.

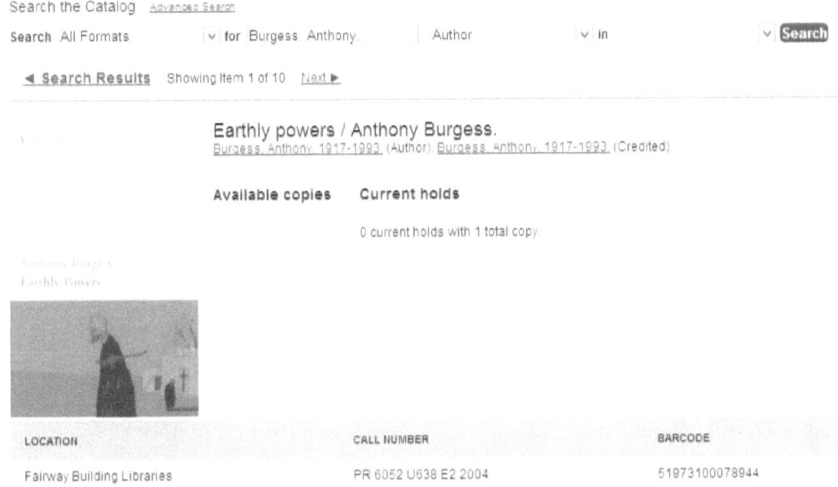

Search the Catalog   Advanced Search

Search All Formats   ∨ for Burgess, Anthony.   Author   ∨ in   ∨ **Search**

◄ **Search Results**   Showing Item 1 of 10   Next ►

Earthly powers / Anthony Burgess.
Burgess, Anthony, 1917–1993. (Author) Burgess, Anthony, 1917–1993. (Credited)

Available copies   **Current holds**

0 current holds with 1 total copy.

LOCATION	CALL NUMBER	BARCODE
Fairway Building Libraries	PR 6052 U638 E2 2004	51973100078944

Figure 3.3. Author Search with Author Links Displayed.
TAMUCT WarriorCat.

Julian Barnes is unusual because he is relatively well known as an author using both his pen name and his given name. More common are authors who are best known for their pseudonyms, like Anthony Burgess, born John Anthony Burgess Wilson; James Herriot, the pen name of John Alfred Wight; or Alice Ellis, Anna Haycraft's pseudonym. In cases where the pseudonym is the most likely name that a researcher would use to find an author, it is probably used to catalog the writing of that person, instead of the given name.

Conversely, in cases where both a pseudonym and the person's given name are famous for separate works, researchers must locate the author under both terms. Because postmodern authors are, in many cases, still publishing, the name authority record for both is retained, so that people can find items using the name best known for that title. Ruth Rendell (Babara Vine) and Peter Berresford Ellis (Peter Tremayne and Peter MacAlan) are examples of authors who have successful current publishing careers under two names, with authority records existing for both. Another complicated situation is a shared pseudonym. Edward Pygge, for instance, was a pseudonym shared by several people, including Barnes. A simple "see also" cross reference would not be appropriate because Barnes is not the only author who wrote with this persona, although he is certainly connected to it. The pseudonymous Pygge has its own authority record because this persona is a unique conglomerate, not a single person. In all of these cases, finding the author's authority record is an important step that clarifies the relationship between various appellations by recommending that the scholar "search also." This information would not be provided through a simple catalog search. LC name authority records are available for free online through the LC Linked Data Service (id.loc.gov). This database is used to find names, titles, and subject headings authorities.

TITLE SEARCH

Title searches in library catalogs are also fairly easy because of advances in the way they work. Some catalogs will find main titles for items, as well as names of sources in anthologies and series. Others will only retrieve main titles, and a keyword search for items in anthologies or a series title query for a specific grouping of resources is also required. As with all the examples listed here, knowing the catalog will enable a determination about how information is being retrieved.

Before beginning a title search, you might want to identify the highest-quality edition of the work available. Usually, when literary scholars think about finding the standard edition of a text, they think of books printed hundreds of years ago, when variant forms were more common and printing practice ensured that one run was different from the next. Though postmodern scholars do not face the same problems, thinking about the edition is still important. Authors might reissue a work with changes, or might correct mistakes in an original version. The Internet also makes pirating a bigger consideration now than it was forty years ago, especially for well-liked titles. Consider the wildly popular Harry Potter series, which produced hundreds of knockoffs on the Internet preceding the publication of the seventh installment of the series. Authors might also publish some part of a book online before it is edited. Another factor to think about is government or publisher censorship. Burgess's *A Clockwork Orange* was originally released in the United States without chapter 21, at the request of the publisher. The omission or inclusion of this chapter greatly changes the way the reader might interpret the work. This is one example of how the American edition of a book might vary from the British edition, though there might be smaller differences. For instance, spellings might be dissimilar or even words, like lorry used instead of truck or lift instead of elevator. The British edition might be difficult to understand for some American readers, but it might be truer to what the author actually wrote. For all of these reasons, the edition is pivotal.

When picking the edition, figure out which version of the book is considered standard among scholars and if the differences between various published instances are substantial. For older works, scholarly editions created after a serious study of the title's transmission history are preferred because they provide all of this information and give the reader a reliable copy of the text. However, the vast majority of postmodern titles will not be old enough or canonical enough to warrant this type of study. As a result, scholars must identify the best version for themselves. This can be done by looking at what others choose. If the standard edition is not readily identifiable, the first edition, first printing is generally a good default. The author or the publisher website is also an invaluable tool because often the writer will note if there were substantial changes between forms.

Once an edition is picked, you can move on to a title search. Though title searches are often fairly simple, some, like series titles, might be more problematic. Book series are common in postmodern fiction and can be found using most catalogs. Many allow series names to be located with the standard title query, though some might require a special advanced option. All of the titles in Doris Lessing's Children of Violence series could be retrieved by one of these title searches, for instance, though the series name is quite general. Adding another field to reflect that Lessing is the author would further limit it. This can be beneficial when the series contains many books that are unfamiliar, though trying it with only official series titles is important. For example, Roddy Doyle's novels *The Commitments*, *The Snapper*, and *The Van* are often referred to as the Barrytown Trilogy, but because this is a nickname, it should not be used in a title search. Verifying the official series name is pivotal.

One problem researchers might discover related to the international nature of contemporary publishing is the prevalence of books being printed under variant titles in different countries. Knowing how versions of a book vary from country to country can be quite important. This is particularly common in the past fifty years due to cultural, political, or social mores that drive publishing-industry decisions. Title searching in a local library catalog is complicated by this phenomenon because an academic library could easily own either edition. The book could be famous under the British title but purchased with the American one. An example of this is Ted Hughes's *The Iron Man*, which was released in the United States as *The Iron Giant* in order to avoid confusion with the comic book character. This can happen even with series titles. For example, Michael Carroll's New Heroes series has a different name in the United States, Quantum Prophecy. Checking the publication place in library catalog records can keep researchers apprised of the version they are using.

Finding translations of British writers is also an important skill. The rise of the web and globalization have turned many authors into international figures. Doris Lessing, Salman Rushdie, Ian McEwan, Emma Donoghue, and others have been translated into French, Spanish, German, Japanese, and a host of additional languages. To find translations, querying the author's name and choosing the language of interest in an advanced catalog search is often an option. This bypasses the need to do a title search. Some catalogs will seek the title in English with a different language specified for the item. These catalogs will retrieve the translated edition in the specified language using the English title. If a catalog does not function in this way, or if the title of a novel in another language beyond this type of search is required, use WorldCat, discussed later in this chapter. WorldCat will help identify the foreign title, because it allows use of the English name with a separate language limiter. Looking in national catalogs for France (catalogue.bnf.fr), Germany (www.dnb.de), and other countries to find more editions of translated books is another strategy. You might also simply look at the author's website, if there is one. Usually it will list the editions of the author's work in English and in other languages. Many scholars doing reception histories for novels, or who study the various editions of an author's work, must find these translations because they represent a different view than is available in the English version. Often, translations are an interpretation in their own right, since they are generally not created by the author.

Researchers need to consider all the avenues when performing title searches and cannot make simple assumptions about the pedigree of materials with which they are working. *Dr. Strangelove or: How I Learned to Stop Worrying and Love the Bomb* is a good example of a work that has a publication history which might complicate a title search because the material moved between media in unique ways. The movie was based on the book *Red Alert* by the British author Peter George, which was originally released as *Two Hours to Doom* in the United Kingdom under the name Peter Bryant. The novel was re-released under the title *Dr. Strangelove* after the movie was released, with a byline stating that it was derived from the movie, rather than the other way around. This example shows how knowing a little about the publication history for a novel, and particularly as it relates to the title, can help ensure that the right edition of the book or movie is received. If the history of this title was unknown, it would be difficult to make sure all pertinent material related to it were found. During the postmodern era, creative works can move between media in strange and sometimes confusing ways, which often leads to new or altered titles.

Once the item is located in a local catalog, the authoritative title and the edition of the book is identifiable by looking at its MARC record, if the information is not displayed in the initial entry. As is evident in figure 3.4, the 245 field contains the title, subtitle, and author. The 250 field indicates the edition. Use this information to make sure the right edition is found and to help search for other versions with the correct title.

```
050 0 0  ‡a PR6023.E833  ‡b G69 2003
082 0 0  ‡a 823/.914  ‡2 22
100 1    ‡a Lessing, Doris May,  ‡d 1919-
240 1 0  ‡a Novels.  ‡k Selections
245 1 4  ‡a The grandmothers :  ‡b four short novels /  ‡c Doris Lessing.
250      ‡a 1st U.S. ed.
260      ‡a New York :  ‡b HarperCollins Publishers,  ‡c 2003.
300      ‡a 311 p. ;  ‡c 24 cm.
505 0 0  ‡t The grandmothers --  ‡t Victoria and the Staveneys --  ‡t The reason for it --  ‡t A love child.
520      ‡a Presents four short novels by award-winning author Doris Lessing, featuring the title work about two wom
         Child."
650    0 ‡a Short stories, English.
856 4 2  ‡3 Publisher description  ‡u http://catdir.loc.gov/catdir/description/hc041/2003056990.html
938      ‡a Baker & Taylor  ‡b BKTY  ‡c 23.95  ‡d 17.96  ‡i 0060530103  ‡n 0004306608  ‡s active
938      ‡a Baker & Taylor  ‡b BKTY  ‡c 13.95  ‡d 10.46  ‡i 0060530111  ‡n 0004358210  ‡s active
938      ‡a Baker and Taylor  ‡b BTCP  ‡n 2003056990
938      ‡a YBP Library Services  ‡b YANK  ‡n 2010988
```

Figure 3.4. MARC Record for Doris Lessing's The Grandmothers: Four Short Novels.
TAMUCT WarriorCat.

Though title searches are frequently straightforward, avoiding easy assumptions about the origins of works can help make retrieval more accurate. Derivative works, items moving between media, and other similar phenomena characterize globalization and the rise of new technology during this period. As a result, attention to publication history is important. The LC title authority databases can help researchers find the right item, though a keyword search in the authority database is usually the most successful strategy. If a title cannot be found elsewhere, this database is recommended as a starting place.

SUBJECT SEARCHES

Subject headings should be identified early in any research project. They are helpful when moving between catalogs because they are the same at all libraries that have the LC system. You can start by identifying the subjects, and then using them to complete initial enquiries, or let research interests dictate the categories that are relevant by drawing subjects from works already found. Either way, they are a powerful means of detecting many books about the same topic accurately and quickly.

Searches using subjects are one of the most efficient queries researchers can perform in a catalog. Most libraries use the LC subject headings as their controlled vocabulary for organizing materials by topic. When performing a subject search in a catalog, most of the items that have been assigned to that category are retrieved. This is important, particularly when concepts have multiple words that could accurately describe them. For instance, when looking for books about women in postmodernism, *women, females,* or *gen-*

der might be employed, retrieving different results each time. By searching within the subject heading "Women in literature," with the truncated keyword *postmodern**, all of the item records in the catalog that contain the word *postmodern*, or its variants, and are assigned to the category "Women in literature" are retrieved, even if the author uses gender or females to describe this phenomenon. "In literature" is frequently applied in conjunction with other terms to describe how a group, concept, or object is depicted in fiction. Similarly, "in motion pictures" refers to topics in film, and "in the arts" can denote artistic topics more broadly.

Headings might be found with several different methods. The easiest way is to do a simple keyword search for a topic, and then click on a link for a subject heading contained in the records for the most appropriate resources retrieved. Usually, the subject headings are located next to the word *subject*, and often they appear as a link, which will find everything else assigned to that category. One caution, however: be wary of subject headings that are overly general. Remember that the broader a search, the more material to wade through to discover the essential scholarship. If this is not successful, a keyword search for subject headings in the Linked Data Service, a database of authoritative words for describing library items from the Library of Congress, is another method. A simple keyword search for *postmodernism* reveals over twenty subject headings. "English literature" is the most common, which can be made more specific to genre, such as "English fiction," "English drama," or "English poetry." Subject headings that refer to the author, but are related to the type of writing this artist does, are also quite common, for instance, "Novelists, English" or "Poets, English." Both of these types of subject headings are usually paired with a date range, such as "20th century."

Another subject heading related to British postmodernism is "Postmodernism (Literature)--Great Britain." This is a complex subject that limits the topic "Postmodernism (Literature)" regionally. One could also employ the general topic "Postmodernism (Literature)," or use the broader "Postmodernism (Literature)--English-speaking countries." The latter would retrieve books about postmodernism from the entire United Kingdom, but would also include the United States and all other English-speaking countries, which might make the search broader than one would like. "English literature--20th century" is also a possibility, though it is much more general. There is a subject heading for postmodern Irish literature, "Postmodernism (Literature)--Ireland," and "Canada" or "Australia" can be substituted as well. These searches will retrieve works about postmodernism in general, or as it is reflected in national literature.

Author subject headings will find scholarship written about a writer. As with author searches, individuals who use pseudonyms or change their names while publishing can make finding everything about them difficult. Because criticism about postmodern literature has not had as much time to mature as other literary periods, finding everything written about an author is even more important. Missing one book might break a study, if it is one of only a few ever written. The easiest way to complete this search is with the writer's authorized name in a subject search. A subject search for *Rushdie, Salman* will retrieve almost everything written about him that the library owns. Also discussed in chapter 1, the subheading "Criticism AND interpretation" can limit a search by entering "Rushdie, Salman--Criticism and interpretation." The same can be achieved by similarly pairing the names of other authors with "Criticism AND interpretation." To more broadly find information about authors, employ the general subject headings mentioned above, "Novelists, English," "Poets, English," "Dramatists, English," and so forth, paired with "20th century" or "21st century."

Because postmodernism defines diverse critical and cultural movements, even more specific headings might be helpful. There is an LC subject heading that is simply "Postcolonialism," though this can also be paired with "in the arts," "in motion pictures," or "in literature." There is also a heading for "Semiotics," as well as one for "Semiotics and literature." Headings like "and the arts" or "and motion pictures" are also promising. They will retrieve semiotic studies of culture, one of the most important trends in postmodern literary analysis. Two different searches might be required to cover fully a topic with varying angles. For instance, the subject "Queer theory" will discover analysis that uses theory about sexuality to frame a discussion, but "Homosexuality in literature" retrieves criticism about gay, lesbian, bisexual, or transgender characters in literature.

Another tactic for retrieving works that base their analysis of literature on the approach of cultural theorists is to pair a subject search for the theorist's name with the keyword *literature*. For instance, *Derrida, Jacques* as the subject, and *literature* as the keyword, seen in figure 3.5.

Search Input

Figure 3.5.   Complex subject and keyword search.
TAMUCT WarriorCat.

This method also works for other difficult-to-define subjects. One instance might be pairing "Literature--Philosophy" or "English fiction--History and criticism--theory, etc." with a keyword, such as *deconstruction*. This can help limit what is retrieved from a general category without losing some of the precision of a subject search.

UNION CATALOGS

Copac National, Academic and Specialist Library Catalogue. Manchester: University of Manchester. copac.ac.uk.
WorldCat. Dublin, OH: OCLC. firstsearch.oclc.org.
WorldCat.org. Dublin, OH: OCLC. www.worldcat.org.

Now that we have discussed searching in the catalog, we should switch gears to talk about different types of catalogs. Of these, the union catalog is one of the most important. A union catalog is a resource that contains the holdings of more than one library. Union catalogs are invaluable for scholars as library budgets decrease, but the proportion of material about postmodern literature increases. Union catalogs can be employed in much the same way as other local catalogs, but they allow users to identify and locate copies of material not held by their home library. Once materials are identified, researchers can often borrow them through interlibrary loan agreements between own-ing libraries and their home organization. They might also be able to check out books with regional reciprocal lending programs that allow patrons from other libraries in the same city, state, county, parish, province, or other re-gional division to loan materials.

The most well-known union catalog in the United States is **WorldCat**, cre-ated by the Online Computer Library Center (OCLC). WorldCat is an online catalog produced collaboratively by libraries internationally in order to help librarians and patrons catalog resources, identify information, and gain access to materials. Approximately seventy-two thousand libraries are represented in WorldCat, with over two billion items. WorldCat contains records from librar-ies in 170 countries and territories in over 470 languages. Because of its size and scope, WorldCat is a powerful tool that can help locate a variety of material about a topic, including books, videos, articles, CDs, and archival materials.

We recommend using WorldCat's subscription interface if it is available through your home library. In addition to a basic keyword search, WorldCat offers an advanced option that allows searching of common fields like sub-ject, date, language, and title, as well as journal title, ISSN, ISBN, and World-Cat accession number (assigned when the item is added to the database).

Searching is available within one library, or many. The default ranking for WorldCat results is by number of owning libraries, so that those items owned by the most will appear first. For scholars, this ranking might not be efficient, because academic books are often not widely held outside of specialized research libraries. To get better results, change rankings by relevance based on the number of times keywords appear in proximity to one another, or by date published. When an item of interest is found, the record will look much like those of a local catalog, except that they will include a list of libraries that have the item. Your local library should be at the top if it owns the resource.

Because WorldCat contains records for thousands of libraries, limiting the search might be required. One way to do this is to choose the type of item from books, visual materials, computers files, Internet resources, serial publications, sound recordings, archival materials, articles, musical scores, and maps. WorldCat has multiple records for items because they are added by libraries worldwide, and cataloging might be different. When resources are found, the entry will be detailed and should provide a complete view of the bibliographic information for the item. Once this record is visible, advanced options to follow a hyperlink to similar works or other content related to the same author are available.

Despite the large number of items represented, remember that WorldCat is not an exhaustive resource. This catalog only contains records for resources uploaded by libraries who participate in the program. Extremely new materials or those that are rare, for instance, might not appear because a library has yet to catalog them. There is no single database that will retrieve everything about any topic.

Access to **WorldCat.org** is available through a public interface. WorldCat. org is not as exhaustive as the subscription WorldCat because many libraries have opted not to subscribe to the commercial version, and therefore their library holdings are not represented in the freely available database. Additionally, the public interface does not search using Boolean operators and other advanced techniques. The advanced search does give many options to define fields, such as author, ISBN, ISSN, and titles. Limiters for year, audience, content, format, and language are also available in advanced options. When completing a search in WorldCat.org, the results will be ranked by relevance rather than number of libraries. Findings can be narrowed in the results screen using facets. WorldCat.org provides some article-level retrieval for JSTOR, MEDLINE, ERIC, the British Library's Inside Serials, the GPO Monthly Catalogue, and the OCLC Article First database. Part of the MLA International Bibliography is also searchable in WorldCat.org.

Through WorldCat.org, OCLC offers a mobile app, and regularly allows patrons to test-drive new services currently under development, including visual search options, user tagging, or enhanced browsing. These types of programs are helpful because they allow bibliographic data to be viewed and manipulated in novel ways. Personal accounts can also be set up through WorldCat.org to allow users to tag items, make lists, and export citations for marked records into citation managers.

Copac National, Academic and Specialist Library Catalogue is useful for researchers who might need to find specialist or academic material from libraries in the United Kingdom or Ireland because it contains records for most of these. Some libraries might not have cataloged rare materials yet. Collections represented include the British Library, the British Museum, Oxford University, and Cambridge University. Copac is similar to WorldCat in that it contains records for many libraries across a specific geographic area, though Copac does not function as an interlibrary loan platform. The primary purpose is to show what member libraries own. Though WorldCat might also contain some of these records, items retrieved through Copac are generally unique. Featuring large research libraries and specialist libraries, Copac is aimed at scholars trying to find material that might not be available through a local library. Copac allows for searching in ways similar to WorldCat, with the addition of a map search that lets researchers find maps from a distinctive period for a geographic location. Information gained from Copac might be of special interest to those looking for British postmodern literature because British libraries tend to have a wider selection of newer novels. This might also help identify big collections of particular authors across the United Kingdom and Ireland. Copac might not contain all items from each library, so visiting the library's website is a good next step.

NATIONAL LIBRARY CATALOGS

British Library. British National Bibliography (BNB). London: British Library Board. bnb.bl.uk.
———. Explore the British Library. London: British Library Board. explore.bl.uk.
Library of Congress Online Catalog. Washington, DC: Library of Congress. catalog.loc.gov.
Llyfrgell Genedlaethol Cymru: The National Library of Wales. Ceredigion, UK: National Library of Wales. cat.llgc.org.uk.
Main Catalogue. Edinburgh: National Library of Scotland. main-cat.nls.uk.
National Library of Ireland Catalogue. Dublin: National Library of Ireland. catalogue.nli.ie.
United States Copyright Office Catalog. Washington, DC: Library of Congress. cocatalog.loc.gov.

In addition to union catalogs, national library catalogs can also be quite important. National libraries are established by a government to act as the official repository for the state or country they represent. Often, they aim to collect all items published in the region they serve, and sometimes they have responsibilities related to copyright. As a result, national library catalogs are usually exhaustive lists of items published within a country, making them important to researchers studying the literature of that region. Frequently, these libraries also have many rare archival collections related to important historical events and people in the nation, which will be discussed further in chapter 8. One important note is that, though the LC is listed here and though it plays the role of a national library in some limited respects, the U.S. federal government has never codified this, and the primary responsibility of LC is as the repository for the U.S. Congress.

Though items in a national library generally appear in the union catalogs listed earlier, becoming familiar with the collections at these libraries can help identify major trends in research across a country, as well as important authors who contribute to the nationwide conversation about a subject. National libraries also feature broad digital collections specific to the history and culture of the country that might be useful to scholars. These collections are often historical in nature or feature highlighted content based on a recent election or other event.

For postmodern British literature, the British Library is the most important resource in that category. With over 150 million items and three million new items every year, the British Library is a large repository of information. The library actually offers several catalogs, and users should utilize the one most appropriate to their inquiry. These catalogs include the main catalog, Explore the British Library, the Archives and Manuscripts Catalog, the British National Bibliography, and the Sound and Moving Image Catalog. In addition to the various catalogs, the British Library also offers a browse feature, where patrons can look through lists of authoritative names, subjects, or titles.

The main catalog, called **Explore the British Library**, can search all print holdings available in the main collection, as well as digital items, including thirty-seven million electronic journal articles. This catalog does not access records for rare materials, sound recordings, or newspapers unless they are digitized. The main search is a simple keyword query that functions in a way similar to the catalogs discussed earlier. The options for the advanced search are fairly standard, though they do allow researchers to look through user-generated tags, in addition to other, more common choices, such as author, keyword, subject, and title. The advanced search also enables the choice of material type, which might help when hunting for books or another specific format, such as audio or an archived website. The results are sorted by relevance, which is ranked based on the number of times queried terms appear and the proximity of words to one another. The results list provides options for refining searches based on limiters such as authors, publishers, publication dates, collections, genres, and language. The date function is of particular use to postmodern scholars because results for holdings at larger libraries with collections that span centuries can be quickly narrowed.

In addition to Explore the British Library, several specialized catalogs are also available. These are identical to the main catalog in many ways, though each has certain features that are worth noting. The **British National Bibliography** (BNB), Archives and Manuscripts Catalog, and Sound and Moving Image Catalog are also useful. The BNB holds records of journals and books published or distributed in the United Kingdom and Ireland since 1950. These dates line up perfectly with postmodernism, making this an ideal resource. The Sound and Moving Image Catalog will be discussed with more depth in chapter 9 since most of the resources are from the mid- or late twentieth century, and the Archives and Manuscripts Catalog will be discussed in chapter 8.

The **Library of Congress Online Catalog** is another resource that might be used in a way similar to the national catalogs mentioned here. Though the main function of the LC is to support the United States Congress, the library has one of the largest collections in the world, with over 34.5 million books, in addition to films, journals, sound recordings, maps, and other materials. The catalog is fairly straightforward. The main options are the basic and the advanced searches, with the latter providing limiters and Boolean connectors. The search field choices are extensive also and include geographic subject, ISBN/ISSN, corporation or meeting name, and content notes. There is a browse function where the beginning of a query can be entered to see what comes before and after results in an indexed list. For instance, you could find "Subjects Beginning With" *postmodern* to see all of the available subject categories starting with that term, and to browse what comes before and after them. Clicking on the subject link shows everything assigned to that subject category. The results are sorted by relevance, though they can be re-sorted with date, title, or author.

Like the British Library, the LC has separate catalogs for its rare collections, including those that are digital. Choosing the appropriate search category is important. Though copious digitized collections exist online, many are not related to the late twentieth century, or they are specific to United States history. Sound recordings and the moving image archive might be more relevant. One catalog that could be of great use for identifying American editions of British books is the **United States Copyright Office Catalog**. With copyright records back to 1978, this catalog represents copyright registration paperwork, which most works should have on file.

Though the LC is an American library, U.S. editions of British books are likely to be represented in its holdings. Books by U.S. nationals about British literature are also part of the LC collection. Another benefit is that the LC is the standard cataloging source in America, which means that the records should be high quality. For all these reasons, checking LC collections will be worthwhile.

Though the British Library and the LC are the largest in this category, there are others worth mentioning. The National Library of Ireland is the primary depository for materials related to Irish history and has over eight million items. Seven catalogs contain different formats, so researchers have many options for retrieving information. Catalogs include the main catalog, called the **National Library of Ireland Catalogue**, a newspaper catalog, a manuscript source catalog, a manuscript collection list, and three photograph catalogs. The library separates materials into three distinct categories: print, manuscript, and visual. The main catalog contains records for both the primary print collection and digitized material from all library collections.

The National Library of Scotland has roughly fifteen million items, with archival material related to Scottish history. Some items are digitized, and others must be viewed on-site. Several catalogs provide access to material in the library, such as the **Main Catalogue**, a manuscript catalog, a rare books catalog, and a theater program catalog. Researchers with an interest in Scottish literature should familiarize themselves with the collections at this library and choose the appropriate tool to access their desired content.

Llyfrgell Genedlaethol Cymru: The National Library of Wales preserves the culture of Wales, including documents related to important current and past people, events, places, and ideas. Of particular value, the national library has started to digitize pieces of its collection for use by scholars, making these important artifacts available to a larger number of individuals.

ONLINE TOOLS

Google Books. Menlo Park, CA: Google. books.google.com.
Google Scholar. Menlo Park, CA: Google. scholar.google.com.
HathiTrust Digital Library. Ann Arbor, MI: HathiTrust. www.hathitrust.org.
Internet Archive. San Francisco: Internet Archive. archive.org.
Open Library. San Francisco: Internet Archive. openlibrary.org.

Though traditional library catalogs are still a primary research tool in the humanities, new online resources are also increasingly beneficial. These make the collections of many libraries accessible electronically in different

ways, and any modern researcher needs to stay current by becoming familiar with them. While traditional catalogs can often only query the record
and sometimes a book summary, HathiTrust, Internet Archive, and Google
Books make it possible to search the entire text of a book for a single string
of terms, similar to the new capabilities available with ebooks through library
discovery systems. This capability makes finding a chapter or even a page
about a specific topic much easier than it has ever been in the past. Similarly,
Google Scholar makes it possible to discover articles using one query, even
those articles not indexed in a database to which your library subscribes. By
partnering with publishers, Google ensures that the resources they include
are academic in nature. Because these search many different sources for content, allowing researchers to canvas a greater number of articles, books, and
reports, they represent a powerful method of surveying the available sources
beyond the limited databases and catalogs of the past decade. That said,
though their convenience and importance cannot be overlooked, they are by
no means perfect. With big data, the possibility for large errors abounds. Remember that these are not meant to substitute for standard editions, and that
they are not evaluated for quality and accuracy to the same degree as content
in a library database or print collection.

Google Books is a database that contains the text of millions of books
scanned by Google and made searchable via optical character recognition
(OCR), which converts textual image files to searchable word documents.
Google Scholar searches the full-text scholarly literature for most academic
fields. Both of these are similar to catalogs in that they offer records for items
located elsewhere, either on the web or physically in a library. Notably, both
Google Books and Google Scholar proffer advanced search options not available in most web searches, and even some catalogs, such as title, author, or
citation metrics. They might also let you set a home library as the default. For
Google Scholar, setting a library allows users to link into the online databases
available at the institution, if it has made this feature available. This allows
Google Scholar to function like a general catalog for your online databases,
similar in some ways to a discovery tool, though not as tailored or accurate.
For instance, when searching for Jeanette Winterson in Google Scholar, many
articles and books about Winterson appear, but there are also extraneous resources that might not have much to do with Winterson's body of work, such
as Sarah Water's *Tipping the Velvet*. This points to one drawback of both
Google searches: much is retrieved, but there is a large potential for resources
that are not directly relevant. One positive note is that you gain breadth when
using Google Scholar or Google Books since items not available through
your library will still appear in your results. One example of when these
tools are useful is researching the less well-known Welsh writer Bernice

Rubens. Through Google Books and Google Scholar, even small mentions of Rubens's work can be found in unexpected places, like a book about autism, *Autistic States in Children*, by Frances Tustin.

Like Google Books, **HathiTrust Digital Library** is a database of digitally converted research materials from sixty partner institutions. This database allows scholars to search the full text of these items via OCR, and lets them see which libraries own the materials. The HathiTrust website includes both a catalog search and a full-text search, in addition to browsing options. Items that are out of copyright are made visible online to all users, and patrons of member institutions have even greater access. These scans are high quality and intended to preserve resources, in addition to making them more widely available. One note about HathiTrust related to postmodern writers, though: searching someone like Colum McCann will retrieve many results, but they might have the same problem as Google Scholar and Google Books. Because so much full text is searched, extraneous results are often retrieved, such as the quote collection, *Eyes Like Butterflies: A Treasury of Similes and Metaphors*. This title is unlikely to be especially valuable in a study about McCann.

Another drawback for all of these resources is that the full text will often be unavailable. These are primarily tools for identifying what is available, not for finding a copy. Generally, the resource itself is only offered when it is out of copyright or is available open source from the author or publisher. To find documents that are freely available, use the **Internet Archive**, a digital resource with the goal of making information accessible to everyone. The Internet Archive contains many works that are in the public domain, including videos, images, documents, audio files, software, television news, and archived websites through a service called the "Wayback Machine," which allows the tracking of different versions of websites, such as author sites as discussed in chapter 11. **Open Library**, the Internet Archive's sister site, is another resource for finding a myriad of texts, many of which are available online. By becoming an Open Library patron, you can access and check out ebooks using the searchable catalog, for instance, recent books by Jeanette Winterson and Julian Barnes. This can be helpful, especially for those without digital access to a research library.

CONCLUSION

All library catalogs have unique characteristics. Each is different because catalogers have some discretion in how they interpret the guidelines. Not all catalogs will search exactly the same fields when a category is chosen.

Though best practices can be defined, taking the time to know your local catalog remains invaluable to successful item retrieval. With this said, remember that most catalogs will operate on the same principles. They will have a standard vocabulary, and they will attempt to accurately represent the items they contain with error-free bibliographic data. Looking for authorized names and titles is usually the best way to start. Moreover, the need for highly accurate bibliographic indexes that represent resources available to patrons of one library or of a system of libraries will not change, even though the way these catalogs function and the items they contain might be different. Large-scale discovery tools that search a library's entire holdings, including full-text resources, are likely the future, but they require the same level of accuracy and the same skills described here.

Chapter Four

Print and Electronic Bibliographies, Indexes, and Annual Reviews

Bibliographies, indexes, and annual reviews identify the relevant books, book chapters, journal articles, reviews, dissertations, reference works, unpublished manuscripts, and other resources that you might need for your research. Many will encompass both primary and secondary sources, making them valuable when locating contemporary scholarship or uncovering obscure items about an author, such as unpublished manuscripts, rare editions, or recordings. Since no bibliography, index, or annual review can ever be completely comprehensive, knowing how to discover and utilize more than one is a prized skill. The scope can vary greatly, so two bibliographies about the same topic can focus on different time periods or be centered on authors from different countries. They might also vary in the kinds of sources examined and the amount of information included. Because these are so pivotal to literary research, we will spend this entire chapter explaining how to locate these kinds of sources and explain the most effective ways to use them.

A bibliography is a collection of citations that point to resources about a particular topic or theme, or those within a discipline. Pages at the end of a journal article, book chapter, full-length work, or even a database can all be bibliographies. Some are general collections of sources on a topic, theme, or genre, while others are centered on a very specific topic, like an author bibliography. They can be enumerative, which means they are a list of resources that provides citations and detailed bibliographic information. Their primary purpose is to record and catalog, often aiming to be comprehensive, containing all items in a category. Descriptive bibliographies, on the other hand, give description and analysis in their annotations, which allow a scholar to evaluate the importance of the work. Though you can find these as full-length monographs for older literary periods, postmodern scholars might have a harder time as a result of shifting trends in publishing. They are becoming less common due to the increased reliance on online searching in databases and search engines, but older bibliographies and those that are still being published are worth consulting and hold a wealth of information not readily available elsewhere.

In contrast, indexes are traditionally published serially and function as broad guides to the literature of a specific discipline, a genre, or a particular format, such as periodicals, but they are different from bibliographies because they provide access to the contents of individual items or multiple publications by means of entry points, such as title, author, or subject. Abstracts, or short summaries of individual works, are a common feature of many records found in indexes. More recently, these tools have evolved into the online subscription databases that scholars search today. They are easier to maneuver than some of the large print volume sets (large in terms of size of individual volumes and in terms of numbers of volumes) that used to be the form that indexes would take. In most cases, online databases are also updated more regularly than their print counterparts.

As bibliographies and indexes are increasingly found online, the distinction between the two becomes blurred. For this reason, this chapter will cover general literature bibliographies and indexes together. In the digital context, resources like the *Modern Language Association International Bibliography* (*MLAIB*) and the *Annual Bibliography of English Language and Literature* (*ABELL*) are simultaneously bibliographies and indexes. Since they are general literary resources, they will not focus specifically on postmodernism, but they do comprise all time periods and genres that fit within the scope of the resource. Publications like the *MLAIB* and *ABELL* tend to include secondary sources but not primary ones. In addition to these more traditional indexes and bibliographies, this section will also discuss JSTOR and Project Muse. While not actually bibliographies or indexes, they are often used by researchers in the same way. They usually do not provide the same level of depth and breadth of treatment as traditional subject bibliographies and indexes, but they are relatively easy to navigate and have the added benefit of allowing access to full-text articles.

This chapter will also examine more specific kinds of resources, such as monographic bibliographies on topics like postmodern literature and culture, twentieth-century literature, and British history, as well as specific author bibliographies and annual reviews. While specialized bibliographies will aid a scholar in identifying sources that explicitly focus on different aspects of British postmodern literature and thought, annual reviews are overviews of secondary sources published during a given year. They are beneficial for identifying important literary trends, determining gaps in the research, and learning about the significant contributions being made by scholars. Some annual reviews, such as the valuable *Year's Work in English Studies*, are published by associations. In other cases, individual journals devote one issue each year to an annual review.

Though we discuss tips associated with finding and exploiting these resources throughout the chapter, some general advice can be applied in many situations. Most importantly, before deciding which tools to use, read the introduction of a bibliography or the description of an index to find out what kinds of resources are included and to learn about what kind of coverage is provided by the source. The introduction or overview will also help you understand how the source is arranged, how to employ the index, learn why some sources were excluded, and discover how (or if) the resource will be updated. Many of the publications described here are accessible as an online subscription database, but your library might have a print or microform version instead, so you will want to check to see what is available.

GENERAL LITERATURE BIBLIOGRAPHIES AND INDEXES

Annual Bibliography of English Language and Literature (ABELL). Leeds: Maney Publishing for the Modern Humanities Research Association, 1921–. Annual. Available online via www.chadwyck.com.

JSTOR: The Scholarly Journal Archive. New York: JSTOR, 1995–. www .jstor.org.

Modern Language Association International Bibliography of Books and Articles of the Modern Languages and Literatures (MLAIB). New York: Modern Language Association of America, 1922–. Annual. Available online through multiple vendors. For more information go to www.mla.org/ bib_electronic.

Project MUSE. Baltimore, MD: Johns Hopkins University Press, 1993–. muse.jhu.edu.

The literature bibliographies and indexes discussed in this section are today's principal literary research tools. Several have their roots in print publications, though they are now primarily online. Depending on the coverage available digitally, you might still need to refer to the older print versions at times. You will find it useful to review the search tips outlined in chapter 2 as you explore these resources.

One standard index that is fundamental to academic research in the humanities is the **Modern Language Association International Bibliography of Books and Articles of the Modern Languages and Literatures**. Today the *MLAIB* indexes books, articles, electronic resources, and dissertations on modern languages and literatures, linguistics, and folklore. Beginning in 1921 as a record of American literary scholarship, it was published under the title *American Bibliography* as part of the journal *PMLA: Publications of the Modern Language Association of America*. International scholarship was first included in 1956. A stand-alone four-volume bibliography appeared in 1969 and eventually became a five-volume set arranged into the following subject areas: (1) British and Irish, Commonwealth, English Caribbean, and American literatures; (2) European, Asian, African, and Latin American literatures; (3) linguistics; (4) general literature, humanities, teaching of literature, and rhetoric and composition; and (5) folklore. Additionally, a subject index encompassing the contents of all five volumes was published as its own volume. The print bibliography was available to libraries and individuals until 2008. Learning the history of standard bibliographies like the *MLAIB* is a best practice in case you need to refer back to some of the older print editions. Also, identifying the general arrangement of former print volumes will give you an idea of what will be covered in the online version.

The Modern Language Association created its own standardized descriptors for the works included. These heading are unique to the *MLAIB* and do not match the Library of Congress (LC) subject headings or other controlled vocabularies, as they have their own structure and syntax in order to uniquely reflect the needs of humanities scholars. This makes *MLAIB* optimal for literary research and demonstrates one particular benefit of a subject index compared to, for instance, a discovery tool from your library, which simultaneously searches most of the possible resources in the majority of the database available to you (described in greater detail in chapter 3). Subject indexes are tailored to and designed for an academic discipline, making their headings more intuitive and better rooted in the nomenclature associated with that area of study. Examples of descriptors found in the *MLAIB* records demonstrate this principle: "film adaptation," "relationship to postmodernism," "pastiche," "intertextuality," "treatment of Great Britain," and "relationship to postmodernism." Each of these is taken from the practice of literary criticism, reflecting trends and terms common in the field.

The online version of the *MLAIB* delivers access to resources from the 1920s to the present and is available from several different vendors, such as EBSCO, Gale Cengage, ProQuest CSA, and ProQuest–Chadwyck-Healey. In this chapter, the descriptions and examples are based on the platform provided by EBSCO, but regardless of the vendor to which your library subscribes, the content will be the same. One important detail to note is that the *MLAIB* only supplies citations to sources and is not a full-text resource, though depending on your library's vendor agreements, you might find some full text or links to articles in, for example, JSTOR and Project Muse. Many libraries will have a link resolver, which is software that links a record of information about a source to other resources available at the library. As a result, the user will be able to find out if a library has access to the full text of an article or have a book in their holdings with the click of a button. Some platforms, including EBSCO, also offer access to the *MLA Directory of Periodicals*, as well as a name and subject thesaurus. The *MLA Directory of Periodicals* is a tool to identify relevant journals, as discussed in chapter 5.

Using the "Advanced Search" page in EBSCO to search *MLAIB* allows you to select a variety of different options from a drop-down menu, such as all text, author, subjects, date, editors, genre, ISBN, ISSN, journal title, literary technique, literature topic, period, primary subject author, reviewed by, and scholarly theory or discipline. For more suggestions on searching techniques, see chapter 1. Records can also be limited by publication date, language, period, publication type, and genre. Under "limit your results," you can select boxes that specify peer-reviewed articles, electronic publication, or references available, or you can also exclude dissertations from the query. These options are the result of excellent indexing, which allows you to create very specific searches. The results screen presents brief citations in order of relevance, which can be re-sorted by date, author, or source. Many libraries have the ability to link to the full text from *MLAIB*, even though it is not a full-text database. From that screen you can also further refine your results by taking advantage of facets for categories such as source types, subject, and publication. There are options to save results in a folder or to create an e-mail or RSS alert to assist you in keeping track of your searches and favorite journals. Always remember to take advantage of the "Help" option to learn how to use a specific feature, such as saving searches.

Individual records provide general subject areas, such as subject literature, period, primary subject author, and genre. Figure 4.1 is a good example of what a typical record will look like, complete with fields such as general subject area and period. This one was retrieved by doing a Boolean search for *Neil Gaiman* AND *fantasy*. In addition to being in the title of the article, the term *fantasy* also appears in the genre field as "fantasy story," which, when clicked on, finds more stories that fit in this genre. Generally, you will not find abstracts, though *MLAIB* is beginning to offer some publisher-supplied abstracts.

The ***Annual Bibliography of English Language and Literature*** (*ABELL*) is the British counterpart to the *MLAIB*. It can be productive to do searches in both bibliographies to ensure thoroughness because, though there is some overlap, original content still appears in both sources. *ABELL* has more cita-

Title: The Double-Edged Nature of Neil Gaiman's Ironical Perspectives and Liminal Fantasies
Authors: Klapcsik, Sandor
Source: Journal of the Fantastic in the Arts (JFA) 2009; 20 (2 [75]): 193-209. [Journal Detail]
Peer Reviewed: Yes
ISSN: 0897-0521
General Subject Areas: *Subject Literature:* English literature
          Period: 1900-1999
             Primary Subject Author: Gaiman, Neil (1960-)
          Genre: short story; fantasy story
Subject Terms: irony ; relationship to liminality ; postmodernism
Document Information: *Publication Type:* journal article
       Language of Publication: English
       Update Code: 201101
       Sequence Numbers: 2011-1-7259
Accession Number: 2011030582
Database: MLA International Bibliography

Figure 4.1.   Modified MLAIB record for "The Double-Edged Nature of Neil Gaiman's Ironical Perspectives and Liminal Fantasies."
MLAIB, via EBSCO.

tions to criticism originating in British journals and books, which is useful for research on postmodern literature from the United Kingdom. First published in 1920 by the Modern Humanities Research Association (MHRA), *ABELL* indexes sources such as books, collections of essays, critical editions, book reviews (which are not found in *MLAIB*), journal articles, and dissertations. The scope is international but limited to English-speaking countries. Topics covered include literature in English, the English language, bibliographic topics (such as the study of publishing history), and traditional cultures (such as custom, belief, narrative, song, and dance). Today *ABELL* is available online through ProQuest as either a stand-alone product or as part of Literature Online (LION) and is also still available in print. The online version is updated monthly, while the print edition is published annually.

Though *ABELL*'s search interface in the Chadwyck-Healey platform is simpler than *MLAIB*, it provides a lot of good search options, such as fields for keywords, title keywords, subjects, authors/reviewers, publication details, journals, and ISBN/ISSN. You can select from a list of possible terms, or just enter terms into the appropriate field. You can also limit your results by selecting latest updates, publication years, and resource types (such as articles, books, and reviews). Each citation on your results screen gives information about the author, title, publication, year, ISSN or ISBN, subject reference number, and additional search terms. You can save your searches and e-mail, print, or download your citations. Like *MLAIB*, *ABELL* is not a full-text database, so articles might or might not be offered or linked, depending on your library's vendor agreements.

As mentioned earlier, JSTOR and Project Muse, the next two resources, are not traditionally bibliographies or indexes, but they are often utilized by scholars in a similar manner. In addition, Google Scholar and HathiTrust sometimes function in a comparable way. Though you can find information and search tips for Google Scholar and HathiTrust under "Online Tools" in chapter 3, JSTOR and Project Muse will be explained here.

JSTOR is a well-known nonprofit journal repository that began in 1995 as a way to archive academic journals in order to save institutions space while also increasing access to scholarship. Currently, it archives nearly two thousand titles from the humanities, sciences, and social sciences. Instead of publishing journals, JSTOR has agreements with university presses, commercial publishers, scholarly and professional societies, independent journals, museums, and libraries to distribute content produced by these entities. Since the main purpose of JSTOR is to serve as a repository, it mostly has back files of journals. Current issues are not generally available, though this is changing as JSTOR has started adding newer content over the past several years through its Current Scholarship Program. JSTOR has also started to expand its platform to contain some ebooks from university presses. Almost everything in JSTOR is full text, and usually starts with the first volume, ending three to five years ago depending on the "moving wall" agreement with the publisher. A "moving wall" is a period of time during which new content cannot be made available. This "moving wall" agreement is put in place so that scholars and libraries will continue to subscribe to the latest issues through the publishers. The California Digital Library and the Harvard Depository serve as paper repositories to back up JSTOR's digital content. Access to content varies depending on what your library purchases. Your library might have the complete package, several multidisciplinary collections, or several discipline-specific collections.

The content in JSTOR can be browsed by subject, title, or publisher, or searches can be performed. Browsing is especially important when locating journals relevant to the topic that you want to explore. Large subject areas include area studies, arts, business and economics, history, humanities, law, medicine and allied health, science and mathematics, and social sciences. Several thousand peer-reviewed journals encompass the language and literature collection, including relevant titles such as *boundary 2*, *Contemporary Literature*, *Critical Inquiry*, *Modern Language Quarterly*, *New Literary History*, and *Twentieth-Century Literature*. Searching in JSTOR can be a little like searching for a needle in a haystack because its main purpose is to be a journal repository, rather than an index, so it does not have subject headings.

You can search the full text of journal articles using keywords, or search in author, article title, abstract, and caption fields. Doing a keyword search in the full-text article means you might retrieve results that have little to do with your topic, since everything is queried, including footnotes and other asides. Using the term *science fiction*, for instance, will return results from a wide variety of subjects, such as science journals, as long as those two words appear somewhere in the text. Limiting to the search fields can make your results more precise, but you can also miss important results. Narrowing by item type (articles, books, pamphlets, reviews, miscellaneous), date range, language, publication title, and ISSN might also prove to be successful. In addition, results might be limited by discipline or publication title, which can help avoid the above example regarding the return of science journals when you look for *science fiction* articles.

An "Advanced Search" is advisable with JSTOR because there are more options for narrowing results. For example, if you want to find articles that explore British poet laureate Carol Ann Duffy's connection to LGBT litera-ture, you would enter *Carol Ann Duffy* and *queer theory* in separate fields in the advanced search, or possibly *Carol Ann Duffy* and *LGBT literature* or *lesbian literature*. You can experiment with different strategies to retrieve relevant results, and it is advisable to use the "Help" feature for hints. If you already have a citation, using "Citation Locator" under the search will retrieve the specific article because you can look for the title, author, ISSN, volume, issue, start page, month/season, day, and year. The nature of the journal repository makes the "Citation Locator" one of the more valuable tools in JSTOR since it reduces the number of results you get with simpler searches. That said, the ability to search through so many resources in such a comprehensive way can be a benefit of JSTOR when you are not able to locate items in other databases. If a piece of information is a true "needle in a haystack," JSTOR might well be the only tool you have to find it, and this is when the repository shines.

Project Muse also has full-text access to journals, but it differs from JSTOR in that it focuses on delivering current access to over four hundred peer-reviewed journal titles and three thousand book titles in the humanities and social sciences. Maintained by Johns Hopkins University Press, it is a collaboration between libraries and publishers. Libraries subscribe to differ-ent levels of access, so yours might not have access to every journal offered through Project Muse.

Research areas, titles, publishers, books, and journals can be browsed in Project Muse, or the database can be searched. Like JSTOR, browsing is use-ful for locating relevant publications in your field, such as "Area and Ethnic Studies," "Creative Writing," "Literature, Philosophy, and Film," "Theater," and "Performing Arts." Both basic and advanced search options are presented. You first must do a basic query before seeing the advanced screen. Facets allow narrowing by content type, research area, author, publisher, journal name, language, and year. You can also do an advanced search with content, title, author, and publisher as your fields, or you could utilize certain operators to narrow and broaden your searches. Selecting "ALL" is equivalent to a Boolean "AND," while "ANY" is similar to a Boolean "OR," and "NONE" is like a Boolean "NOT" search. Though searching Project Muse tends to be more precise than JSTOR, you still need to experiment with your terms because indexing is not provided at the same level as in *MLAIB*. Your results will deliver basic citation information and a snippet of text with your search terms in bold. Selecting a result will lead you to the article itself. Results might be sorted by relevance, oldest first, or newest first.

BIBLIOGRAPHIES FOR BRITISH
LITERATURE, CULTURE, AND HISTORY

Howard-Hill, T. H. *Index to British Literary Bibliography*. 9 volumes. New York: Oxford University Press, 1969.

Richardson, R. C., and W. H. Chaloner. *British Economic and Social History: A Bibliographical Guide*. 3rd edition. Manchester: Manchester University Press, 1996.

Robbins, Keith. *A Bibliography of British History, 1914–1989*. New York: Oxford University Press, 1996.

Slater, John. *Bibliography of Modern British Philosophers*. 2 volumes. New York: Continuum, 2004.

Sweeney, Patricia E. *Biographies of British Women: An Annotated Bibliography*. Santa Barbara, CA: ABC-CLIO, 1993.

This section covers bibliographies that involve literature, history, and culture in order to provide useful context for researchers of the twentieth century and earlier. Though some of the works in this section are older, they still have value because understanding the historical events that preceded the postmodern era is necessary since many postmodern authors are responding to what happened in earlier times.

The *Index to British Literary Bibliography*, a nine-volume set published by Oxford University Press, contains checklists and bibliographies for specific topics and time periods, which scholars can employ to find more specific bibliographies about their areas of study. The titles in the set are *Bibliography of British Literary Bibliographies*, *Shakespeare Bibliography and*

Textual Criticism, British Bibliography to 1890, British Bibliography and Textual Criticism (two volumes), the *Index to British Literary Bibliographies, 1890–1969, British Literary Bibliography, 1970–1979, British Literary Bibliography, 1980–1989*, and *British Literary Bibliography, 1990–1999*. These include works on British literature, bibliography and textual criticism, general and period bibliography, regional bibliography, book production and distribution, forms, genres, and subjects. The introduction in each book explains what is covered in a particular volume, and the table of abbreviations serves as the key to information in the entries. Annotations are not provided, but the set does have a comprehensive list of sources. The entire series is beneficial for researchers because of the history and context it explores, though those interested in British postmodernism will want to pay special attention to the last three volumes, as they contain authors from the time period being studied. Use the index of subjects found in the back of each volume to identify relevant authors and themes.

Part of the History and Related Disciplines Select Bibliographies series, the **British Economic and Social History: A Bibliographical Guide** is compiled by R. C. Richardson and W. H. Chaloner and is now in its third edition, which is much revised and enlarged. The guide has 7,400 entries that begin with resources on historiography and methodology and then are divided into four principal sections comprising the periods 1066–1300, 1300–1500, 1500–1700, and 1700–1980, along with separate sections on Wales, Scotland, and Ireland. Researchers of British postmodern authors will find 1700–1980 most interesting, but other sections might also prove significant, depending on the information needed to provide background. Topics of note in the 1700–1980 section are population, the working classes, leisure, the press and broadcasting, religion, and women, and sources include reference works, journal articles, books, and primary materials. Learning more about the economic and social history of England will sometimes be advantageous when interpreting references to historical events or a character's economic status, such as the middle-class existence of Veronica Hegarty in Anne Enright's *The Gathering*. Some entries have very brief annotations and cross-references to guide users among the different sections of the book. There is an index of authors and a general index.

A Bibliography of British History, 1914–1989, edited by Keith Robbins, was published in 1996 by Oxford University Press and is part of a series that covers different time periods. As explained in the preface, this bibliography is intended to be helpful to scholars in a wide range of disciplines, including literature. The 27,264 entries are divided into twelve main sections: "General," "Constitutional and Political History," "The Economy and Industry," "British Society," "Religion and the Churches," "External Relations," "War and the Armed Services," "Transport," "Urban and Rural Life, Standard of Living, Housing, and the Environment," "Medicine and Health," "Education," and "Culture, Recreation, Leisure, and Sport." The last section has categories such as "Books and Publishing," "The Press," "Writers and Literature," "Theatre," and "Comedy." The great variety of topics will aid a scholar trying to understand the contextual elements in literature, for instance, Ian McEwan's backdrop of World War II in *Atonement*. Entries are numbered and contain a citation to the work, but there are no annotations. An extensive index supports researchers in locating people, topics, and places.

Researchers of British postmodern literature will find the two-volume set *Bibliography of Modern British Philosophers* by John G. Slater a valuable resource because many contemporary authors study philosophical theorists and cultural critics. Published in 2004 by Continuum, this bibliography is mostly concerned with the primary writings of the philosophers, but some secondary sources are noted too. The major and minor philosophers, who write on a variety of topics, are recorded in alphabetical order, with their individual works itemized chronologically. No annotations are provided, but the citations are thorough, indicating page numbers and editions, among other useful information. This book can be hard to navigate because there is no index and only a short introduction at the beginning, but if you have a particular philosopher that you want to research, it will be a helpful tool. Since the listings of primary writings are exhaustive, incorporating monographs, articles, pamphlets, lectures, and more, this bibliography can aid in locating all the works of a particular philosopher.

Patricia E. Sweeney wrote *Biographies of British Women: An Annotated Bibliography* in 1993, and it has 2,014 entries for the biographies of seven hundred British women in a variety of fields in the United Kingdom (England, Ireland, Scotland, and Wales). The primary emphasis is on biographies, but there are also memoirs, portraits written by family and friends, and books evaluating each woman's career. Since creative nonfiction and memoir are particularly important genres of contemporary literature, reference works like this can be significant for scholars. Even in postmodern film, the memoir can have an impact, as in the 2001 *Iris*, based on memories from Iris Murdoch's husband, John Bayley. *Biographies of British Women* has the added benefit of focusing on important female subjects, a group sometimes overlooked. This book is arranged alphabetically by women's names and has cross-references. Annotations provide scope, methodology, strengths and weaknesses, and any special features. An appendix at the end lists women by professions and categories, such as artists, authors, poets, royalty, scientists, and others, and an index identifies book titles and relevant names. While scholars will find postmodern authors such as the aforementioned Murdoch and Doris Lessing, this book is also effective for locating resources that give biographical information about the key female thinkers and activists that influenced the twentieth century, including those who broke ground in new professional and social spheres during the women's rights movement of the 1970s.

BIBLIOGRAPHIES ON POSTMODERNISM
LITERATURE AND CULTURE

Madsen, Deborah L. *Postmodernism: A Bibliography, 1926–1994.* Amsterdam: Rodopi, 1995.
McCaffery, Larry, ed. *Postmodern Fiction: A Bio-Bibliographical Guide.* New York: Greenwood Press, 1986.

The following are two examples of bibliographies that address the postmodern period specifically. They are helpful because they are more narrowly focused than a general literary index. Though they cover postmodernism, they do not simply feature British authors or literary texts. This larger scope makes these resources valuable for understanding the context surrounding the literary period.

Postmodernism: A Bibliography, 1926–1994 by Deborah Madsen is part of the Postmodern Studies series published by Rodopi, which identifies articles and monographs that are either theoretical or practical in nature. Madsen's book records sources from a variety of disciplines in many languages, published primarily from 1970 to 1994, although she notes several earlier sources that discuss postmodernism, including a monograph from 1926. Deborah Madsen writes about books, journals, journal articles, working papers, and exhibition catalogues, but very few primary documents. The book is organized chronologically. Sources are listed alphabetically by year. Though annotations are not provided with these entries, information such as author, title, publisher, LC number, and document type is included. Author and subject indexes are also present, which identify particular topics and authors of note. The strength of this work is how comprehensive it is, and the sources from many different disciplines (anthropology, cultural studies, feminism, fiction, legal studies, literary theory, poetry, religion, sociology, and more) can be helpful for a researcher trying to connect literature to other aspects of culture and society, one important strain in current literary theory.

Larry McCaffery's *Postmodern Fiction: A Bio-Bibliographical Guide*, part of the Movements in the Arts series published by Greenwood Press, focuses specifically on fiction and covers the period between 1960 and 1986. The book begins with an introduction by McCaffery, and each chapter is written by a different scholar. Part 1 has an overview of articles on postmodern fiction and postmodern criticism, covering topics such as experimental realism, metafiction, and postmodern poetry. Each topic has an essay and a bibliography of primary and secondary sources. Part 2 is an alphabetical list of international authors (J. G. Ballard, John Fowles, Salman Rushdie, and more) and critics (Roland Barthes, Paul de Man, Jacques Derrida, Stanley Fish, Geoffrey Hartman, Ihab Hassan, Fredric Jameson, Tzvetan Todorov, and others) of postmodern fiction. Each entry includes a brief biography, a description of the writing style, and a bibliography of primary and secondary sources. An appendix of selected postmodern criticism and a subject index conclude the volume. While the subject index can be used to find specific British authors discussed in the book, the selected bibliography is expedient for identifying relevant books and articles to be read.

These two bibliographies give a fairly full view of common issues in postmodernism since together they span three decades and encompass not just literary sources but also several different disciplines.

BIBLIOGRAPHIES FOR TWENTIETH-CENTURY BRITISH LITERATURE

English Association. *A Critical Bibliography of Twentieth-Century Literature Studies*. 4 volumes. Oxford: Blackwell, 1998.

Somer, John L, and Barbara E. Cooper. *American and British Literature, 1945–1975: An Annotated Bibliography of Contemporary Scholarship*. Lawrence: Regents Press of Kansas, 1980.

Stanton, Robert J. *A Bibliography of Modern British Novelists*. 2 volumes. Troy, NY: Whitston, 1978.

Temple, Ruth Z., and Martin Tucker. *Twentieth Century British Literature: A Reference Guide and Bibliography*. New York: Ungar, 1968.

Some of the books in this section are slightly dated, but they can be still be worthwhile for researchers because they illustrate the literary history surrounding postmodern authors. Also, while some postmodern authors are still writing today, others were at their peak in the 1970s, 1980s, and 1990s, such as John le Carré, making older scholarship potentially noteworthy.

A Critical Bibliography of Twentieth-Century Literature Studies is a four-volume set, published for Britain's English Association by Blackwell. Though the bibliography discusses more than just British literature, it focuses on all English-language writing. Drawn from *The Year's Work in English Studies*, which is examined below in the "Annual Reviews" section, this

set specifically considers twentieth-century literature studies and has essays
organized by years. Covering the period from 1954 until 1994, the essays
are written by literary scholars working in fiction, poetry, and drama. A comprehensive index is supplied, which identifies relevant authors and topics,
including Martin Amis, poetic artifice, experimental poetry, Philip Larkin,
montage, John Osborne, postmodern fiction, short story cycles, Third World
fiction, and Jeanette Winterson.

John Somer and Barbara Cooper's *American and British Literature,
1945–1975: An Annotated Bibliography of Contemporary Scholarship*,
published in 1980, was originally intended to help literature teachers and
professors investigate criticism about contemporary writing in order to plan
classes, but researchers will find it useful because they can learn about contemporary scholarship across three decades, which will assist in creating
context for the works they are studying. British and American literature are
mixed together throughout the book, so you will need to utilize the index to
find references to specific British writers such as Iris Murdoch, J. G. Ballard,
and Ted Hughes. This book is divided into two parts, studies of contemporary
literature and study guides. The first section involves general studies, drama,
fiction and prose, poetry, critical theory, and work published after 1975. The
guides have research tools such as abstract, summary, and excerpt collections; bibliographies; biographical guides and directories; and handbooks
and guides. Each chapter itemizes its resources in alphabetical order by
author and has annotations that are brief, nonevaluative descriptions of the
work. This book focuses on secondary sources, so it is especially important
for identifying relevant literary criticism and reference works that will aid in
understanding postmodernist literature.

Though *A Bibliography of Modern British Novelists* was published in
1978, it is still valuable because several prominent British authors, such as
Doris Lessing, Iris Murdoch, and Jean Rhys, are discussed in this two-volume
set. In addition to a chapter on each author, there are chapters called "Books
and Dissertations Referring to Two or More of the Novelists" and "Periodical
Articles Referring to Two or More of the Novelists," which are both arranged
alphabetically. These are especially important for a recent generation of writers, since the first scholarship that appears about an author often compares
him or her to an older, more established artist. Each chapter devoted to an
author begins with a list of all of the writings by that person arranged chronologically, including novels, short stories, plays, poems, and miscellaneous
writings. The next part of each chapter details scholarship about each author,
arranged alphabetically, such as overviews of his or her canon and life and
reviews of individual works. A variety of sources, such as newspaper articles,
reviews found in magazines, and reference works, make up this bibliography.

Brief annotations (often one-sentence long) are provided for some entries, and there are cross-references throughout, though there is no index.

The dated *Twentieth Century British Literature: A Reference Guide and Bibliography* by Ruth Z. Temple and Martin Tucker, published in 1968, will not be very helpful for the entire century, but it will facilitate identifying writers, works, themes, and styles through the 1960s. British authors are defined here as writers of English, Irish, Welsh, Scottish, or Commonwealth origin. This bibliography includes modernists as well as postmodernists. The index of authors leads to specific writers such as William Golding, Harold Pinter, and Philip Larkin, all of whom might be of interest to researchers looking at the latter half of the twentieth century. The secondary sources in the first part of the book comprise sections on bibliographies; sources for biography; reference books; journals; histories; special studies of modern literature; autobiographies; collections of essays, theory, and special studies of criticism, drama, the novel, and poetry. Each section is in alphabetical order by writer. Some entries have brief annotations. The second part records about four hundred British authors in alphabetical order with all of their creative works listed chronologically by date of publication. Covering both well-known and more obscure authors, this is a wealth of information about primary sources. The variety of materials found in this bibliography will make it a very useful tool for anyone wanting to research mid-twentieth-century British literature.

POSTMODERN AUTHOR BIBLIOGRAPHIES

Baker, William, and J. C. Ross. *Harold Pinter: A Bibliographical History*. New Castle, DE: Oak Knoll Press, 2005.

Fletcher, John, and Cheryl B. Bove. *Iris Murdoch: A Descriptive Primary and Annotated Secondary Bibliography*. New York: Garland, 1994.

Gekoski, R. A., and P. A. Grogan. *William Golding: A Bibliography, 1934–1993*. London: Andre Deutsch, 1994.

Kuortti, Joel. *The Salman Rushdie Bibliography: A Bibliography of Salman Rushdie's Work and Rushdie Criticism*. Frankfurt am Main: P. Lang, 1997.

Pringle, David. *J. G. Ballard: A Primary and Secondary Bibliography*. Boston: G. K. Hall, 1984.

Bibliographies for individual authors have traditionally been a common kind of scholarly work, though they are rare for those still living. The likelihood that you will find one for a contemporary author will depend on how prolific the individual is and how much criticism exists about him or her. When searching for a bibliography for a writer in your library catalog, search for the author as a subject and then browse through the subject headings to find the term *bibliography*. You can also add *bibliography* to your subject search (Burgess, Anthony, 1917–1993--Bibliography). If you just search for the name and the word *bibliography* as a keyword search, you might retrieve many results that are not actually full-length bibliographies. If a book on any topic includes a bibliography, then the catalog record will show that information in a notes or description field, which will be part of the results of a keyword search, as discussed in chapter 3.

Bibliographies for individual authors can contain different kinds of sources. While many bibliographies list both primary and secondary materials, some only focus on one or the other. They might cover a specific time in a writer's life, or they might only examine a particular theme or genre of his or her work. Many bibliographies have annotations or evaluations of the works, while others provide only a checklist. The titles described here are examples of different kinds of monographic bibliographies. You might also find bibliographies for specific authors in journals or on websites.

William Baker and John C. Ross published ***Harold Pinter: A Bibliographic History*** with Oak Knoll Press in 2005, three years before Pinter's death. A thorough overview on the works written by Harold Pinter is given. The book has eleven main sections: plays and sketches for the stage, radio, and television; screenplays; poetry; fiction; prose nonfiction: essays, articles, and published speeches; published letters to newspapers and magazines; interviews printed in newspapers or magazines; miscellaneous (minor pieces, collaborative writings, and editing); editions of collected works or selected works; sound items; and audio-visual materials. Each entry inventories different editions of a published work and has detailed descriptions of the physical objects and their contents. Other special features are a chronology of Pinter's life, color plates of a few published works, and appendixes of his individual literary works, textual revisions, and promptbooks. There is an index of Pinter's works, in addition to a general index that helps locate collaborators, relevant places, and important topics. While this book would not be convenient for finding secondary works, it can benefit a researcher trying to trace Pinter's artistic evolution and to understand his place in history.

Iris Murdoch: A Descriptive Primary and Annotated Secondary Bibliography by John Fletcher and Cheryl Bove, part of the Garland Reference Library of the Humanities, aims to furnish sources for Murdoch's entire career and contains both published and unpublished works. Iris Murdoch died in 1999, so while there is some gap, most of her life is covered. Part 1 discusses her works: separately published works and critical essays, reviews, contributions to books, letters, poems, and some images. Part 2 examines criticism, including interviews, books and journals devoted entirely or in part to her, dissertations and theses, selected notes, allusions, miscellaneous items, brief references to her, articles, broadcasts, reviews of works by or about her, selected sources of biographical information, and principal bibliographical sources. The appendixes provide an alphabetical inventory of Murdoch's principal works and a key to the abbreviations, manuscripts and correspondences, lists of translations, and periodicals and newspapers in which writings of Iris Murdoch and criticism of her work have appeared. There are indexes for names and titles. The value of this bibliography lies in the detailed descriptions and annotations: in Part 1 information about format, editions, pagination, contents, binding, and notes is given, and in Part 2 annotations for most of the criticism are offered.

William Golding: A Bibliography, 1934–1993 by R. A. Gekoski and P. A. Grogan spans most of that writer's life, is divided into seven sections, and has an index. Section A enumerates first British and American editions of books and pamphlets by Golding. Section B shows the first British and American editions of books that have contributions by him, while section C gives his contributions to periodical publications. Section D itemizes in chronological order radio and television broadcasts either by Golding or about his works. Section E has translations of his works arranged alphabetically by country. Section F lists literary criticism written about his work in English and other languages, while section G incorporates reviews of his works in major publications. Entries do not have annotations. Of interest is the fact that Golding himself wrote the foreword, an extraordinarily rare occurrence for this type of scholarly work. Another unique feature are the images of original book covers of his works.

Joel Kuortti's *The Salman Rushdie Bibliography: A Bibliography of Salman Rushdie's Work and Rushdie Criticism* aimed for full coverage of Rushdie's work up to its publication in 1997. Part 1 records bibliographic citations for various editions of the author's writings and offers references to reviews and studies of the work, which are assigned numbers like "CA75-1." Kurthi employs an alphanumeric system for cross-references between sections so that a broadcast of an interview can be found under both the interview (I) and broadcast (T) sections, while "CA" refers to critical articles and "CB" to critical books. The introduction has an explanation for what each part of the label means. The first two digits indicate the year, and the last digit describes where it will be in the genre list for that year. The next six sections are composed of short stories and parts of novels, essays and articles, reviews, interviews, discussions in which he has participated, poems, and television, radio, and video appearances. Each entry in these six sections supplies the title followed by all the places where it was published. Section eight has reference works that examine Rushdie's life and works, and section nine includes miscellaneous materials. Part 2 notes criticism of his works, cataloged chronologically and marked with the aforementioned labels. There are no annotations, though there is an index. The final sections present some related websites, but unsurprisingly some of these URLs are no longer current. If the URL does not work, try to do an online search for either the title of the website or the name of the author or organization.

David Pringle's *J. G. Ballard: A Primary and Secondary Bibliography* is part of the Masters of Science Fiction and Fantasy series published by G. K. Hall. Often a monographic bibliography is part of a series, so if you find one useful title in a series, it might be beneficial to seek out other volumes in the series because other relevant authors might be covered. Completed in 1984, it does not span Ballard's entire canon but is helpful because it focuses on both primary (fiction, miscellaneous media, and nonfiction) and secondary (criticism and bio-bibliographical studies) works, which provides valuable biographical information and points to more resources. Both the primary and secondary sections are divided by years, so it is possible to look up what Ballard published in a given time period and then see what criticism was published that same year. The secondary sources are annotated, describing the theories and arguments in the scholarship. This book also includes a checklist of books and an interview with Ballard, appendixes that record foreign-language editions and his nonfiction written in French, and indexes, which will help researchers discover his writings, his critics, reviewers, interviewers, and people referred to in his works.

ANNUAL REVIEWS

English Association. *The Year's Work in Critical and Cultural Theory.* Oxford: Oxford University Press, 1991–. Available online via subscription from Oxford University Press at ywcct.oxfordjournals.org.
———. *The Year's Work in English Studies.* Oxford: Oxford University Press, 1921–. Available online via subscription from Oxford University Press at ywes.oxfordjournals.org.

The Year's Work in English Studies (*YWES*), an annual publication published by the English Association, began in 1921 and continues today. The first few years of the annual did not list criticism about twentieth-century literature and lacked a separate section for twentieth-century literature until the 1950s. The literature review essays, written by experts in the field, are composed of overviews and evaluations of major criticism and scholarship published during the year, covering all genres and periods of literature written in English. Sections usually have a general overview and then further subdivisions, such as "Post-1945 Fiction" and "Post-1950 Drama." Each volume has indexes to critics, writers, and subjects, which can assist in locating references to criticism about individuals and texts and provides a valuable overview of what was published during a given year and a good historical perspective of the changing nature of literary studies. *YWES* also has informative descriptions of works, including critical or theoretical approaches taken, so that you can decide whether or not to use a particular item.

The Year's Work in Critical and Cultural Theory is an annual publication that began as a companion volume to *The Year's Work in English Studies*. The field of critical theory grew enough so that it became its own separate series in 1991. Though a primary focus of this annual is literature and literary criticism, it also incorporates critical theory pertaining to art history, popular music, and media studies. Most volumes have a narrative bibliography that itemizes and evaluates both books and articles on specific aspects of critical and cultural theory and current theoretical discussions. Usually each volume contains a chapter devoted to "Modernism and Postmodernism." Other topics of interest are deconstruction, psychoanalysis, postcolonial theory, and film theory. Each volume has an index that can be utilized to find specific theories and theorists referenced that year. The online versions of both *The Year's Work in Critical and Cultural Theory* and *YWES*, available by subscription through Oxford University Press, provide advanced search options that allow a scholar to look for a particular topic or author across years.

CONCLUSION

When searching some of the general online databases like *MLAIB*, you might be tempted to assume that a single source is enough to ensure that you have done an exhaustive exploration of materials available about a topic, but that is not always the case. Utilizing more specialized bibliographies and indexes makes you more confident that you have not missed a relevant source that might not be retrieved by subject or keyword searches in a general database. In particular, older bibliographies can be helpful in identifying primary sources that might not be listed in general indexes. This chapter only examines a small percentage of the relevant bibliographies and indexes for a given topic, so it is important to understand some of the strategies outlined in the section on postmodern author bibliographies to find other useful bibliographies and indexes.

Chapter Five

Scholarly Journals

Scholarly journals are a good way to monitor current research because they are published more quickly than monographs. Many academics will first publish a new idea about their field of study in a journal and then later expand the ideas and research on that topic in a full-length book. This creates certain fields where articles are generally more important than the books that follow, particularly the sciences and social sciences. Though monographs and book chapters are still usually the most significant resources in the humanities, often the cutting-edge research will be in periodicals, especially from early-career scholars, who usually first write articles for journals. Another benefit of periodicals is that they are able to cover topics that might not support an entire book. As a result, sometimes you can find extraordinarily specific literature in journals about topics that might otherwise seem too narrow or hard to find. The bibliographies and indexes covered in chapter 4 are vital for searching for articles in scholarly journals. You can use tools like *MLAIB* to search for a particular topic instead of having to search the tables of content of individual issues. You will also find full-text articles in online databases and journal collections like Academic Search Complete, JSTOR, and Project Muse.

In addition to searching for articles in databases and indexes, you might want to identify a couple of journals to read on a regular basis. Regularly reading journals that feature articles on topics relevant to your research will help you learn more about your field and discover new theories and ideas being discussed by scholars. This will also help you identify the key researchers in your field and understand the "conversation" they are having through their articles about topics associated with your discipline. You can discover journals in sources like the MLA Directory of Periodicals or Project Muse that list journals by subjects. In most cases, you can also look in your library catalog for specific journal titles. Keeping up with new issues in relevant journals is now as easy as setting up table-of-content alerts that will inform you when a new issue has been issued. Many databases and journal websites offer directions on how to create these alerts in their help sections. The alert is usually sent to your e-mail address, or it can come through a Really Simple Syndication (RSS) feed.

In addition to literary criticism about authors and texts, some scholarly journals also include letters and book reviews, which describe new monographs or other tools you might want to use in your research. This helps you discern which books or online resources are going to be the most important in the next few years. The titles chosen and the details highlighted in the review also tell you a lot about the field in which you are working. Often, materials are selected by either the journal or the reviewer because they are by a significant academic or because they are about an important topic. The issues in a book that the reviewer has positive or negative reactions to give insight into what a subfield prizes, what scholars respond to favorably, and what serious mistakes might be made that should be avoided. One caveat though: due to periodical distribution cycles, it often takes several months for the items to appear in journals, so a review might not be printed in time to be of much help soon after the book first debuts. On another note, reviews are also one of the first publishing opportunities for many young academics. Peer-reviewed journals, sometimes called refereed journals, are the gold standard for quality in academic publishing. This is because these resources require that articles go through a blind review by several experts in the field who determine the quality of its methodology and research and decide if the work adds anything to the scholarship. This blind assessment provides rigorous oversight for the papers in journals that use this process. All peer-reviewed journals are scholarly, but not all scholarly journals are peer-reviewed. Though peer-reviewed journals are generally considered to be higher quality, regular scholarly journals also help researchers gain greater understanding about a topic. You can utilize tools like the MLA Directory of Periodicals and Ulrich's Periodicals Directory to determine whether a journal is peer-reviewed or not. You can also sometimes find information about a journal's submission rates using these same tools. Information about the selectivity of the journal is often covered on the journal's website as well.

This chapter lists journals that will be of interest to researchers studying postmodernism and is divided into the following areas: twentieth-century and contemporary literature journals, postmodernism journals, author-specific journals, general literature journals, and non-literature-related journals. Each entry includes a brief description to help you decide if this item will be relevant to your work. The descriptions cover the scope of the journal, information about indexing and selectivity, and examples of relevant articles and topics found in recent issues. The journals covered here are scholarly in nature and are mostly concerned with literary criticism. Contemporary reviews and literary magazines will be discussed in chapter 6.

TWENTIETH-CENTURY AND CONTEMPORARY LITERATURE JOURNALS

Contemporary Literature. University of Wisconsin Press, 1960–. Quarterly. ISSN: 0010-7484. Former title: *Wisconsin Studies in Contemporary Literature*, 1960–1967. uwpress.wisc.edu/journals/journals/cl.html.

Critique: Studies in Contemporary Fiction. Taylor & Francis, 1956–. Quarterly. ISSN: 0011-1619. www.tandfonline.com/loi/vcrt20.

Modern Fiction Studies. Johns Hopkins University Press, 1955–. Quarterly. ISSN: 1080-658X. www.press.jhu.edu/journals/modern_fiction_studies/index.html.

Twentieth-Century Literature: A Scholarly and Critical Journal. Hofstra University, 1955–. Quarterly. ISSN: 0041-462X. www.hofstra.edu/academics/Colleges/HCLAS/ENGL/engl_tcl.html.

Scholarly journals that cover a broad time period are often the touchstone for research in a specific literary era. They contain a wide variety of topics, garnering attention from many different corners of a discipline. They can be especially important because they help researchers stay current in diverse subfields that are interrelated or that are connected to a primary disciplinary interest. These journals can also be significant for graduate students or early-career academics who are not totally sure in which subfield they wish to specialize. Being widely aware of what is being published in the larger conversation about a literary period can help narrow down thesis or dissertation topics or allow scholars to see connections to areas they might otherwise miss. Another benefit of writing for these periodicals is that, because they are so multifunctional and because they often choose from the best literature being written across a wide selection, they are generally well respected and well known for quality by many individuals in the humanities.

For the current period of British writing, one such journal is the quarterly peer-reviewed **Contemporary Literature**, published by the University of Wisconsin Press since 1960. Called *Wisconsin Studies in Contemporary Literature* until 1967, it prints essays, interviews, profiles, reviews, and literary criticism on all aspects of contemporary literature. Articles on multiple genres, including poetry, the novel, drama, creative nonfiction, new media and digital literature, and graphic narrative are preferred by the journal. The journal seeks to feature the full diversity of critical practices and favors articles that frame their analysis of texts within larger literary, historical, theoretical, or cultural debates, which reflect many of the central concerns of postmodern literature. Indexed by *MLAIB* and *ABELL*, articles range between twenty-five to thirty-five pages. Sixteen to twenty articles are selected out of the roughly 175 articles that are submitted every year. Examples of articles about specific British postmodern authors are "Satirizing the Carnival of Postmodern Capitalism: The Transatlantic and Dialogic Structure of Martin Amis's *Money*" and "Memory's Fragile Power in Kazuo Ishiguro's *Remains of the Day* and W. G. Sebald's *Max Ferber*."

Critique: Studies in Contemporary Fiction, circulating since 1956, is a quarterly peer-reviewed journal that has essays on contemporary fiction. Specifically, *Critique* accepts critical essays on the fiction of significant emerging writers from any country. This journal is selective, only taking twenty of the one hundred articles that are submitted each year. It is indexed in *MLAIB*, and articles are between ten and twenty pages. Recent articles include "The Public Burning, Utopia, and the Limits of the Postmodern Imagination," "Rebels, Conspirators, and Parrots, Oh My! Lacanian Paranoia and Obsession in Three Postmodern Novels," and "'Aren't You Haunted by All This Recurrence?': Spectral Traces of Traumatized Childhood(s) in Doris Lessing's *The Sweetest Dream*."

Johns Hopkins University Press's *Modern Fiction Studies*, which began in 1955, publishes peer-reviewed articles on a quarterly basis. Papers about modern and contemporary fiction from theoretical, historical, and interdisciplinary approaches are the focus. The journal selects twenty-five of the three hundred submissions it receives yearly and is indexed in *MLAIB* and *ABELL*. Issues alternate between general and special, which consider a specific topic or author. In addition to scholarly articles, there are also book reviews about "The Americas," "British, Irish, and Postcolonial Literatures," and "Theory and Cultural Studies." Some recent special issues that might be worth browsing are "Postmodern Narratives" and "New British Fiction." Some examples of relevant recent articles are "The Anxieties of Authenticity in Post-2000 British Fiction," "British Black Box: A Return to Race and Science in Zadie Smith's *White Teeth*," and "Ishiguro's *Inhuman Aesthetics*."

Hofstra University began publishing the quarterly *Twentieth-Century Literature: A Scholarly and Critical Journal* in 1955. This journal has peer-reviewed articles about modern and contemporary literature as well as some book reviews. An annotated bibliography of current scholarship was included in every issue until 1981. Highly selective, it accepts only 10 percent of the approximately two hundred submissions received every year and is indexed by *MLAIB* and *ABELL*. Several issues have been devoted to postmodernism, such as in Fall/Winter 2011 issue, "Postmodernism, Then," and Fall 2007, "After Postmodernism." Although these issues mostly examine American postmodernism, they covered concepts helpful for research on British literature as well.

POSTMODERNISM JOURNALS

boundary 2: An International Journal of Literature and Culture. Duke University Press, 1972–. Three issues per year. ISSN: 0190-3659. Former title: *boundary 2: A Journal of Postmodern Literature and Culture*, 1972–1990. boundary2.dukejournals.org.

Kritikos: An International and Interdisciplinary Journal of Postmodern Cultural Sound, Text, and Image. Intertheory Press, 2004–. Six issues per year. ISSN: 1552-5112. intertheory.org/kritikos.

Postmodern Culture: An Electronic Journal of Interdisciplinary Criticism. Johns Hopkins University Press, 1990–. Three issues per year. ISSN: 1053-1920. www.press.jhu.edu/journals/postmodern_culture.

In addition to broad journals that cover a literary period, you will also find those that specialize in a topic or subfield. In this case, publications that focus on postmodern theory and culture will be likely to print articles of interest. There are generally a few high-quality publications in each subfield that are the bedrock of research for that area, and these become essential reading for a scholar as he or she establishes a professional reputation and narrows down his or her interests. As a result, identifying these journals as you begin to concentrate and specialize is invaluable.

The journal ***boundary 2: An International Journal of Literature and Culture*** is published by Duke University Press. It was known as *boundary 2: A Journal of Postmodern Literature and Culture* from 1972 until 1990. Produced three times a year and peer-reviewed, it contains articles that approach problems in the areas of literature and culture from a number of political, historical, and theoretical perspectives. Articles are about fifteen pages long and are indexed in the *MLAIB*. Though it changed its name to broaden beyond a purely postmodern focus, most of the articles in *boundary 2* are still about postmodernism. Also note that this journal does not take unsolicited manuscripts because the aim is to exclude articles that fall within "the standard professional areas" and instead only solicited pieces are published, and only those that "identify and analyze the tyrannies of thought and action spreading around the world and that suggest alternatives to these emerging configurations of power." As a result, the publication has an antiestablishment viewpoint, which is directly related to postmodernism.

Kritikos: An International and Interdisciplinary Journal of Postmodern Cultural Sound, Text, and Image began in 2004 and is published online six times a year. Articles mostly center on cultural theory, art, and criticism. Works that are concerned with the currency of the postmodern period are sought. The journal is peer-reviewed and accepts about half the submissions that are received every year. Articles are between one thousand and two thousand words, and book reviews are included. Indexed in the *MLAIB* as part of the Directory of Open Access Journals, one of the strengths of this publication is that it examines other texts and media besides literature, so anyone seeking research about multimedia works will want to monitor it.

Johns Hopkins University Press has distributed *Postmodern Culture: An Electronic Journal of Interdisciplinary Criticism* since 1990. Beginning as a groundbreaking experiment in online scholarly publishing, it has become an electronic journal of interdisciplinary thought on contemporary cultures. Commentary, criticism, and theory on subjects ranging from identity politics to the economics of information are covered, and it includes still images, sound, animations, and full-motion video as well as more traditional articles. This journal is produced three times a year and is indexed in *MLAIB*. Accepting only fifteen to twenty of the roughly one hundred submissions it receives, it is highly selective. Articles are between three thousand and eight thousand words. The journal has book reviews as well as peer-reviewed articles and covers postmodern culture in many countries, including the United Kingdom.

AUTHOR-SPECIFIC JOURNALS

Anthony Burgess Newsletter. Anthony Burgess Centre, 1999–2004. Biannually. Open Access. www.masterbibangers.net/ABC/index.php.
Doris Lessing Studies. Doris Lessing Society, 1976–. Biannually. ISSN: 1541-8596. Former title: *Doris Lessing Newsletter*, 1976–2001. cstl-cla. semo.edu/raschke/doris_lessing_society/dls.htm.
Jean Rhys Review. University of Tulsa, 1986–2001. Semiannually. ISSN: 0889-759X.
Pinter Review. University of Tampa, 1987–. Annually. ISSN: 0895-9706. www.haroldpinter.org/pinterreview/index.shtml.
Ted Hughes Society Journal. Ted Hughes Society, 2011–. Annually. ISSN: 2051-7270. www.thetedhughessociety.org.

Though many journals have a general focus on a time period or a literary style, some concentrate on a specific author. They might contain articles on other individuals and texts, but most of the other authors will be from the same time period or have some other relationship to the primary person of interest. Societies dedicated to an individual often are the ones that sponsor these author-specific publications. In many cases they start off as newsletters for these societies and maintain some of this function, such as including information about upcoming conferences and news about members. Since these journals and newsletters are often managed by societies, the publishing rates for these journals can be a bit more sporadic. You might find that there are several-year gaps between issues. Sometimes the societies might cease publication entirely or will suspend it for several years. The resources listed here as examples are all sponsored by writer-centric societies.

The ***Anthony Burgess Newsletter*** was an online journal published by the Anthony Burgess Centre biannually from 1999 to 2004. The center hopes to revive this newsletter in the future. The website has full-text content as well as a table of contents for some of the issues. Though it is now defunct, the articles that were published still have value for anyone wanting to do in-depth study of Anthony Burgess's work because they included original articles, reminiscences, announcements of work in progress, reviews, interviews, notices of performance, and other events. One value of examining a source like this is that a researcher can frequently identify the major scholars studying that particular author since they are likely to have written regularly in these sources.

Originally called the *Doris Lessing Newsletter*, ***Doris Lessing Studies*** has been produced by the Doris Lessing Society since 1976. It is published biannually and is peer-reviewed. Essays about her writing, life, and politics; reviews of books by or about Lessing; reviews of her lectures or interviews; news about members' works on Lessing, bibliographies; announcements, explorations of classroom experiences; and translations of Lessing interviews are included. Occasionally, the journal has special issues on themes related to her work, such as trauma, approaches to teaching, aging, and postcolonialism. Articles are fourteen pages or shorter. The *MLAIB* indexes *Doris Lessing Studies*, and about half of the submissions that are received are accepted.

The ***Jean Rhys Review*** began in 1986. The current status for this journal is unclear. Ulrich's Periodicals Directory describes it as unresolved, and the *MLAIB* has not indexed it since 2001, though it is marked as actively indexed. The unclear status of this publication is a good example of how author-specific periodicals can have sporadic print histories. When it was regularly issuing updates, this journal was peer-reviewed and was published on a semi-annual basis. A forum for research in progress, bibliography, critical articles, reviews, and announcements of forthcoming studies and conferences related to the work of Jean Rhys were provided. One of the more useful features of this publication was the continuing bibliography published in many issues, which made it very current and quite thorough. Examples of relevant topics in some of the articles are Jean Rhys's relationships to other authors, feminist interpretations, postcolonial theory, Creole identity, and sexuality.

The University of Tampa began the ***Pinter Review*** in 1987 in conjunction with the Harold Pinter Society. Peer-reviewed articles, notes, production reviews, queries, and bibliographical and other details about the work of Harold Pinter are published annually. This journal is indexed in the *International Bibliography of Theatre and Dance with Full Text*. The bibliographies included in many of the issues are especially helpful for discovering more sources about the writer. Some of the issues focus on a specific topic or theme related to his work. For example, a memorial issue that covered the years 2009–2011 appeared shortly after Pinter's death to commemorate his legacy.

The Ted Hughes Society began publishing the peer-reviewed ***Ted Hughes Society Journal*** online in 2011. A subscription is required to view these articles on the website, and it is not indexed anywhere. Mini-essays on Hughes's life and works are an example of some of the limited free content available. The maximum length of an article is five thousand to seven thousand words. Book reviews are welcomed, though the aim for this journal is to promote scholarly engagement with the works of Hughes and to support the study of his life. In addition to the scholarly articles, the journal website has a section for news, which features newspaper articles about Hughes and information about conferences and calls for papers relevant to scholars in this area. Information about archives and the Ted Hughes Online Resources (THOR) project are also a part of the website. THOR aims to collect as many online articles on Hughes as available, offering a central location from which researchers can find information about the poet. Categories include "Ted Hughes Websites," "Manuscripts and Archives," "Criticism," "Biographical Works," "Information about Hughes and Sylvia Plath," "Interviews," "Miscellany," and "Media." These extra sections are a good example of the special features that are often part of author society publications.

As these newer digital resources about Hughes indicate, it is likely that this type of periodical will eventually find better, more sustainable paradigms online. Because they have always been mostly small and sporadic publications, with tenuous existences and highly specialized audiences, author-specific journals have long struggled to produce print editions according to publishing models constructed by larger, better-funded academic journals. Easing the pressure to produce a full issue twice annually, and publishing high-quality articles online as they are received and selected, could solve many of the problems that plague this category of resource.

GENERAL LITERATURE JOURNALS

Critical Inquiry. University of Chicago Press, 1974–. Quarterly. ISSN: 0093-1896. criticalinquiry.uchicago.edu.

diacritics. Johns Hopkins University Press, 1971–. Quarterly. ISSN: 0300-7162. www.press.jhu.edu/journals/diacritics.

ELH: English Literary History. Johns Hopkins University Press, 1934–. Quarterly. ISSN: 0013-8304. www.press.jhu.edu/journals/english_literary _history/index.html.

English: The Journal of the English Association. Oxford University Press, 1935–. Three issues per year. ISSN: 0013-8215. english.oxfordjournals.org.

Essays in Criticism: A Quarterly Journal of Literary Criticism. Oxford University Press, 1951–. Quarterly. ISSN: 0014-0856. eic.oxfordjournals.org.

Modern Language Quarterly: A Journal of Literary History. Duke University Press, 1940–. Quarterly. ISSN: 0026-7929. mlq.dukejournals.org.

Modern Language Review. Maney Publishing, 1905–. Quarterly. ISSN: 0026-7937. Former title: *Modern Language Quarterly*. www.mhra.org.uk/ Publications/Journals/mlr.html.

New Literary History: A Journal of Theory and Interpretation. Johns Hopkins University Press, 1969–. Quarterly. ISSN: 0028-6087. www.press.jhu .edu/journals/new_literary_history/index.html.

PMLA: Publications of the Modern Language Association. Modern Language Association of America, 1884–. Six issues per year. ISSN: 0030-8129. Former title: *Modern Language Association of America: Transactions and Proceedings*, 1884–1888. www.mla.org/pmla.

Journals in this section are concerned with many different aspects of literature, instead of one time period or topic, though there is a particular emphasis on journals that concentrate more heavily on English literature. As with the journals broadly related to time periods, these have strong reputations among scholars because of the institutions they are associated with and because many of these journals have a very long publication history. Furthermore, they appeal to so many different scholars in varying disciplines that they are considered to be important journals by many different subfields. One way to think about this is to remember that the more far reaching a journal is, the bigger the pool of submissions the journal will receive. The bigger the pool of submissions, the more selective a journal can be with what it accepts. Reading these general publications will help you ensure you are staying current on the important trends and scholars from across a wide variety of literary studies.

Critical Inquiry has been published quarterly by the University of Chicago Press since 1974. This journal is interdisciplinary, peer-reviewed, and highly regarded for its articles about literary theory. Essays on different areas related to literary criticism and lists of recently published books of critical interest are included. Articles are no more than 7,500 words. The journal is highly selective, accepting only twenty-four of the approximately 360 articles that are submitted each year. *MLAIB* and *ABELL* both index *Critical Inquiry*. Articles focus on theory, method, and the exploration of critical principles in the fields of literature, music, visual arts, film, philosophy, and popular culture. Researchers of British postmodernism will be interested in the articles about multimedia texts, cultural critique, exploring theory, and popular culture, among other topics.

The journal *diacritics* began in 1971, and Johns Hopkins University Press distributes it quarterly. Best known as a forum for rethinking the aims and methods of the humanities, it also includes book reviews. Peer-reviewed articles compare and analyze books on specific theoretical works and develop their own positions on the theses, methods, and theoretical implications of those works. Articles are about eight thousand to ten thousand words, and about twenty-five of the eighty submissions it receives annually are taken. The *MLAIB* indexes it, but not *ABELL*. Recent articles of interest are "The Criticism of Culture and the Culture of Criticism: At the Intersection of Postcolonialism and Globalization Theory," "Contemporaneity and Its Discontents," and "Listening Eye: Postmodernism, Paranoia, and the Hypervisible." One of the more interesting aspects of this journal is that many of the issues include images of an artist's work at the end, such as images of the paintings and collages of Sarah Slavick in volume 41. Sarah Slavick is a mixed-media artist who is interested in representing organic forms. Images are accompanied by a brief biography of the author and a description of his or her work, methods, and philosophy. The themes and topics examined by these artists are often similar to what postmodern authors are exploring.

ELH: English Literary History concentrates on history, criticism, and theory related to English and American literature. Beginning in 1934, it is published quarterly by Johns Hopkins University Press. Each issue has about ten peer-reviewed articles that are between eight and fourteen thousand words. Author-supplied abstracts are provided, and the final issue of a volume has a table of contents. Letters and reviews are not included. *ELH* is fully indexed in both *ABELL* and *MLAIB* and is highly selective, accepting about 10 percent of the 350 submissions it receives. Though this journal focuses more on literary history, researchers will find some articles about postmodern authors, texts, and topics. For example, the 2011 article "Games People Play: Metafiction, Defense Strategy, and the Cultures of Simulation" is concerned with American fiction, but the concepts of metafiction and simulation are very useful for understanding postmodern concerns. Reading some of the articles in this journal might also help you to learn more about the work that preceded postmodern texts, since many of them respond to previous writers and thinkers, especially those associated with modernism. To this end, recent articles about modernism have been "Sociability in the Metropole: Modernism's Bohemian Salons" and "'Swastika Arms of Passage Leading to Nothing': Late Modernism and the 'New' Britain."

English: The Journal of the English Association began in 1935 and is published by Oxford University Press. Distributed quarterly, it includes peer-reviewed literary criticism, book reviews, and some original poetry. Articles average between five thousand and nine thousand words and are selectively accepted, with only about seven to nine of the roughly eighty to one hundred articles submitted each year actually appearing in the journal. While *English* is indexed in *MLAIB*, *ABELL*, and Periodicals Index Online, the journal also provides open access to its scholarship on the publisher's website. Book reviews might be especially helpful for a researcher deciding on whether to pursue certain scholarly monographs. For instance, the 2007 book review "Postmodern Exhaustion" gives a lengthy review of *Postmodern Literature* by Ian Gregson and *The Cambridge Companion to Postmodernism* edited by Steven Connor and examines how each author handles the complexity of studying this topic.

Also published by Oxford University Press, *Essays in Criticism: A Quarterly Journal of Literary Criticism* has been issued since 1951 and covers English literature from Chaucer to the present day. *Essays in Criticism* is concerned with balancing original interpretations and rigorous scholarship. Peer-reviewed articles, book reviews, and the "Critical Opinions" sections are accepted for publication through a highly selective process. Only fourteen to sixteen of the 80 to 120 articles submitted every year are published. Journal articles average between six thousand and eight thousand words. *MLAIB* and *ABELL* index *Essays in Criticism*. The "Critical Opinions" sections are highly recommended for new researchers seeking to understand more about some of the major discussions that have taken place in literary studies.

Duke University's peer-reviewed journal *Modern Language Quarterly: A Journal of Literary History* began in 1940 and has articles about literature and literary studies as a profession. Theoretical reflections on the relationship of literary change and cultural critique are provided. *Modern Language Quarterly* is distributed four times a year and covers all literary periods from the Middle Ages to today. Occasionally, special issues on different topics such as world literature, realism, and postcolonialism appear. The journal is selective, accepting sixteen out of seventy-five to one hundred submissions. Articles are about seven thousand to ten thousand words in length. The journal's website offers access to the table of contents for individual issues, a list of upcoming articles, and abstracts. *MLAIB* and *ABELL* index this journal. Researchers will find the theoretical reflections included in some issues insightful. Examples of recent articles that might be of interest are "1966 Nervous Breakdown; or, When Did Postmodernism Begin?" and "Cultivating a Common Literary Heritage: British Histories of English Literature since World War II."

The major journal of the Modern Humanities Research Association is *Modern Language Review*, which began in 1905 and is issued quarterly. It has broad coverage, including all modern European literatures, languages, and cultures from the Middle Ages to the present, consisting of general and comparative literature. About five hundred book reviews are also published each year. About two-thirds of the journal article submissions that are received are used. The journal does not have any letters or advertisements. *MLAIB*, *ABELL*, and Book Review Index Plus Online index it. Researchers will find many relevant peer-reviewed articles, such as articles about specific authors like Martin Amis and John Fowles. The book reviews will also be helpful in evaluating monographs about postmodernist theory and criticism.

New Literary History: A Journal of Theory and Interpretation is published by Johns Hopkins University Press and is concerned with questions of theory, method, interpretation, and literary history. The peer-reviewed articles discuss literatures from around the world and from all time periods. Issued quarterly since 1969, selected essays are about eight thousand words long, and it accepts forty of the approximately 120 articles submitted each year. *MLAIB* and *ABELL* provide indexing. Each issue has a list of books received. The emphasis on theory will be valuable for research on postmodernism. Many issues focus on a specific theme, such as recent special issues on topics like "In the Mood," which had several articles about philosophy and moods. One issue had articles about "The State of Postcolonial Studies," while another issue asked "What Is an Avant-Garde?"

PMLA: Publications of the Modern Language Association is the major journal of the Modern Language Association, and, as a result, it is the major publication for American studies of national and international literatures. *PMLA* began in 1884 and is published six times per year. Scholarly articles, professional notes, and letters are included in the first four issues every year. The fifth issue is a directory of members, and the sixth is the program for the annual convention. Book reviews are not part of this publication. The journal has articles about languages and literature from all time periods and from many different countries. Articles are between 2,500 words and 9,000 words and are indexed in *MLAIB* and *ABELL*. This periodical is very selective because it only accepts submissions from MLA members, and of the 200 to 320 articles submitted during a twelve-month period, only twenty-five to thirty-five appear in the journal. You will find articles about British postmodern authors like Caryl Churchill, J. G. Ballard, and Salman Rushdie.

OTHER NONLITERARY JOURNALS

Cultural Studies. Taylor & Francis, 1987–. Six issues per year. ISSN: 0950-2386. www.tandfonline.com/loi/rcus20.

English Historical Review. Oxford University Press, 1886–. Six issues per year. ISSN: 0013-8266. ehr.oxfordjournals.org.

Historical Journal. Cambridge University Press, 1923–. Quarterly. ISSN: 0018-246X. Former title: *Cambridge Historical Journal*, 1923–1957. journals.cambridge.org/action/displayJournal?jid-HIS.

Journal of British Studies. University of Chicago Press, 1961–. Quarterly. ISSN: 0021-9371. Former title: *Albion*, 1961–2005. www.journals.uchicago.edu/toc/jbs/current.

Literature Film Quarterly. Salisbury University, 1973–. Quarterly. ISSN: 0090-4260. www.salisbury.edu/lfq.

Philosophy and Literature. Johns Hopkins University Press, 1976–. Biannually. ISSN: 0190-0013. www.press.jhu.edu/journals/philosophy_and_literature.

Social History. Routledge, 1976–. Quarterly. ISSN: 0307-1022. www.tandf.co.uk/journals/titles/03071022.asp.

Twentieth Century British History. Oxford University Press, 1990–. Quarterly. ISSN: 0955-2359. tcbh.oxfordjournals.org.

The final section of this chapter lists nonliterary journals that might be helpful for those doing research on British postmodernism. Many of these provide excellent context for the study of writing from this period. Often, academics have a tendency to become so isolated in their small specialty that they miss important connections to other fields and interests. Remaining aware of the value of these types of periodicals as you narrow your interests can help ensure you do not develop the "tunnel vision" common to some midcareer researchers.

Also, many fields are becoming more interdisciplinary in their focus, so research outside of one's own area is one common way to gain different perspectives on a topic and become familiar with new methodologies. To that end, you might also want to consult the appendix of this book for more resources of this nature, though neither this chapter nor the appendix will provide you with a comprehensive list of resources for your research, so you should consider consulting the databases and indexes that are specific to the related discipline. You might also find it beneficial to contact a librarian who is a specialist in the subject area to learn more about what is available to you.

Cultural Studies has been distributed by Taylor & Francis since 1987. The journal is produced six times a year and includes articles, reviews, critiques, photographs, and other forms of "cultural" and "intellectual" production. This publication is an international journal that is interested in the relationship between cultural practices, everyday life, and material, economic, political, geographical, and historical contexts, with, for instance, recent articles such as "Black British, Brown British, and British Cultural Studies," "Children of Empire," and "Space for Cultural Studies." Special issues on different topics occasionally appear. Articles are no longer than thirty-five pages, and they are peer-reviewed and indexed in the *MLAIB*.

Published six times a year by Oxford University Press, the ***English Historical Review*** is chiefly concerned with British history. European and world history from the classical period to the present day are also examined. This peer-reviewed journal has been circulating since 1886, which makes it the oldest scholarly historical studies journal written in English. Notes and documents, review articles, book reviews, and articles are published regularly, and notices of periodicals and occasional publications are listed each year, providing short annotations of scholarship. Articles are fifteen thousand words at the most, while notes and documents are no more than 7,500 words. Historical Abstracts indexes the entire journal, but *ABELL* indexes it selectively. You will find articles about topics like postcolonialism, postwar England, and gender relations in the United Kingdom.

The ***Historical Journal*** is published by Cambridge University Press and focuses on British, European, and world history from the fifteenth century to the modern age, though it is primarily concerned with British history. From 1923 to 1957, it was called the *Cambridge Historical Journal*. This peer-reviewed periodical has research articles, scholarly responses to previous articles, historiographical reviews, and review articles. Issued quarterly, it includes both new and established scholars. Articles range from twenty to thirty-five pages. Historical Abstracts indexes this journal from the beginning, while *ABELL* indexes it selectively starting in 1935. Roughly thirty-five articles a year are accepted. Recent articles have covered topics of interest such as Labor Party history between the 1930s and the 1960s, men's involvement in the 1970s British women's liberation movement, and Britain's decline as a world power.

The University of Chicago Press has been publishing the ***Journal of British Studies*** since 1961. This journal is the official publication for the North American Conference of British Studies, merging with *Albion: A Quarterly Journal Concerned with British Studies* in 2005. In addition to having peer-reviewed articles from all time periods of British history and culture, it has a large book review section. Topic areas include art, economics, gender studies, literature, political science, and religion. Articles of recent interest are on postwar politics, capital punishment, British propaganda during World War II, and British sexual culture in the 1940s and 1950s. Sometimes this quarterly journal has a roundtable of viewpoints on a specific issue or on someone's scholarship. Articles are about twenty to thirty pages. Historical Abstracts indexes it, while *MLAIB* and *ABELL* also have some coverage.

Starting in 1973, the **Literature Film Quarterly** has been published by Salisbury University. This journal has peer-reviewed articles on individual motion pictures; interviews with directors, screenwriters, and literary figures; reviews of current film adaptations of literary works; reviews of books concerning film; and responses to articles and reviews. There is a particular focus on film adaptations. Usually articles are between 5,000 and 6,500 words and are selectively chosen, with about forty to fifty articles accepted from two hundred to three hundred submissions. The International Index to Film Periodicals, the Film Literature Index, and the annual PMLA Bibliography provide indexing, but it is also represented in *Abstracts of English Studies*, *ABELL*, and the Humanities Index. As demonstrated in other chapters of this book, postmodernism is frequently concerned with adaptations and the connections between different media, so this journal will be of special interest to scholars of British postmodernism. Film adaptions of works by authors such as Harold Pinter, John Fowles, and Anthony Burgess are discussed in some articles. Relevant articles about postmodern film such as "Texts, Technologies, and Intertextualities: Film Adaptation in a Postmodern World" and "Postmodern Mirrors" will also be of interest.

Philosophy and Literature has been published biannually since 1976 by Johns Hopkins University Press. This journal explores the dialogue between literary and philosophical studies, and topics such as the aesthetics of literature, theory of criticism, philosophical interpretation of literature, and literary treatment of philosophy are included. Articles are no more than 7,500 words. Some examples of interesting articles are "From Postmodernism to Postmodernity: The Local/Global Context," "The Postmodern Posture," and "Postmodern Critique: A Philosophical-Literary Dialogue." Essays, notes, and reviews are present, some peer-reviewed, and are indexed in both the *MLAIB* and the Philosopher's Index. *Philosophy and Literature* is highly selective, accepting only fifteen to twenty-five of the roughly two hundred submissions received every year.

An interdisciplinary journal published by Routledge since 1976, **Social History** focuses on the social and cultural histories of all geographic regions from every time period and is interested in issues of class, gender, and ethnicity. This peer-reviewed quarterly publication includes abstracts, articles, reviews, short notices, and lists of books received. Sometimes scholarly discussions, review articles, and conference reports are featured. There are usually two to five articles that are about fifteen to thirty pages long. This journal is indexed in Historical Abstracts. Recent topics covered in the journal have been about the expansion of automobiles from the 1950s to 1970s, juvenile delinquency in England from the 1940s to 1970s, and the British popular press in the twentieth century.

Twentieth Century British History began in 1990 and is distributed quarterly by Oxford University Press. Every aspect of twentieth-century British history is covered, and it aims to cross traditional disciplinary boundaries to facilitate the study of patterns of change and continuity across the twentieth century. Recent articles have been "Working Class Heroes: Rock Music and British Society in the 1960s and 1970s," "Blood, Sweat and Toil: Remaking the British Working Class, 1939–1945," and "Unequal Britain: Equalities in Britain since 1945." This peer-reviewed journal has about four or five articles in each issue that are about twenty to thirty-five pages long, and some book reviews. Review articles, obituaries, lectures, and notes are sometimes published. Historical Abstracts provides indexing. Scholars researching British postmodernism will find it especially helpful because of its focus on contemporary culture and history.

CONCLUSION

This chapter identifies and describes important journals in literary studies and other related fields that are relevant to British postmodernism. The journals discussed here are not a complete list of what is available; rather, they are meant to be a sample of major journals that will help you see the possibilities of using these kinds of sources in your research. Bibliographies and indexes, like those covered in chapter 4, will aid you in locating specific articles and identifying new titles. Research is becoming more interdisciplinary, so you might need to look outside of your own field to enhance your arguments. You will want to consider using bibliographies and indexes for other disciplines, such as Historical Abstracts and Philosopher's Index. Also, take a look at the appendix at the end of this book for more resources.

The first five chapters of this book have been mostly concerned with identifying print and online resources that will point you to secondary sources. Though you can use some of the resources that have already been covered to find primary sources, you will need to utilize other more specialized tools to do a more thorough search for primary documents. The next chapters will introduce you to strategies and resources for finding these primary sources. They will cover contemporary reviews and literary magazines, period journals and newspapers, digital collections, and manuscripts and archives.

Chapter Six

Contemporary Reviews

Since postmodernism is a relatively recent literary moment, a scholar might find contemporary reviews more plentiful than scholarly articles, especially in cases where academic works about a text have yet to be written. Contemporary reviews also represent one of the most important resources for conducting reader-response research, a common school of criticism that attempts to frame a piece of writing based on the way an audience responds to it. For both these reasons, contemporary reviews are a vital source for literary scholars.

Reviews from the period in which a book was published are considered primary sources because they illustrate how a title was received by critics and the environment in which the author wrote. You can even discover how popular a book was based on whether it appeared in mainstream publications and how many different places reviews were published. The political bent or artistic mission of the publications that print reviews might reveal information about an author's political or artistic intent, or at least the way his or her perspective was viewed at the time. Academic criticism written shortly after the publication of a text can reflect the initial reactions of scholars, which can differ greatly from later studies that might take into account other titles in a writer's canon. Reviews can also give you a sense of what a work means in its own moment, something that the distance of time can obscure. For instance, Chris Cleave's award-winning *Incendiary*, about a terrorist attack at a sporting event, was received against the backdrop of the London Underground bombings, which occurred on the day it was published, July 7, 2005. A review of the novel during this period would no doubt be affected by the immediacy of this event. For this reason, reviews can help scholars understand writing in the terms under which it was created, rather than those we might impose without the perspective that contemporary views can offer. Recognizing the importance of contemporary reviews, this chapter will provide examples of relevant review publications and suggest some useful places to look for them.

NEWSPAPER AND MAGAZINE REVIEWS

Contemporary Review. Contemporary Review Company, 1866–. Quarterly. ISSN: 0010-7565. www.contemporaryreview.co.uk/home.htm.

Guardian Books Online. Guardian News and Media, 1821–. www.theguard ian.com/books.

London Magazine. London Magazine, 1954–. Monthly. ISSN: 0024-6085. http://thelondonmagazine.org.

London Review of Books. NYREV, 1979–. Bimonthly. ISSN: 0260-9592. www.lrb.co.uk.

New York Times Book Review Index, 1896–1970. 5 volumes. New York: Arno Press, 1973.

New York Times Books Online. New York Times Company, 1851–. www .nytimes.com/pages/books/index.html.

Spectator. Spectator Ltd., 1828. Weekly. ISSN: 0038-6952. www.spectator .co.uk/books.

Times Literary Supplement Index, 1902–1990. 6 volumes. Reading, UK: Research Publications, 1978–1986. www.the-tls.co.uk/tls.

World Literature Today. University of Oklahoma, 1977. Six issues per year. ISSN: 0196-3570. Former title: *Books Abroad*, 1927–1976. www.ou.edu/ worldlit.

This list has examples of the kinds of sources that might contain reviews for postmodern authors. Though this is not an exhaustive list, many types of sources that carry reviews are represented. Being able to identify these is important, since they are both multiple and varied. Developing a habit of regularly reading publications that print reviews will make you aware of the latest books being written, which is especially helpful for many postmodern authors who are still alive and working. Advice on how to locate other pertinent sources for reviews will be covered in the next section of this chapter.

One particularly important type of publication when searching for reviews are magazines primarily dedicated to this genre. Though these are becoming increasingly rare with the advent of the Internet, relevant back issues are still available. The most important of these related to our literary period is the **Contemporary Review**, a British magazine that began in 1866 as a monthly, and later became a quarterly publication. Sharing a fate similar to other sources like it, publication ceased in 2012, and as of 2013 the publisher was considering online alternatives. A researcher will still discover value in reading the reviews of British authors found here. When the magazine was active, essays, literary criticism, literary supplements, and short reviews were all accepted. An average of 120 new titles were reviewed or noticed in the reviews section of each issue.

Another source for reviews are local or national newspapers. Though they will be discussed more thoroughly in the next chapter, their usefulness for finding reviews is worth noting. Of this group, one of the best known is the *New York Times* (*NYT*), which has an extensive book review section. You can utilize the ***New York Times* Books Online** to locate many of the reviews written in this paper. Obviously, the *NYT* is an American publication, but it includes reviews for authors writing internationally, such as the June 20, 2013, assessment of Colum McCann's *TransAtlantic*. The *NYT* is also important because it deeply influences publishing in the United States and the United Kingdom. The reach for this publication is very large, with a daily circulation of 1.87 million (as of April 2013) and more than 30 million unique visitors to its website (as of January 2011). You can search for book reviews on the *NYT* website from 1981 to the present. Older reviews can be found through the five-volume set of the ***New York Times Book Review Index, 1896–1970***. Each volume is a separate index: author, title, byline (author of the review), subject, and category (e.g., poetry or short stories). The beginning of each index has an introduction and an abbreviation key to help navigate the source and understand the entries. The reviews themselves can be found in a digital interface or a microform collection, depending on your library's holdings.

The *Guardian* is a well-known British newspaper with a book review section. Published since 1821, this newspaper is now available in print and online, with a combined reach of nine million readers (as of August 2013). The "Books" subsection (under the "Culture" section) of the website is called ***Guardian* Books Online**. It has many valuable features, such as editors' picks, latest reviews, latest news, hot topics, reader reviews, videos, a bookshop, and more. Books can be searched by search all (title, author, or ISBN), title only, or author only, resulting in reviews from the *Guardian*, the *Observer* (a sister publication), and users. For example, an author search for Neil Gaiman shows that the recent *The Ocean at the End of the Lane* has a five-star user rating and six user reviews, along with the official *Guardian* and *Observer* reviews. Many libraries will have print and electronic subscriptions to this publication and might have access to older issues through microfilm.

The British *Times Literary Supplement* (*TLS*) is an influential source, which, according to its website, is "the leading international forum for literary culture." *TLS* is worth mentioning because its primary focus is the publication of reviews about both fiction and nonfiction. Finding a *TLS* review can give you a strong insight into a book's initial reception. Some postmodern authors even write reviews of other people's works in *TLS*. For instance, Julian Barnes wrote a review of the book *Cezanne: A Life* by Alex Danchev on December 19, 2012. Access to the full text of the *TLS* archive is included in a current subscription, but you can do some limited searching on their website without a subscription. You have more options with a subscription, including searching by book title, author, contributor, keyword, or ISBN. Some libraries have full-text access to the *TLS* Historical Archive through Gale Cengage, which dates from 1902 to 2007. Each volume in the ***Times Literary Supplement Index, 1902–1990*** features a different time period. Within the volumes there are separate categories for the entries, which are listed alphabetically. Distinct typefaces help to indicate the categories (personal names, titles, and subjects). The main entries will have a list of titles with reviews, followed by the page number and the year written.

Similar to *TLS* in both scope and genre, the ***London Review of Books*** has been published since 1979. The bimonthly issues contain up to fifteen long reviews and essays by academics, writers, and journalists, along with shorter art reviews, poetry, and letters. Notably, the circulation for this title is the greatest of any literary magazine in Europe, with 59,265 subscribers, making it a particularly influential publication. Martin Amis, Doris Lessing, Salman Rushdie, Julian Barnes, Kazuo Ishiguro, and many others have contributed to this publication at one time or another.

Other resources that often contain reviews of new literature are those that broadly discuss contemporary culture. One famous example from the United States is *Harper's*, which often reviews British novels. The ***Spectator***, a weekly magazine that has been in print since 1828, is one British publication that fits this description. The *Spectator* is especially important because it is the oldest continuously published magazine in the English language. Featuring articles from British journalists, critics, authors, and cartoonists, you will regularly find book reviews in the "Books and Arts" section of the magazine, including reviews of the works of many British postmodern authors. Sometimes the *Spectator* also publishes critical essays or blog posts that delve into topics related to postmodern writers. Camilla Swift's blog post "Jeanette Winterson Is Not the Only Artist to Have Enjoyed Killing Animals" is one instance, which uses a tweet by Winterson about eating a rabbit that was becoming a nuisance to explore the killing of animals in fiction.

Another good example of this kind of publication is ***London Magazine***, which began in 1732 as a publication of arts, literature, and miscellaneous interests. Though the magazine has had some gaps in its publications years and has changed ownership several times, a form of it is still in existence today. The magazine is published six times a year and is available with a digital subscription. Without a subscription, you can view the titles and authors of the articles and reviews. Postmodern authors such as Harold Pinter and Ted Hughes have been featured. Some libraries might have access to older editions either in special collections, in the microfilm format, or through a source like ProQuest, though look out for name changes and different publishers since it has changed ownership and focus several times For example, at one point it was called *Harmsworth's Monthly Pictorial Magazine*.

Some review publications offer broad coverage in many different regions and languages. One instance is **World Literature Today**, which has articles, essays, and criticism about recent literature written in all the major and minor languages of the world. Beginning as a publication called *Books Abroad* in 1927, it expanded to become *World Literature Today* in 1977. The international emphasis gives it an interesting perspective, particularly in terms of postcolonial literature, such as the review of Indian English writer Tabish Khair's *How to Fight Islamist Terror from the Missionary Position*, which explores complex concepts related to terrorism and prejudice. The University of Oklahoma publishes it six times a year, with most issues featuring a "World Literature in Review" section that provides useful book reviews. JSTOR gives full-text access to older issues.

LOCATING REVIEWS AND CRITICISM IN TWENTIETH-CENTURY AND CONTEMPORARY PERIODICALS

Book Review Digest Plus. New York: H. W. Wilson. www.ebscohost.com/public/book-review-digest-plus-h.w.-wilson.

Book Review Digest Retrospective: 1905–1982. New York: H. W. Wilson. www.ebscohost.com/academic/book-review-digest-retrospective.

Book Review Index Online. Detroit: Gale Cengage Learning. Available online at www.gale.cengage.com.

Contemporary Literary Criticism. Detroit: Gale Cengage Learning, 1973.

Farber, Evan I., ed. *Combined Retrospective Index to Book Reviews in Humanities Journals, 1802–1974*. 10 volumes. Woodbridge, CT: Research Publications, 1982–1984.

Lane, Denis, and Carol M. C. Lane. *Modern Irish Literature*. New York: Ungar, 1988.

Readers' Guide Retrospective: 1890–1982. New York: H. W. Wilson. www.ebscohost.com/archives/wilson-archives/readers-guide-retrospective.

Readers' Guide to Periodical Literature. New York: H. W. Wilson, 1900. www.ebscohost.com/academic/readers-guide-to-periodical-literature.

Twentieth-Century Literary Criticism. Detroit: Gale Cengage Learning.

Though keeping up with book review publications is best practice, at times you will want to do a thorough search for all reviews or contemporary criticism published about a particular title. Consulting a variety of indexes and digests such as the ones listed in this section will make you more likely to find all the possible reviews, though it is usually impossible to guarantee that you have discovered everything. For more information about indexes, please review chapter 4.

The *Book Review Digest* is a source for locating book reviews that is available online and in print. The online version has two parts: the ***Book Review Digest Plus***, which covers 1982 to the present, and the ***Book Review Digest Retrospective: 1905–1982***. It was created by H. W. Wilson, but EBSCO now hosts it, with reviews for more than three hundred thousand books in over five hundred popular magazines, newspapers, and professional sources. Fiction, plays, and poetry are reviewed. Each entry has a brief synopsis of the text followed by citations for the reviews. There are usually short excerpts from the reviews, so a researcher can get a feel for the article before pursuing it. Review sources like the *Times Literary Supplement*, the *New York Times Book Review*, *Booklist*, the *New Republic*, and the *Nation* are included.

The **Book Review Index Online** is similar to the *Book Review Digest*, though it does not contain reviews for texts published before 1965, and in this source you can find reviews in academic journals. Gale Cengage offers access, with more than five million review citations from thousands of publications, including refereed journals, general interest publications, and newspapers. The index is searchable by the author evaluated, title of the book reviewed, publication date, reviewer, title of the review, review length, journal, refereed publications, and reading level. For example, an author search for Colum McCann results in eighty-two articles. You can also set limits by dates, review type, length, and publication format, among other options. Only citations are given, but usually you will obtain an excerpt or other information to help you decide if the review will be useful. Many libraries provide a link resolver so you can find the review if your library subscribes to the source publication.

The ***Combined Retrospective Index to Book Reviews in Humanities Journals, 1802–1974*** indexes more than five hundred thousand reviews from 157 humanities journals. Coverage only goes until 1974, so newer works are not contained, but it is still a valuable source for older titles. The author index is arranged alphabetically by the writer's last name and spans the first nine volumes. The titles of individual works are listed alphabetically under the author's name and have brief citations for each review source. There are no summaries. Volume 10 is the title index for all works. It refers you to the author's name so you can then find him or her in the other volumes. Each volume has a "Quick-Reference User's Guide" at the beginning to help you navigate this index.

The *Readers' Guide to Periodical Literature*, which is discussed in more detail in chapter 7, is available as an annual print index and an online database. It is available online as two different products: the **Readers' Guide Retrospective: 1890–1982** and the **Readers' Guide to Periodical Literature**, which covers 1982 to the present. It was created by H. W. Wilson, but it can now be found on the EBSCO platform. The main focus of the *Readers' Guide* is popular magazines rather than scholarly articles, indexing 375 general interest periodicals published in the United States. Though you will find overlap with many of these other tools, it does list some publications not found elsewhere. In the online versions you can specify document type, which could be article, book review, poem, or short story. You can then limit your searches to just book reviews. For example, if you look for *Midnight's Children* by Salman Rushdie and limit by book review, you will have six results, all dating from 1981. You will not have full-text access to these articles, but if your library has a link resolver, you might be able to locate them.

Contemporary Literary Criticism and **Twentieth-Century Literary Criticism** are both published through Gale Cengage. Some libraries might have online access to these sets through their Literary Criticism Online platform. Other libraries have the print volumes. Each print volume of both of these series has profiles of about six to eight novelists, poets, playwrights, and other writers and provides full-text or excerpted criticism in chronological order from books, magazines, literary reviews, newspapers, and scholarly journals. Full citations are given, so you can locate the original criticism. Each volume includes cumulative author name (Julian Barnes, Neil Gaiman, Philip Larkin, John James Osborne, Jeanette Winterson), topic (cyberpunk, disease and literature, graphic narratives, postcolonialism, postmodernism, science and modern literature), and nationality (Australian, English, Irish, Scottish, Welsh) indexes, as well as a volume-specific title index. A cumulative title index for the entire series is available separately. While *Contemporary Literary Criticism* discusses authors who are currently active or who died after 1959, *Twentieth-Century Literary Criticism* covers 1900–1999.

Another series similar to the Literary Criticism series published by Gale Cengage is A Library of Literary Criticism, published by Ungar. The titles listed in these resources tend to be older, and they are not cumulative, but they do focus on bringing together selections of criticism about individual authors such as John Banville, Samuel Beckett, Seamus Heaney, Iris Murdoch, and John Millington Synge. One example is **Modern Irish Literature**, which examines eighty-seven authors from both the north and south of the country who are poets, dramatists, novelists, or essayists, or who work in other genres. Entries begin with a brief overview of an author's work and then contain criticism that is arranged chronologically to help a researcher trace the trajectory of an author's career. The full-text or excerpted criticism listed under an author's name includes a complete citation to assist you in locating the original publication. Bibliographies for each author can be found at the end of the book, along with an index to critics.

AUTHOR-SPECIFIC CRITICISM SOURCES

Beedham, Matthew. *The Novels of Kazuo Ishiguro: A Reader's Guide to Essential Criticism*. New York: Palgrave Macmillan, 2010.
Heusel, Barbara S. *Iris Murdoch's Paradoxical Novels: Thirty Years of Critical Reception*. Rochester, NY: Camden House, 2001.
Holmes, Frederick M. *Julian Barnes*. New York: Palgrave Macmillan, 2009.
Watt, Donald. *Aldous Huxley: The Critical Heritage*. London: Routledge & Kegan Paul, 1975.

Though it can be fairly easy to read reviews and criticism in newspapers and magazines, having a book-length work that gathers together criticism for a specific writer can be a good way to ensure you are thorough. Generally, only major authors are given this kind of treatment, and many postmodern authors are not yet well enough established, so it is entirely possible that you will not find a work like this for the author you are researching. What follows are examples of what might be available. You should also take a look at chapter 4 for other full-length bibliographies that include annotations for secondary works.

Matthew Beedham's *The Novels of Kazuo Ishiguro: A Reader's Guide to Essential Criticism* is a recent addition to Palgrave Macmillan's Reader's Guides to Essential Criticism series. This book outlines the initial critical response, in the form of reviews, interviews, and scholarly articles, to the novels of Kazuo Ishiguro and explores some of the essential themes of his work. Each chapter examines a specific novel, providing a survey of the key scholars and perspectives taken. *Remains of the Day* gets the most extensive treatment, with three chapters devoted to exploring its reception and narration, historical and postcolonial readings, and interdisciplinary approaches. In addition to these chapters, the book has an introduction and conclusion that provide background and analysis about the author, a select bibliography, and an index. A scholar using this guide would gain a thorough knowledge of the critical reception that Ishiguro has received.

Iris Murdoch's Paradoxical Novels: Thirty Years of Critical Reception by Barbara Heusel is part of the Literary Criticism in Perspective series published by Camden House. Each book in this series traces literary scholarship and criticism for major as well as neglected authors. The publisher's website explains that the aim is to "reveal the workings of academic criticism itself and how trends in the academy and in society at large affect it." This particular volume was published in 2001. The six chapters each have a different focus, such as "A Philosophical Novelist? Early Dialogues" and "Postmodernist Experimentation." Each one discusses how different reviewers and critics approached Murdoch's writing in relation to that theme. Reading these chapters will give a researcher a strong understanding of the major scholars who study Murdoch and their interpretations of her work. The book also has an introduction that gives valuable background about the author, a bibliography, and an index.

Julian Barnes by Frederick M. Holmes was published in 2009 and is part of the New British Fiction series from Palgrave. Each book in this series serves as an introduction to writers who emerged during and after the 1970s, such as Ian McEwan, Zadie Smith, Jeanette Winterson, and Salman Rushdie. This volume has a timeline, biographical information, a brief analysis of his major works, and an index. The third section, called "Criticism and Contexts," is primarily concerned with the reaction to Barnes's writing, outlining the critical reception he received in a lengthy essay that compares reviews of his works from different publications and offers explanations for some of these responses. For instance, Frederick M. Holmes explains that even with his first novel, *Metroland*, a few reviewers already had high expectations of his work because he had a reputation for being a good writer due to his articles as a journalist. A bibliography at the end of the book will help a researcher locate the reviews mentioned in the critical reception essay.

An example of Routledge's Critical Heritage series is *Aldous Huxley: The Critical Heritage* by Donald Watt, which begins with an introduction that explains the materials covered in the book and discusses the author's initial reception by critics. A list of Aldous Huxley's major works is also provided. Each entry in the book examines the reviews of one of Aldous Huxley's texts, starting in 1920 and ending in 1962. The entry has either the full text or excerpts from individual reviews contemporary to the book's publication. Each review has a brief biographical note about the reviewer. For instance, *Brave New World* has fifteen reviews starting with Rebecca West's in the *Daily Telegraph* from February 1932 and ending with Winfield H. Roger's essay in the *Sewanee Review* from July–September 1935 called "Aldous Huxley's Humanism." Appendixes include "References for the Introduction," "Translations," and "Collected Works Sales." A bibliography and an index finish the book.

CONCLUSION

An important consideration for doing literary research is the fact that literary scholarship is cumulative. Instead of replacing older research, the new scholar responds to and builds on what has come before he or she puts pen to paper. The resources in this chapter will help you discover the early critical reactions to works, which will allow you to build a foundation for comparing later works and understanding the critical reception of an author over time. You have been given many of the tools that can be used to find the criticism and reviews that were written during an author's lifetime. More details about the newspapers, magazines, and literary magazines where reviews can appear will be given in the next chapter, including more in-depth strategies on how to find these publications.

Chapter Seven

Newspapers, Periodicals, Literary Magazines, Zines, and Microforms

The postmodern periodical press in Britain is defined by a few different trends, which determine how the task of finding these resources should be approached. One is the consolidation of mainstream news outlets under fewer corporate owners, as a result of mergers and the globalization of media markets, which were concentrated locally or regionally prior to the late twentieth century.[1] Another is the proliferation of alternative media outlets, especially in the more recent past with the advent of new technologies such as the Internet.[2] The third is the cultural and social upheaval in British society from the 1960s forward, and particularly changes related to class, gender, and race. In combination, these trends profoundly altered the nature of periodical publishing in the United Kingdom, and internationally.

Of these three trends, the consolidation of the mainstream press and the concatenate rise of other media has had the biggest effect on the way news is reported and perceived in Britain. Between 1962 and 2006, there was a 20 percent decrease in the number of daily newspapers sold in the UK,[3] while fifty-three newspapers closed in 2009 alone.[4] In contrast, between 2002 and 2009, television viewership in the UK rose from 3.54 hours daily to 3.75.[5] Additionally, the print readership now trends toward tabloid magazines that are primarily concerned with entertainment updates, such as the *Sun*, the best-selling daily in the UK as of January 2012.[6] This change impacts researchers because it is not enough anymore to find a handful of influential newspapers in order to determine the cultural meaning of an event. Radio, TV, print, and even Internet sources that reflect modern reactions to historical or cultural occasions should be identified.

The variety of responses related to the wedding of Prince William and Kate Middleton in 2011 is a good example of this trend. An estimated 34.7 million viewers watched coverage of the nuptials on one of the BBC stations at some

point during the proceedings.[7] In addition, print newspapers, magazines, radio stations, dedicated blogs, Twitter feeds, and many other forms of media
covered aspects of the wedding. To research the cultural impact of this event
on Britain, you would need to discover multiple types of news media, some
better vetted and more trustworthy than others.

The changing nature of news led in many ways to the second important
trend in periodical publication: the rise of alternative press, literary magazines, and Internet forums. All of these types of press are outside mainstream
markets, but as new modes of publication blossomed in the late 1960s and
traditional news failed to tackle issues important to a more diverse postmodern underground, alternative publications flowered. These promoted subver-
sive culture and questioned mainstream politics, particularly through the San
Francisco–based global network of alternative publishers, the Underground
Press Syndicate, which disseminated periodicals like the *San Francisco
Oracle* and the *East Village Other* in London and other major cities.[8] Alternative publications also started in London, most notably the *International
Times*.[9] Though this initial alternative press movement had already started to
fall apart by the mid-1970s,[10] dissent in underground and alternative media
continued. Famous examples include publications associated with the do-
it-yourself-focused punk movement of the 1980s and, more recently, those
online sources, such as blogs and social media accounts, which were against
the Iraq War and the London Olympics. These are important to artistic and
cultural movements and range from zines or smaller, self-published magazines to underground periodicals and blogs.

One benefit to researchers is that scholarly finding aids grew up with these
new types of periodicals, making this era one of the best documented. Indexes, serial bibliographies, and other tools abound to track down resources
that might not have been easily identifiable had they been published a century ago. Even the Internet is a boon. A lot of born-digital content is tailored
to Internet searching, which provides access to a broad range of items that
would have survived in only one or two rare archives previously, if at all.
Where once we had the ephemeral pamphlets of the Enlightenment, we now
have millions of blogs, indexed and viewable online, though these are also
ephemeral, sometimes changing names, URLs, and other information rapidly.
While this is extremely important for researchers, it also makes the task of
wading through available material much more difficult. As a result, abstracts
and other annotated bibliographic sources are more useful than ever.

Underscoring both of these printing transitions, the social changes in
Britain during and following the 1960s encouraged new perspectives on
class, race, gender, sexuality, and other diverse topics.[11] The social changes
described here led to a thriving alternative press and to new publications dedi-

cated to issues that were emerging in "Swinging London."[12] Publications like this focused on broad or narrow special topics related to issues that were not explicitly explored in the past. As a result, scholars studying postmodernism have access to a much wider variety of views on the news of the day.

Though all of these changes make the amount of documentation related to postmodern periodicals much larger, the sheer volume of available research requires special skills. Indexes and bibliographies are key to successful retrieval of potential resources, if for no other reason than to help define keyword searching. Title lists, in particular, are important to help scholars identify what they should be looking for in a tidal wave of disparate materials. The task of researching is much quicker and more efficient when you know how to use these tools properly. To help narrow the field, individuals might want to start their periodical research with the *Bibliography of Serial Bibliographies*, a resource that lists the available references at the time of its publication.

NEWSPAPERS AND OTHER NEWS SOURCES

Access World News. Naples, FL: NewsBank. www.newsbank.com.

BBC. London: British Broadcasting Corporation. www.bbc.com.

BBC Archive. London: British Broadcasting Corporation, 2013. www.bbc .co.uk/archive/.

The Bibliography of British Newspapers. London: British Library Publishing Division, 1991.

British Pathé. London: British Pathé Ltd. www.britishpathe.com.

The Encyclopedia of the British Press, 1422–1992. New York: Palgrave Macmillan, 1993.

Financial Times Historical Archive, 1888–2008. Farmington Hills, MI: Gale. www.gale.cengage.com.

Guardian. London: Guardian Group. www.theguardian.com.

Guardian (1821–2003). Ann Arbor, MI: ProQuest. www.proquest.com.

Illustrated London News, 1842–2003. Farmington Hills, MI: Gale. www .gale.cengage.com.

InfoTrac Newsstand. Farmington Hills, MI: Gale. www.gale.cengage.com.

Irish Times (1859–2008). Ann Arbor, MI: ProQuest. www.proquest.com.

LexisNexis Academic. Dayton, OH: LexisNexis. www.lexis.com.

Listener Historical Archive, 1929–1991. Farmington Hills, MI: Gale. www .gale.cengage.com.

London Broadcast Company/Independent Radio News Audio Archive. London: British Universities Film & Video Council. bufvc.ac.uk/tvandradio/lbc/.

News on Screen: The World's Leading Resource for the Study of Newsreels and Cinemagazines. London: British Universities Film & Video Council. bufvc.ac.uk/newsonscreen.

Observer. London: Guardian Group. observer.guardian.com.

Observer (1791–2003). Ann Arbor, MI: ProQuest. www.proquest.com.

ProQuest Historical Newspapers. Ann Arbor, MI: ProQuest. www.proquest.com.

ProQuest Newsstand. Ann Arbor, MI: ProQuest. www.proquest.com.

Scotsman (1817–1950). Ann Arbor, MI: ProQuest. www.proquest.com.

Sunday Times Digital Archive, 1822–2006. Farmington Hills, MI: Gale. www.gale.cengage.com.

Times Digital Archive, 1785–2006. Farmington Hills, MI: Gale. www.gale.cengage.com.

Times Literary Supplement, 1902–2007. Farmington Hills, MI: Gale. www.gale.cengage.com.

Times. London: News UK. www.thetimes.co.uk.

Weekly Irish Times (1876–1958). Ann Arbor, MI: ProQuest. www.proquest.com.

Because the postmodern period saw an explosion of news reporting in diverse media, the field of inquiry is much larger than in previous literary eras. Print and broadcast sources are of competing cultural importance and should be researched in parallel. Gossip magazines also proliferated in the postmodern period and sometimes appear as news sources alongside Britain's more traditional media. Though these sources are not always considered reliable, they might be of importance to cultural scholars since the blurring of lines between entertainment and news has had a profound impact on British society.

British newspapers are important to literary research because they represent windows into the current cultural events that shape the stories told by postmodern authors. For instance, when researching the fictional events in Doris Lessing's *The Good Terrorist*, British newspapers could provide information about political terrorism during the 1980s or historical events that occurred in the book, such as Margaret Thatcher's policies and the reaction on the left to her tenure. Reports of terrorism in both the UK and outside of this region could elucidate Lessing's writing. Newspapers might also give insight into the historical periods and places that postmodern fiction explores. Ruth Prawer Jhabvala's *Heat and Dust* takes place in 1920s India and deals with issues of gender and colonialism. Reading newspaper accounts from this time and place would be important to understanding the novel. Newspapers might additionally contain reports of a book's reception and how it impacted British culture.

Before looking at individual newspapers, we should consider how to find articles using the Internet and library resources, both current and archival. When researching a literary period from the past, recent issues are not important, but postmodernism is a contemporary trend, and so recent news will be just as useful as periodical archives. Because there are so many newspapers, there are also many companies that provide access to them online, most importantly Gale, ProQuest, LexisNexis, and NewsBank. This can cause some confusion. Even more confusing, the platforms that include the current editions of a newspaper might not host the archives for that same title. For this reason, scholars who do a lot of research in current events will need to be quite familiar with a wide variety of pertinent resources.

Though many of these publications are online, some will only be accessible through a subscription. This makes the task of finding news more difficult if you do not have a personal subscription. Libraries tend to get newspapers from a mix of vendors, such as those just listed. As a result, the publication you need for a specific region of the UK might not be readable on any of these platforms, or it might be available in multiple products for varying date ranges. Even when some articles are posted online through a newspaper's website, having it through a library will usually provide fuller access to historical content and better options for searching since most databases have advanced indexing and interfaces that are richer than the simple search box available on websites. For these reasons, scholars might prefer using the library for news, even though finding the right database is more difficult than simply clicking on the publisher's website.

One example of a newspaper platform with a more robust search interface is Gale's **InfoTrac Newsstand**. InfoTrac offers access to the better-known British and Irish daily newspapers, and is included in Academic OneFile, Gale's comprehensive periodical database. the *Times*, *Financial Times*, *Guardian*, *Daily Mail*, and *Irish Times* are represented, in addition to many regional publications. In fact, the wide array of Commonwealth newspapers contained distinguishes InfoTrac from other newspaper platforms, many of which only carry the major newspapers. Fewer have more localized titles, as InfoTrac does. These newspapers are important because they cover regional stories that might not be picked up nationally, and they give a different perspective. For instance, coverage of the Saville Inquiry into the Bloody Sunday shootings could vary depending on local perspectives of the event. If there is one particular regional publication that is of interest, for instance, the *Chichester Observer* or the *Isle of Man Today*, identify the database that has access to the most complete date ranges. InfoTrac is one of the better places to start in this process.

In addition to wide coverage of Commonwealth titles, the interface for InfoTrac is similar to other Gale products, and researchers who are already familiar with this utility might prefer it over some of the others listed here. You can search based on subject, keyword, publication title, or the entire article. Advanced search options are available that focus on headlines, date ranges, authors, or newspaper sections. This granularity in the interface makes InfoTrac particularly useful for scholars of literature and other humanities subjects.

Gale also offers several historical newspaper archives, and especially the *Times Digital Archive*, which is discussed later in this chapter. Other archive titles are the *Financial Times Historical Archive, 1888–2008*, the *Illustrated London News, 1842–2003*, the *Times Literary Supplement, 1902–2007* (discussed more in chapter 6), the *Listener Historical Archive, 1929–1991*, and the *Sunday Times Digital Archive, 1822–2006*. Though these are smaller papers, they all have some national appeal and therefore might have broad applications for researchers. For each of these newspapers, a simple keyword search is an option, as is an advanced Boolean query with date and document-type limiters. When viewing a page of the paper, a list of the articles on that page is presented. Browsing through a newspaper on a specific historical date is also possible.

Another important current news platform for researching British post-modernism is **ProQuest Newsstand**. Though traditionally ProQuest was better known for historical news content, while companies like LexisNexis or NewsBank have dominated the current periodical market, ProQuest has added many of the best-known titles to their platform, for instance, the *Times*, *Guardian*, *Observer*, *Financial Times*, *Daily Mail*, *Daily Record*, *Daily Telegraph*, and *BBC Monitoring* from the United Kingdom. The *Irish Times* and *Irish Independent* are also available.

The default query for ProQuest Newsstand is a basic keyword search that looks through the full text of articles. The advanced option enables Boolean searching or subject queries in a robust array of indexes, such as companies, people, subjects, locations, or creative works. Scholars can also set date ranges and choose document types. Document-type searching might be of special interest, since it allows advertisements, birth or death notices, correspondence, commentary, cartoons, and other types of special content to be targeted. For those who study advertisements or other hard-to-get-at genres, these advanced limiters are important. As demonstrated in figure 7.1, choosing to search announcements for the creative work *Life of Brian* with the document type "advertisement" will retrieve print ads for this movie. Though this example is taken from ProQuest Newsstand, the same techniques can be used in other newspaper products from ProQuest. Results can be sorted by

Figure 7.1. ProQuest Newsstand search for Life of Brian advertisements.
ProQuest Newsstand.

relevance or date. Another interesting feature with the ProQuest platform is the "find similar" option, which allows a researcher to paste content to find other articles that might have the same keywords or structure.

This interface is also used for **ProQuest Historical Newspapers**, another resource with older articles. Historical Newspapers is more of a brand than a single database since it is not a collection of resources but rather the name of a series of individual titles that libraries purchase or subscribe to independently. As a result, a library's holdings for Historical Newspapers will change based on what they actually decide to license. Many important international publications are made available through Historical Newspapers, including the *Guardian* and the *Observer*, which we will discuss later. The ***Irish Times***, ***Weekly Irish Times***, and the ***Scotsman*** are also offered. These digital archives demonstrate one drawback that postmodern researchers might discover as they look for material: while a wide variety of content is born digital, all of it is still in copyright, making access problematic and often costly.

LexisNexis Academic is a well-known source with a long reputation for giving current news, containing articles and transcripts from broadcasts. For the United Kingdom, you will find many of the same titles that are available through ProQuest Newsstand and InfoTrac, including the *Times*, *Guardian*, *Daily Mail*, and *Irish Times*. The drawback with LexisNexis is that the search interface is targeted at business researchers, so it might not be as easy to use as some others, lacking as it does the more advanced options offered by Gale and ProQuest. Also, LexisNexis only has text for the articles, rather than the PDF scans offered by their competitors. As a result, pictures and layout for original article are not available. The basic search can be performed across all news, foreign-language items, or broadcast transcripts. To use this search, click on "Search the News" and type in keywords, such as *Hay Festival of Literature and Arts*, an event held annually in Wales. This search will retrieve newspaper, magazines, trade press articles, and other resources related to this event, often called the "Woodstock of the mind." The advanced search allows researchers to identify desired date ranges, to choose sources, or to build a complex search by segments, if you wanted to find, for instance, information about one year of the *Hay Festival*. An index can also be used to create a more pinpointed query. Most content in LexisNexis Academic only goes back to the 1990s or 2000s, so it will not help much when older stories are required.

Though **Access World News** contains many of the widely known daily newspapers offered by the other platforms, including the *Times*, *Guardian*, and *Daily Mail*, this NewsBank database is better known for local and regional newspapers, primarily in the United States but also internationally. As a result, Access World News is an excellent place to look for resources when the events or individuals for which information is needed are more prominent in one particular jurisdiction with highly regionalized periodicals. For instance, if you are interested in a regional writer like H. E. Bates, who lived in Rushden and then Kent for much for his life, newspapers related to those locations would be likely to carry more information pertinent to his career.

The interface for Access World News can be set as a map of a region, or searched with multiple fields for different information. Advanced searching allows the limiting of results by date, location, and source type. One particular limitation of Access World News: Research Collection, which is the subscription most academic libraries have, is that it does not contain newspapers from Ireland. There is a separate subscription that some libraries might provide called Access U.K. and Ireland Newspapers that does have the *Irish Times*, the *Irish Independent*, and the *Sunday Times*, yet even this is a limited list considering the vast number of regional publications for England, Scotland, and Wales.

There are other databases that contain newspapers, but these are the major ones that should cover most sources from national, regional, and local publications available electronically. Familiarizing yourself with each of these is a good way to make sure you are finding everything available. Of course, no database can substitute for knowing the newspapers that are most important to an area of study, including their historical importance, where they are accessible, and their reputation. Despite the fact that we cannot list all the myriad of national, regional, and local newspapers here, we will endeavor to provide the basic information pertinent to a few of the most current and important national news sources in England.

The *Times*, formerly the *Times of London*, is the first major newspaper in Britain of which one should be aware. Beginning in 1785, the *Times* is the best-known daily, national newspaper and is recognized for taking moderate or conservative-leaning positions. The *Sunday Times* is also worth mentioning, as its sister publication. Current access to the *Times* is available with a subscription on the publication's homepage, or from InfoTrac Newsstand (1985–present), ProQuest Newsstand (1992–present), LexisNexis Academic (1985–present), and Access World News (1985–present). The *Sunday Times* is accessible in LexisNexis Academic (1985–present) and Access World News (1985–present). The *Times* has a long history of being indexed in both *Palmer's Index to the Times* and the *Official Index to the Times*. Though *Palmer's Index* is of little use to postmodern researchers because it is limited to pre-1905 publications, the *Official Index* runs from 1906 to 1980 and is available electronically as the *Times Digital Archive* through Gale Digital Collections. The index includes the ability to search for authors by byline or by a subject list that places articles into broad categories.

The *Times Digital Archive* from Gale covers 1785–2006 and defaults to a basic keyword search that scans through the entire text of the articles. An advanced search interface is also available that lets you home in on specific types of documentation, such as advertisements, editorial commentary, obituaries, stock exchange tables, pictures, or people. The advanced search also allows limiting by date ranges, keywords, titles, and authors. The results are ranked by relevancy, based on the frequency with which terms are used. The twenty-year addition to the earlier release of this product adds content from 1985 to 2006, which includes articles from the *Times2*, a daily supplement of mostly feature articles. This is a massive database, containing over eleven million items, and essential for British newspaper research.

The ***Guardian*** and its sister publication, the ***Observer***, also play significant roles in the postmodern era. They are the left-leaning newspapers in Britain, a counterpoint to the more conservative *Times*. The current issue of the *Guardian* can be viewed online, and recent issues are available with InfoTrac Newsstand (1990–present), ProQuest Newsstand (1996–present), LexisNexis Academic (1984–present), and Access World News (1998–present). The current *Observer* is also available from its website, or through InfoTrac Newsstand (1993–present), ProQuest Newsstand (1995–present), LexisNexis Academic (1990–present), and Access World News (1998–present). An archive of indexed, searchable content from the *Guardian* and the *Observer* is found on the ProQuest Historical Newspapers platform, with coverage until 2003. Access to a similar historical archive can be purchased online through the website for those without subscriptions through a library.

The British Broadcasting Corporation is another profoundly influential institution during the postmodern period, and discussing the *Times* and the *Guardian* without mentioning the BBC would be inappropriate. In addition to the current news site, simply called **BBC**, the British Broadcasting Corporation also produces various news programs for radio and television, such as *BBC News Hour*, which is most commonly aired on radio in the United States. Digitization for the **BBC Archive** should be completed by 2015, and much of the digitized content is now available for free online through the archive's website back to 1930. The content is queried through a basic keyword search in the top right-hand corner of the screen, and limiters can narrow down the type of content on the results page. This website also features a catalog of programs and episodes, as well as author and subject indexes. Text is linked, making indexed contributors, topics, program names, and other data easily navigable. These links are also used to make recommendations for other videos of interest. The sheer volume of content alone makes this archive profoundly important for postmodern researchers, but these linking features are a powerful tool to discover new aspects of the social and cultural history of Britain over the past fifty years, especially for those interested in authors and literary critics, who are well represented in programs like *Monitor*, which ran from 1958 to 1965 and featured interviews with Aldous Huxley and Kingsley Amis. One big drawback is that the archive does not have a specific advanced search dedicated to its content. This makes finding materials more difficult.

In addition to the BBC Archive, two digitization projects from JISC, formerly the UK's Joint Information Systems Committee, are also quite useful for researchers who wish to study broadcast news: News on Screen and the London Broadcast Company/Independent Radio News Audio Archive. **News on Screen: The World's Leading Resource for the Study of Newsreels and Cinemagazines** is an index of digitized news broadcasts from multiple sources, some of which might be available online and some that might require subscription logins or are otherwise limited. One particularly important set of resources indexed in News on Screen comes from the Digital Newsreel Archive, which has the British Movietone News series. For most of the British Movietone videos, a low-resolution clip will play without a login since the database is primarily there to act as a licensing agent for the newsreels. The search interface for News on Screen allows you to choose fields, such as summary, location, footage, written source, issues number, title, researcher comments, version, credits, company reference, NoS number, or keyword. Date ranges, series titles, video source, and type are also potential limiters. There are specialized searches through the News on Screen databases that contain production documents, information about people, and series histories. The **London Broadcast Company/Independent Radio News Audio Archive** contains commercial radio recordings from 1973 to 1996. Most recordings will not be available for those unaffiliated with UK institutes of higher education, though the database has value as an index of recordings for all researchers. Some of the recordings might link to transcripts of the audio—for instance, those of Margaret Thatcher's speeches and interviews. Though researchers in the United States often do not have access to all of the media available through these two resources, the content they index is rare, which makes them valuable tools, despite their limitations.

Another database that might be of use when looking for documentaries or newsreels is the commercial **British Pathé**. Though its main purpose is to license vintage footage to contemporary producers, the database still provides nine thousand items with 3,500 hours of film. The resource can be searched or browsed by archive or program name. This content is valuable when researching pop culture. For instance, a keyword search for the *Rolling Stones* retrieves twenty-five films made between 1964 and 1970 as the band rose to popularity in the UK and toured throughout the Commonwealth. A sliding button at the top of the page allows patrons to limit results by year, and several other options let visitors further focus their query. An advanced search is available and includes fields such as tape, canister number, sound, color, group, decade, category, and excluded terms. The videos are free to "preview" online, though licensing is required to reproduce the clips for new video productions.

As mentioned earlier, we cannot list every news source that might be important. We can only make some suggestions about where you might find these items and supporting information about them. One of your best resources is the British Library, discussed further in chapter 8, which has a comprehensive collection of newspapers published in the UK, particularly for the postmodern period. British Library collections include mainstream newspapers like the *Manchester Evening News* or the *Liverpool Echo*, in addition to more erudite materials on film, music, and other cultural phenomena, covered later in chapter 9. Collections located at the library can be searched in the catalog, Explore the British Library, described in chapter 3, though the full text is only available in print if you visit the library. To target newspapers, researchers can choose "Newspaper Library" from the drop-down menu next to the search box in the default keyword query, or they can use advanced options. Though this is not an index of individual articles, the catalog is useful for identifying regional or local newspapers and for discovering publication frequency, dates, publishers, title variants, and other key information. Because the British Library has an extensive collection of newspapers from the entire United Kingdom, and because as a national library it is charged with collecting items published across the country, a record for most newspapers pertinent to contemporary British history will likely be found.

Outside of these large-scale digitization projects, researchers can also turn to more traditional tools to find smaller regional news sources that might have been closed due to consolidation. Often these can only be requested through interlibrary loan or by traveling to archives that hold them, as discussed in chapter 8. **The Bibliography of British Newspapers** indexes British newspapers by region and is useful for finding defunct publications. This might be especially important in cases where the research interest is someone like William Golding, who grew up in Cornwall, which is one of the regions covered in volume 6 of this bibliography. By identifying local newspapers from the period of the author's childhood, local stories about the author or about themes discussed in his writing might be discovered. Entries give the name of the publication, the publisher, addresses, name changes, dates, mergers, and location where the newspaper circulated. There is an index for place. Newspapers are divided based on where they were circulated and where they drew their news, and then are listed by date.

The Encyclopedia of the British Press, 1422–1992 can also be of use to those unfamiliar with less well-known figures in British publishing. Focusing on people and publications, this resource has short entries on journalists, editors, publishers, and titles. The volume also includes lengthier essays about the history of newspaper publishing, from Caxton to the early 1990s. As always, whenever you work with unfamiliar media, it is good to have a handy reference to guide you through those parts that might be unclear.

In addition to the resources listed here, nontraditional media might also be important for finding news. Blogs, Twitter, and other forms of mass communication that occasionally fill the role of a news source in contemporary culture are discussed further in chapter 11, though these technologies are worth noting as we end our discussion. Well-known authors or other media figures might regularly post information about their daily lives and events going on around them in much the same way they once wrote letters to the editor. Increasingly, and even more significantly, these sources might be the only form of information available from a censored or restricted political class, as happened during the Arab Spring, when those opposing entrenched governments in the Middle East took to the Internet to coordinate and disseminate information. In both these cases, social media could prove pivotal to the completion of a research project. Remember, though, that despite the willingness of some to believe whatever they read online, these sources are often not corroborated and should be handled with the appropriate level of skepticism and care.

JOURNALS

Aesthetica. York: Aesthetica Magazine Ltd. www.aestheticamagazine.com.
BHI: British Humanities Index. Ann Arbor, MI: ProQuest. www.proquest.com.
Chapman: Scotland's Quality Literary Magazine. Edinburgh: Chapman Publishing. www.chapman-pub.co.uk/home.php.
Literary Review. London: Literature Review. www.literaryreview.co.uk.
New Welsh Review. Aberystwyth, UK: New Welsh Review Ltd. www.newwelshreview.com.
New Yorker. New York: Condé Naste. www.newyorker.com.
Ulrichsweb. Seattle: Serial Solutions. ulrichsweb.serialssolutions.com.

Though critical journals are covered more completely in chapter 5, current magazines and literary journals might also be of worth to scholars, and there are some unique resources that focus on these publications. Popular cultural magazines are particularly beneficial because many publish new creative works, such as **The New Yorker** in the United States, or **Literary Review**, **Aesthetica**, and the **New Welsh Review** in the United Kingdom. Often they are the preeminent venue for poets and fiction writers to debut new pieces, making them important to literary researchers. Unfortunately, because these publications often include a conglomeration of news, criticism, and original works, it might be difficult to identify which magazines and which issues deserve attention.

One way to identify the journals that are likely to carry original work is to look them up in **Ulrichsweb**, formerly Ulrich's International Periodicals Directory or Ulrich's Periodicals Directory. This database provides information about three hundred thousand publications, active, suspended, and ceased, published internationally after 1974. ISSN, price, publisher, former titles, publication dates, frequency, available formats, and other useful information are listed in each record. Though not an index of articles, Ulrich's acts as the directory of note for contemporary periodicals and functions like a union title list for serials in the postmodern period. Ulrich's will also tell you where the journal is indexed and abstracted. Ulrich's is of particular use for identifying new periodicals as possible sources for research and verifying that journals are peer-reviewed. Take *Chapman: Scotland's Quality Literary Magazine* as an example, which has been published in Scotland since 1970. By looking this title up in Ulrichsweb, patrons will find how frequently it is published, when it was first published, where it is available online, and a description of what it publishes. All of these pieces of information can be useful for researchers learning about a new area of literary interest.

Another way to find journals or to identify issues to peruse is **BHI: British Humanities Index**. Similar to the U.S. *Readers' Guide to Periodical Literature*, BHI is helpful because it identifies research published in sources with broad subjects. BHI indexes British periodical literature related to a wide variety of art or humanities topics. The database has indexing for 370 academic journals, magazines, and newspapers from 1962 to the present. Now on the ProQuest platform, the interface features keyword searching and advanced options, such as date ranges and subjects. Articles are organized with terms taken from the original print index that the database supersedes, the *BHI Annual*. The online version is updated monthly, adding about 1,500 records each time. Some English-language articles from publications outside of Britain might appear, such as those from New Zealand, Australia, and Canada. *London Magazine* is a good example of the type of resource that makes BHI particularly useful as an index. Printing news, original creative writing, reviews, criticism, and other cultural items, *London Magazine* does not fit easily into any one subject category. By indexing it, BHI ensures that you can identify the criticism, if you want, or the original creative writing, which might otherwise be lost or buried with the rest of the content.

LITERARY MAGAZINES

"Annual Bibliography of Commonwealth Literature." *Journal of Commonwealth Literature*. Newcastle upon Tyne: Sage.

Areté. Oxford: Areté Ltd. www.aretemagazine.co.uk.

Believer. San Francisco: McSweeney's Books. www.believermag.com.

Cambridge Literary Review. Cambridge: University of Cambridge. www.cambridgeliteraryreview.org.

Edinburgh Review. Edinburgh: Edinburgh Review. edinburgh-review.com.

Goode, Stephen H., ed. *Index to Commonwealth Little Magazines.* Troy, NY: Whitston Publishing, 1966–1986.

Granta. London: Sigrid Rausing. www.granta.com.

International Directory of Little Magazines and Small Presses. Paradise, CA: Dustbooks, 1965–.

London Magazine. London: London Magazine. thelondonmagazine.org.

Mslexia. Newcastle upon Tyne: Mslexia Publications Ltd. www.mslexia.co.uk.

New Pages. Bay City, MI: New Pages. www.newpages.com.

Oxford Literary Review. Edinburgh: Edinburgh University Press. www.euppublishing.com/journal/olr.

Paris Review. New York: Paris Review Foundation. www.theparisreview.org.

Poets and Writers. Palm Coast, FL: Poets & Writers Inc. www.pw.org.

Sader, Marion, ed. *Comprehensive Index to English-Language Little Magazines, 1890–1970: Series One.* 8 volumes. Millwood, NY: Kraus-Thomson Organization, 1976.

Short Story Index. Ipswich, MA: EBSCO. www.ebscohost.com.

Sullivan, Alvin, ed. *British Literary Magazines: The Modern Age, 1914–1984.* 4 volumes. Historical Guides to the World's Periodicals and Newspapers. Greenwood, CT: Westport, 1986.

Swallow, Alan. *Index to Little Magazines.* Denver, CO: A. Swallow, 1942–1965.

Writer's Forum. Bournemouth, UK: Select Publisher Services Ltd. www.writers-forum.com.

During the postmodern period, literary magazines, or those that focus on new writing from current authors, went from popular forms of entertainment to the more rarified auspices of academic publishing or small-niche presses, appealing to artistic communities or cultural enclaves. Despite the decreasing popular demand for literature in periodicals, these "little magazines," or small, noncommercial magazines that publish literature and often experimental or nontraditional writing, continued to be extremely noteworthy to the ongoing development of literary trends, techniques, and movements. *Granta*, one of the most significant British literary magazines, is particularly prominent because it publishes established authors and rising stars. *Granta* also circulates a list of up-and-coming British novelists under the age of forty every ten years, which has named writers such as Martin Amis and Kazuo Ishiguro. Because studying a new era in literary history is partly dependent on discovering who will be in the canon, these specialized journals and the awards they confer are helpful. In addition, they often include reviews, special issues edited by already-established writers, and other useful specialty publications. Identifying them is difficult because they ceased to be the mass-market publications that made authors superstars in the earlier half of the twentieth century, but researchers have one advantage. The proliferation of specialized academic reference sources, even as some forms of publishing faded, ensured the creation of finding aids for this type of material that make research much easier.

One of these aids is the biennial *Index to Commonwealth Little Magazines*, which indexed material appearing in approximately fifteen to forty little magazines published in Commonwealth and ex-Commonwealth countries during the years 1965–1993. Though imperfect, this index has magazines not listed elsewhere and has author and subject guides. Entries are listed alphabetically by reviewer's name, author of the work being reviewed, or subject, and contain basic bibliographic information about essays, reviews, primary works, and other content. Many authors and subjects related to postmodernism are listed in the indexes. For example, the 1990–1992 volume has two reviews listed under the postmodernism subject: *Future* Fall: Excursions into Post-Modernity* edited by E. A. Grosz (reviewed in *Southern Review*) and *Myth, Truth, and Literature: Towards a True Post-Modernism* by Colin Falck (reviewed in *Agenda*).

Similarly, the eight-volume *Comprehensive Index to English-Language Little Magazines, 1890–1970* covers a wider variety of publications, though over half of the resources indexed are American in origin. One hundred periodicals are represented, featuring poetry, fiction, and criticism. Many well-known publications, such as *Black Mountain Review*, *Kenyon Review*, *Paris Review*, and *Prairie Schooner*, are discussed, along with less well-known titles, such as *Briarcliff Quarterly* and *Egoist: An Individual Review*. These magazines are listed at the beginning in a section called "List of Magazines Indexed," which gives publisher location, number of volumes, and last known publication date, as well as details on name changes and mergers. Entries have authors, the title of the article, names of translators, the type of article, the title of the little magazine, the issue number, dates of issue, and pages of article. They are organized alphabetically by last name of the contributor or by subject. A search for Anthony Burgess results in a "see also" note for John Anthony Burgess Wilson. This entry lists works by and works about Burgess. For example, a story he wrote called "I Wish My Wife Was Dead" appeared in the *Transatlantic Review* in the Winter 1969–1970 issue.

The *Index to Little Magazines*, which contains the period from 1940 to 1970, is another author-subject index of about thirty to fifty little magazines not held in either the *Readers' Guide* or the *International Index*. Each volume begins with a list of abbreviations and magazines indexed, which also notes if they have ceased or been suspended. Entries are listed alphabetically by author and subject and provide basic bibliographic information. The little magazines are almost all American publications, but reviews and literary works of British authors are included. For example, a search for Philip Larkin in the 1962–1963 volume reveals a poem he wrote called "Faith Healing" that appeared in the Winter 1962 issue of *Shenandoah* and a review of his poetry in the Spring 1962 issue of the *Western Humanities Review*.

The *International Directory of Little Magazines and Small Presses* is the standard directory to identify these periodicals. Updated once each year, this resource covers active small presses that could go unnoticed otherwise. Indexes are available for subject and region. Because the directory has been published since 1965, it is the best resource for recognizing historically active little magazines. Entries supply contact and publication information for listed resources, which are organized alphabetically, regionally, and by subject.

Sullivan's *British Literary Magazines: The Modern Age, 1914–1984* is also of use, with the fourth volume providing essays on literary periodicals and their significance in British publishing from 1914 to 1984, though it does not cover the entire postmodern period. Each entry delivers the name of the literary magazine, the nature of what it published, and an essay on its significance.

Researchers might also want to consult indexes that guide users to resources based on the genre of writing—for instance, short stories published in periodicals in the 1980s. The *Short Story Index* is just such a resource and is available as an online database through EBSCO, containing 1984 to the present. The print version goes back even further to 1974. This resource features British authors, making it useful to find anthologized works by subject, as well as stories from periodicals if they were published in titles indexed by either the *Readers' Guide*, which is specific to the United States, or the Humanities Index, which has international English-language periodicals. These types of indexes are useful for researchers looking to identify primary pieces of literature published originally or republished in periodicals. To use the *Short Story Index*, browse for an appropriate key term in one of the indexes (such as author or subject). Clicking on the term will list short stories that correspond to it. A simple keyword search is also available.

The cultural changes to British society in the 1960s allowed for more varied voices to emerge, and significant strains of postmodernism endeavor to explore issues of postcolonialism, race, gender, and class. Indexes and bibliographies that identify and therefore make this literature accessible were particularly prolific during this era. While not all of them can be listed here, researchers should be aware of this type of resource. One example is *The Journal of Commonwealth Literature*'s **"Annual Bibliography of Commonwealth Literature,"** which is indispensable in this regard, providing a summary of new literature in English with a special focus on postcolonial literature and writing across the varied regions of the Commonwealth. In addition to book-length works, this bibliography covers periodical publications of original work.

For researchers interested in more contemporary British literary magazines, several websites exist that discuss online publications. The biggest of these are *New Pages*, *Poets and Writers*, and *Writer's Forum*. **New Pages** is an online publication that assesses literary magazines in addition to providing directory information about alternative presses. Though it primarily covers those published in the United States, a good number of resources from the UK are also included. **Poets and Writers** is an American nonprofit organization for creative writers that sponsors a directory to British and American literary magazines and small presses. **Writer's Forum** is a publication for British writers that often discusses submission opportunities, literary journals, and other pertinent information related to authors in the United Kingdom, though it is not a directory in the same sense as the other two websites listed here. Many well-known and influential British literary magazines that have long been available in print, such as **London Magazine**, **Areté**, **Cambridge Literary Review**, **Edinburgh Review**, **Oxford Literary Review**, and **Mslexia**, are also now available online, either partially or entirely. Additionally, do not overlook important literary journals published in the United States, such as the **Paris Review** and the newer **Believer**, which often print authors from the UK, for instance, Salman Rushdie and Zadie Smith.

ALTERNATIVE PRESS

Alternative Press Index. Ipswich, MA: EBSCO. www.ebscohost.com.

Alternative Press Index Archive. Ipswich, MA: EBSCO. www.ebscohost.com.

British Library. Explore the British Library. London: British Library Board. explore.bl.uk.

Fredricksson, Carl Henrick, ed. *Eurozine*. Vienna. www.eurozine.com.

Gifford, Dennis. *The Complete Catalogue of British Comics*. Exeter: Webb & Bower, 1985.

Underground and Alternative Press in Britain. Hassocks, UK: Harvester Press, 1974–.

Underground and Independent Comics, Comix, and Graphic Novels. Alexandria, VA: Alexander Street Press. comx.alexanderstreet.com.

Zobl, Elke, ed. *GRRRLZine Network*. Salzburg: Elke Zobl, 2001–2008. grrrl zines.net.

For postmodern researchers, alternative press publications, zines, graphic novels, and underground printing can identify counterculture primary sources, for instance, the writing of John Cooper Clarke, the punk poet, or

Mark Perry's punk zine *Sniffin' Glue*. Because these types of publications are not well known through more traditional means, many resources have sprung up to help interested parties find alternative media.

The most important of these resources is the ***Alternative Press Index***, which started in the radical 1960s to make accessible leftist-leaning English-language publications and currently indexes titles such as the UK's socialist *New Left Review* and cultural *New Formations*, which print literary and cultural criticism from theorists like Stuart Hall and Amit Chaudhari. Available both in print and online, the digital version through EBSCO holds back issues from 1969 to 1990 in the **Alternative Press Index Archive**, as well as the quarterly current publications from 1990 to the present. This is considered the authoritative source for alternative publications. Both the online and print versions index articles by subject and provide publication information to facilitate the retrieval of these articles.

Underground and Alternative Press in Britain is a microform collection that lists print media from 1961 to 1993 and is the best way to access periodicals such as the *International Times*, *Oz*, and *Private Eye*, which shaped much of the underground culture that became British postmodern literature. For many researchers, this is the only way to access this content, which is rare even in archives. The microform collection has the full text for featured periodicals. For those who have never used a microfilm machine, it might be useful to think of it as a type of limited projector. The machine works by stretching the film under the viewing lens, and placing the film reels on pegs to either side of this lens. The film can then be advanced or rewound from frame to frame, allowing patrons to "flip" through pages of an item. Many newer systems allow users to scan the film, then email or print it.

The British Library also offers an invaluable research guide to finding zines, or self-published periodicals with extremely small circulation, and other counterculture publications. The library has an extensive collection of primary sources from across the Commonwealth, such as graphic novels and comic books. Most of these resources are in the main British Library catalog, **Explore the British Library**, though researchers might also need to use the library's comics finding list. Websites also offer an access point to zines and other alternative media, for instance, through the ***GRRRLZine Network***, ***Eurozine***, or other similar resources. Because these resources are so rare and ephemeral, finding online copies or documentation that describes issues of the zines can be much easier than finding the print originals. ***The Complete Catalogue of British Comics*** can help researchers find graphic art and related literature, and contains price and publication information for comics published before 1985. Because graphic literature is such a significant trend in postmodernism, due largely to novels like Alan Moore's *Watchmen* and Neil Gaiman's Sandman series, these resources are increasingly important. Alexander Street Press's *Un-*

derground and Independent Comics, Comix, and Graphic Novels, discussed further in chapter 11, is another a good source for primary graphical documents and has 421 comic series from multiple countries of origin.

CONCLUSION

Though periodical publishing has changed considerably over the past seventy years, a solid understanding of indexes, bibliographies, and digital apparatuses will assist researchers wading through the large amount of information now available. Knowing the right tools and how to use them should make this job easy. Hopefully, over the next several years, online resources making available new content will become even better, particularly for radio and television. While print periodicals have never been more accessible online, radio and television represent a significant portion of the news media published over the course of the postmodern period. These newer mediums are not well represented in available databases and can be costly or difficult to retrieve. The BBC Archive is an admirable and important undertaking to remedy this situation, though it does not yet mirror the robust and versatile nature of search options available for print retrieval. Better tagging and limiting for this archive would be a huge step forward.

NOTES

1. Linda Jean Kenix, *Alternative and Mainstream Media: The Converging Spectrum* (London: Bloomsbury, 2011), 25.
2. Ibid., 26.
3. Edward Turner, ed., *The Statesman's Yearbook 2013: The Politics, Cultures and Economies of the World* (Basingstoke, UK: Palgrave Macmillan, 2012), 1295.
4. Roy Greenslade, "Britain's Vanishing Newspapers," *Guardian*, February 19, 2009, http://www.theguardian.com/media/greenslade/2009/feb/19/local-newspapers-newspapers.
5. BARB, "Trends in Television: 2013," March 2014, http://www.barb.co.uk/trendspotting/data/trends-in-tv?_s=4?_s=5.
6. Turner, *The Statesman's Yearbook 2013*, 1295.
7. Ben Quinn, "Royal Wedding Television Audience Hit 24m Peak in UK," *Guardian*, April 30, 2011, http://www.theguardian.com/uk/2011/apr/30/royal-wedding-television-audience.
8. Simon Rycroft, *Swinging City: A Cultural Geography of London, 1950–1974*, (Farnham, UK: Ashgate, 2012), 84–86.
9. Ibid., 86–91.
10. Ibid., 91.
11. Ibid., 83–84.
12. Ibid., 83–84.

Chapter Eight

Manuscripts, Archives, and Digital Collections

Though many primary sources and archival materials are now available through microform and digital collections, there are still many items that are only available through physical archives and special collections. We are still some time away from a world where all research can be completed online, due to the limitations in the time and money required to digitize everything, as well as the barriers of copyright. Even if a digital reproduction or a facsimile version exists, you should still visit the physical object in order to identify features like watermarks to verify that the reproduction is faithful to the original or to better read someone's handwriting. As a result, original research often requires a visit to an archive.

This chapter discusses how to identify archival collections, along with tips about doing archival research, finding documents, and scheduling time at facilities with these resources. The information provided here will help you be more prepared to visit such an institution, which will make the time spent completing the research more fruitful. Keep in mind that postmodern authors are in many cases still alive, so they might not have donated any of their personal papers or original manuscripts to an institution yet, which probably represents the biggest barrier to archival research of postmodern authors. Still, discounting archival research for any literary period would be a mistake. In many cases, the primary documents held in archives are at the heart of our discipline and should receive pride of place in any serious research project.

DEFINING ARCHIVES AND MANUSCRIPTS

Archives are often housed in libraries, especially in university libraries, but they can also be found in government buildings, businesses, newspapers, historical societies, and museums. Though libraries and archives share many features, they are actually different institutions with unique purposes and a variety of resources. You might find distinctive search methods, and the tools to use them are necessary. Libraries tend to collect secondary sources, and they purchase them through publishers or vendors one item at a time, either through an approval plan (agreement with a vendor to provide for the automatic delivery of new materials) or through a selection process that considers reviews and recommendations. In contrast, archives almost exclusively collect primary sources and often purchase them as one complete collection. A common example of this is when an author's relative donates all of the person's papers after his or her death. Archivists might take many years to organize, describe, and catalogue this collection if it is quite large. As a result, you might have to sort through a lot of documents to find relevant information. This process can be time-consuming and frustrating, though it might also produce serendipitous results.

Libraries usually collect published works, like books and periodicals. Archives are more likely to hold unpublished, unique works such as organizational records, personal papers, notebooks, journals, letters, and oral histories. Formats such as photographs, slides, films, computers, or audio recordings might also be included in archives. Many of these items are one of a kind and worth a considerable amount of money. Literary scholars are primarily interested in the personal papers of authors, but other unpublished materials are helpful as well. For instance, marital, publisher, or military service records can confirm facts about an author's life. Sometimes the content at a library or an archive might be the same, but the format is different. For example, an academic library would hold the collected letters of Harold Pinter as a scholarly edition published by a university press. This book might be edited and annotated by a well-known Pinter scholar. An archive might hold the original letters, complete with coffee stains and torn pages. Clearly, both resources have value, but different research questions will require one over the other.

When a library does not have the item needed, you can usually submit an interlibrary loan request and have the item delivered to your home library for use. If an archive does not have all the papers or manuscripts of a given author, another archive that has those materials will not send those items. Instead, you will be required to make multiple trips to several different institutions. Since archives tend to have closed-stack collections and will not circulate their materials, patrons must utilize the materials in a reading room after a staff member has retrieved them.

These differences can be understood as the result of the different objectives for each type of institution. The goal of most libraries is to acquire the resources needed to help their patrons read, learn, or perform research. They are very concerned with providing as much access to those resources as possible. Archives are also interested in offering access to patrons, but they are just as focused on acquiring and preserving rare materials so that they will still exist for future generations. As a result, archives place many more restrictions on how their items can be handled than most libraries. Visitors cannot browse the stacks in an archive. Instead, they must employ finding aids to identify what is needed and then request access. Finding aids are resources that describe the background and scope of a collection. They also give an outline of the contents, either at the "item level," which means a description of every item in the collection, or at the "box level," which means the general content of every box in the collection is described. Often only a few items may be examined at a time.

Before access is granted to an archive, proof of identification is required. Some archives, especially those in Europe, might even require a letter of introduction from a known scholar who can confirm a visitor's home institution and scholarly interest in their materials. These policies vary greatly from archive to archive, so always check the requirements before arriving. Hours can be limited as well, so plan your trip accordingly. You do not want to budget only one Monday to use a particular archive during a weeklong research trip to England, only to arrive and find that they are not open on Mondays.

While most libraries have online catalogs that can be utilized to search for their materials, archives often have other search methods. Some materials in archives might appear in a library catalog, particularly those special collections located at a university. Even in those cases, not all materials are listed, and the catalog might not give enough information to really know what is contained in the manuscript. Libraries usually employ MARC Records (see chapters 1 and 3) to catalog their materials. Archives, on the other hand, develop finding aids that are described with Encoded Archival Descriptions (EAD). EAD is preferred by archivists because it gives a structure for descriptive information while still offering the flexibility needed to explain the uniqueness of each collection. Finding aids are often posted online and provide valuable information about the individual items found in a unique collection, along with specific details about where to locate it, such as box and folder numbers. Unfortunately, not every collection will have a finding aid. When this happens, you will want to work directly with the archivist, who can help you discover uncatalogued items and learn special techniques for navigating a unique collection.

So far the term *manuscripts* has been mentioned several times in this chapter without a definition. Though the words *archives* and *manuscripts* are both used to describe collections, they are not exactly the same thing.

Manuscripts are donated or purchased from an individual or a family, while archives come from an institution or an organization. Manuscripts can also refer to handwritten or draft documents, and archives often house manuscripts, along with other objects such as photographs and ephemera (fragile items that were usually not intended to last a long time). Having a basic understanding of the differences between these terms can help identify what you are trying to find and use.

UNIQUE CHALLENGES

Be aware that researching postmodern literature can provide unique challenges. As previously mentioned, one challenge is that primary sources such as original manuscripts, correspondence, and diaries might not be available in an archive since many of the authors are still alive. Some living authors donate their papers, but it is not usual for a donation like this to be made while someone is still alive, and obviously it will not be a complete collection since the author will still be creating new content. If you are studying a specific author, it is advised that you monitor the discussions that might be taking place around that author's papers. Pay attention to recent news articles and updates on his or her website. For instance, the National Library of Scotland has been working hard in recent years to acquire the papers of J. K. Rowling, and their efforts have been documented in the news.

A related issue is that traditional British institutions are especially hesitant to collect documents from living authors. As described in Jamie Andrews's article "'Laid Aside'? Collecting Contemporary Literary Archives and Manuscripts," American institutions with deeper pockets are stepping into this void and beginning to acquire British works, potentially leading to the papers of prominent British writers being divided into several different collections or having no representation in Britain. Andrews suggested that "in the face of this trans-Atlantic activity, deliberate intervention was required to shape a new type of collection. British institutions would have to rethink assumptions about how manuscripts were collected, when they should be acquired, and where they should reside, coupled with a new urgency to ensure their swift retention."[1]

Formats can also be a unique challenge since most postmodern authors are not producing their manuscripts by hand and might not even save different versions of their work as it develops. Examining original manuscripts might require access to older versions of Microsoft Word, or machines that are capable of opening floppy disks and other out-of-date media. There is a real risk that some digital formats will be completely lost if the equipment to run the files no longer exists, or if servers and files have become corrupted. E-mail and other forms of social media are especially difficult to use after their original programs are out-of-date, if these objects are saved at all. As Matthew Kirschenbaum argues in *Mechanisms*, the pervasive belief that "none this stuff is going to last" leads to social practices where these types of communication are purged from inboxes and servers with regularity, jeopardizing the ability of future archival researchers who are no longer likely to have stacks of handwritten correspondence and varying versions of manuscripts.[2] Though archival techniques are beginning to adapt to these born-digital materials, the social norms regarding the easy disposal of Internet communication might pose an even bigger risk to postmodern researchers as the many technical problems recede.

Copyright can create real barriers as well. In the United Kingdom, a work qualifies for copyright protection if it was made after June 1, 1957, by a British citizen. Copyright laws in the United States extend even further back, protecting works written since 1923. As many postmodern British authors began working in the 1950s, much of their writing might not be freely available in a digital format due to copyright. Magazine and newspaper articles from the twentieth and twenty-first century are not always available full-text in library databases. As a result, though these newer works might seem like they would be easier to find online, they might actually be more difficult to locate.

BEST PRACTICES FOR ARCHIVAL RESEARCH

As we have already described, libraries and archives have some major differences, and these extend to the type of preparation required for a visit. Generally, visiting an archive requires more advanced planning than using a library because the more planning you do, the more efficient the visit will be. One of the first steps is to gather background information on your research topic. Starting with an initial examination of this information can help you obtain all the necessary context, which will aid in thinking about what kinds of archival materials are essential and how they should be used. Identifying the collections that hold these materials and where they are housed is an important early step. Authors of biographies and literary criticism might assist with this step by citing the archives they visited in their research, which might be the archives you will need to visit. Later sections of this chapter will describe some other sources that could help with this process.

Once you choose the archives you want to visit, spend time on their websites. As mentioned before, determine if they have limited hours or if they have special policies about who can access their collections. Today, digital finding aids might be available, which should give a clear idea of what is actually housed in the collection. If a digital finding aid is unavailable, look for a relevant archivist's contact information. If a printed finding aid is available, you might also be able to purchase a copy of it through the website. Sometimes finding aids clarify that a visit is unnecessary because the archive doesn't have what is needed or that the research can be performed with just a digitized image of an item or from a reproduction requested for a small fee.

In addition to general restrictions about how and when you can view materials, donors can sometimes place restrictions on access to or use of a collection. They might request that only certain researchers be allowed to access the materials, or that specific documents remain sealed until the death of the creator or the people discussed in them, which can be especially common with postmodern authors. Other restrictions might involve how the materials can be utilized or what permissions need to be sought from members of the estate or a designated lawyer to use materials. An archivist can inform you about the restrictions and offer details about who to contact to resolve any potential barriers to access.

Check the website to find out if it is necessary to make an appointment and what kinds of information are required in order to register with the archive. If you contact an archivist before you visit, he or she can sometimes retrieve relevant materials before your arrival, which will save some waiting in the reading room. Many archives will not allow you to bring in personal items like briefcases, book bags, and coats, though they might provide a locker to store such items. Do not expect to be able to bring in food and drinks. Some archives allow laptops and notebooks, but they rarely permit pens because they do not want to risk a stray mark on their materials, so although many archives have pencils on hand, be prepared with your own. Digital cameras are often permissible, but check the rules before your trip because limitations on what can be photographed are common.

Once in the reading room, the locally available search tools can be explored, such as catalogs, printed finding aids, and reference books. After identifying the desired items, write down your requests on a "call slip" with the required information, which usually includes the box number, a reference ID, or some other means of locating and retrieving the item. Some archives allow for requesting items through e-mail or an online form. There might be limits on how many items may be requested at a time. Once a staff member has pulled an item, you can usually examine it for as long as required. Some archives can hold materials for researchers on a special shelf during the duration of a visit, while others require that everything goes back to their collection at the end of the day, to be re-requested the next day. Fragile books might be placed on a foam cradle to prevent damage from excessive handling. Sometimes a weighted cloth "snake" is provided to keep the book open, instead of using your hands to prop it open while you take notes. Archivists might require gloves to handle very fragile material, though policies on gloves vary since many archivists feel that gloves decrease people's dexterity and can result in torn pages, while others require gloves to prevent oils and dirt from getting on the materials. Make sure your hands are clean before handling rare items.

Often, taking notes as you examine the materials is the best option. Depending on the condition or value of the item, you might be able to request photocopies or digital images. Generally, you cannot scan or copy items yourself, but staff might be willing to do it for you. They might allow you to take nonflash photographs yourself or will take photographs for you. One advantage of having the staff make reproductions is that the quality might be higher, though of course higher quality might require you to have enough storage space on your laptop or your external flash drive to store these reproductions. Be certain of the policies related to reproductions, and always ask for permission before copying or photographing. Have cash with you in case there are charges associated with copies. You should also be prepared to wait a certain amount of time to receive your copies.

If you use information from the archives in your published research, it is important to properly cite your sources. Most archives can help you cite their materials and can give a complete name of the collection. If you want to reproduce an image, you need to secure permission from the archive by filling out forms describing the image and how it will be reproduced. You might need to pay permission fees or request permission from an estate.

Special formats, such as films or computer files, might require other preparations. Generally, if archives have special formats, such as 16 mm film or floppy disks, they will have the equipment to view those formats, but check ahead of time to ensure you will be able to view resources on them. If unfamiliar with how to operate the equipment, ask if staff have time to help. If it is possible to obtain a digitized copy of part of a film or photographs, storage space on your laptop or flash drive will become an even more important consideration. There might also be different rules about how to use film stills or original photographs in your published work.

The policies and restrictions of archives can seem daunting for new researchers, but remember that these policies are in place to protect the materials. They are not there to discourage you from using resources. Most archivists are willing to help researchers understand, handle, and make the most of their materials.

THE BRITISH LIBRARY

The United Kingdom's national library is the British Library, which is also one of the largest research libraries in the world. For those exploring British literature, it is often a very important institution, as shown in the descriptions found in chapters 3 and 7 of this book. You will need to do some advanced research to decide if it is necessary to visit this renowned collection, which first opened in 1857. The library originally had a reading room in the British Museum that was famous for its impressive architecture and because of the reputation of people who studied there. In 1997, the collections were moved to a larger space with eleven reading rooms in the St. Pancras area of London. The old reading room is now part of the British Museum and houses special exhibitions. Seven million other research items can be found in Boston Spa in North Yorkshire.

The eleven reading rooms focus on different subjects, such as the African and Asian Studies Reading Room, the Business and Intellectual Property Centre, the Humanities Reading Rooms, the Manuscripts Reading Room, the Maps Reading Room, the Rare Books and Music Reading Room, the Sciences Reading Room, and the Social Sciences Reading Room. The kind of research you engage in will determine which reading rooms should be used, and the next section of this chapter gives details on resources that can be employed to decide what collections are of interest. Generally, the Humanities Reading Rooms (post-1850 printed books and journals) and the Manuscripts Reading Room are the most relevant to literary research.

In the past it was necessary to write ahead to obtain permissions to utilize the British Library's collections and then make an appointment. Now walk-ins are allowed. The only collections that still require appointments are the Sound Archive, the Print Room of the Asia Pacific and Africa Collection, and the Philatelic Collection. Some older manuscripts, like the illuminated manuscripts, might also require advanced permission. Though advanced clearance to visit is not required, you still need to register and receive a Reading Pass. You must bring two identification documents, one to confirm your home address and the other to prove your signature. Proper identification is essential. For instance, bringing just your passport, which does not have a home address, will only result in a day pass, and precious research time will be wasted re-registering every day. Look at the British Library website for more details on what is needed to properly register.

It is necessary to read and agree to the terms of use before gaining access to the collection. No outerwear can be brought into the reading rooms, but lockers are available for a small deposit. Clear plastic bags are provided for carrying personal items into the reading rooms. Only pencils are allowed, though laptops are permitted in certain areas. No food or drink is allowed, and cell phones must be turned off or silenced. Once in the reading rooms, you may order up to ten items a day, four items at a time. The items can only be used in the reading room where they are delivered and must be returned to the same desk. Most of the time, you can obtain copies of items you need, though visitors cannot bring personal cameras. There are guidelines on how to copy or quote materials. In fact, online copies of print and manuscript items can sometimes be requested and mailed, which might save a physical trip.

Though an appointment is not necessary, you might still want to contact the library staff before your visit. They can offer the latest information on their policies and procedures, guide you to relevant resources, and might be able to pull materials to have them waiting for your visit. Once at the library, staff are a vital touchstone who can help you navigate the complexities of archival research, so do not hesitate to ask for advice while you are there. Subject-specific reference teams staff each reading room to aid in identifying helpful resources.

LOCATING MATERIALS IN THE BRITISH LIBRARY

British Library, Department of Manuscripts. *Index of Manuscripts in the British Library*. 10 volumes. Teaneck, NJ: Chadwyck-Healey, 1984–1986.
British Library. Manuscripts Catalogue. searcharchives.bl.uk.
Nickson, M. A. E., and Julian Conway. *The British Library: Guide to the Catalogues and Indexes of the Department of Manuscripts*. 3rd edition. London: British Library, 1998.

As discussed earlier, one of the most important steps in archival research occurs before ever setting foot in the archive: identifying archival items held in a given collection. Though this is often difficult, the British Library has some expert resources that make the process easier and more efficient. This section lists several of these, but remember that in a digital environment, new finding aids are coming online every year.

The *Index of Manuscripts in the British Library* was published between 1984 and 1986. This ten-volume set takes information from the catalogs and indexes of the British Library and the British Museum to describe the manuscript holdings (literary works, journals, letters, deeds, wills, and other legal documents) that were owned until 1950, which might point to early postmodern authors and those writers who influenced the movement. Spelling variants of names are normalized, and holdings compiled from other sources are incorporated into the index. Entries are in alphabetical order by person or place with place-names before personal names. Each entry provides the title of the manuscript and a description, dates when available, as well as a manuscript and a folio number.

Thankfully, in addition to this index, there is also a catalog available that contains more recent manuscript descriptions. The online **Manuscripts**

Catalogue of the British Library offers an index search and a description search. The index search allows queries of names, additional names, descriptive adjuncts, index entries, languages, states, start years, and end years. For instance, a name search for *Harold Pinter* results in records for drafts and manuscripts of his plays, correspondence from Pinter found in other collections, and the Harold Pinter Archive, found in the Western Manuscripts collection. The descriptions search permits keyword searching of manuscript collection descriptions. While most of the manuscript collections are included in this online catalogue, some collections might still need to be searched in print catalogues.

M. A. E. Nickson's third edition of *The British Library: Guide to the Catalogues and Indexes of the Department of Manuscripts* is a valuable source to consult since it describes the collections and resources found in the Department of Manuscripts, some of which cannot be found in the online catalog. The foundation collections of the department (Cotton, Harley, and Sloane) are outlined, as well as closed collections like the Royal, Lansdowne, Hargrave, Burney, King's, Arundel, Stowe, Ashley, Yates Thompson, and Zweig, and collections to which the department is still adding. Collections are listed with a description of the origins and history, information about the contents, and details about any existing catalogs or indexes. An overview of reference books in the Department of Manuscripts and an index are provided.

PRINT AND ELECTRONIC SOURCES FOR LOCATING RELEVANT ARCHIVES AND MANUSCRIPTS

Abraham, Terry. *Repositories of Primary Sources*. University of Idaho. www.uiweb.uidaho.edu/special-collections/Other.Repositories.html.

Archive Finder. Ann Arbor, MI: ProQuest Chadwyck-Healey. archives.chadwyck.com/marketing/index.jsp.

ArchiveGrid. Dublin, OH: OCLC. www.archivegrid.org.

Archives Hub. Manchester, UK: JISC. archiveshub.ac.uk.

British Film Institute National Archive. www.bfi.org.uk/archive-collections.

DeWitt, Donald L., comp. *Articles Describing Archives and Manuscript Collections in the United States: An Annotated Bibliography*. Westport, CT: Greenwood Press, 1997.

———. *Guides to Archives and Manuscript Collections in the United States: An Annotated Bibliography*. Westport, CT: Greenwood Press, 1994.

Dictionary of Literary Biography. Detroit: Gale, 1978–.

Foster, Janet, and Julia Sheppard, eds. *British Archives: A Guide to Archive Resources in the United Kingdom*. 4th edition. New York: Palgrave, 2002.

Harry Ransom Humanities Research Center. University of Texas at Austin. www.hrc.utexas.edu/research/search.

Jean Rhys Archive. McFarlin Library, University of Tulsa. http://www.lib .utulsa.edu/speccoll/collections/rhysjean/index.htm.

Matthew, H. C. G., and Brian H. Harrison. *Oxford Dictionary of National Biography: In Association with the British Academy: From the Earliest Times to the Year 2000*. Oxford: Oxford University Press, 2004.

———. *Oxford Dictionary of National Biography*. Oxford: Oxford University Press, 2004. www.oxforddnb.com.

National Archives. www.nationalarchives.gov.uk.

National Register of Archives. www.nationalarchives.gov.uk/nra.

Sutton, David, ed. *Location Register of Twentieth-Century English Literary Manuscripts and Letters: A Union List of Papers of Modern English, Irish, Scottish, and Welsh Authors in the British Isles*. 2 volumes. Boston: G. K. Hall, 1988.

University of Reading Library, Research Projects Team. Location Register of English Literary Manuscripts and Letters. www.reading.ac.uk/library/ about-us/projects/lib-location-register.asp.

This section has both print and electronic resources. While it is sometimes still necessary to look through print sources to identify the archives where the manuscripts of authors might be located, the Internet is an increasingly important tool for locating archival materials. When deciding on an archive to visit, begin by finding current information and more details on the archive's website. Institutions are also putting their finding aids online more and more and are including archival materials in their online catalogs. Some archival manuscripts have even been digitized, which provides opportunities to search these collections online. There are also online tools available to locate additional relevant archives. This section contains resources that are exclusively devoted to listing and describing archives, while others have a broader concentration but still have information about manuscripts and archives. You can use the information found in this section to identify potential archives to visit.

For a browsable directory listing archives located in a given region, look no further than *Repositories of Primary Sources*, maintained by Terry Abraham at the University of Idaho. This is a free guide to more than five thousand websites for archives, manuscripts, historic photographs, rare books, oral histories, and other kinds of primary sources. The focus is on repositories, so virtual collections and exhibitions are not part of this website. The resources are organized by geographic areas: Western United States and Canada, Eastern United States and Canada, Latin America and the Caribbean, Europe, Asia and the Pacific, and Africa and the Near East. The repository lists do not have descriptions of the major holdings, but they do offer a link to the institution's website. There is no way to do a search, but you can browse by categories. Currently, there is a copyright of 1995–2013, and the website appears to be regularly updated.

Chadwyck-Healey delivers **Archive Finder** to libraries through subscriptions. A descriptive directory of archives in the United States comprising 220,000 collections in 5,750 repositories, it is available as a stand-alone resource or as part of C19: The Nineteenth Century Index, with an emphasis on nineteenth-century materials, though items are listed from as recently as 2006. Information is drawn from the *National Union Catalog of Manuscript Collections* (*NUCMC*) from 1959 to 2006, the *National Inventory of Documentary Sources in the United States* (*NIDS*), the *National Inventory of Documentary Sources in the United Kingdom and Ireland* (*NIDS UK/ Ireland*), with descriptions from repositories and six thousand online finding aids. Archive Finder is the only online source that contains all 115,000 collections of the *NUCMC*. Collections and repositories included are located in England, Ireland, Scotland, Wales, and the United States. The stand-alone version of this resource has options to search collections or repositories by keyword, collection name, repository name, city, town, state, county, country, *NIDS* fiche number, *NUCMC* number, index terms, and collection dates. Repositories can be searched by repository name, city, town, county, country, and holdings keyword.

The freely available **ArchiveGrid**, provided through OCLC, is a database with descriptions of two million collections. OCLC Research supports it as the basis for their experimentation and testing in text mining, data analysis, and discovery system applications and interfaces. The indexed holdings of more than 3,800 archives can be searched. Collections have correspondence, family histories, historical documents, manuscripts, and personal papers. This resource is a good place to find out if any documents related to an author are located in collections primarily devoted to other people, which fills in a gap created by other resources that only list authors with major collections. For example, a search for Neil Gaiman does not yield a collection devoted to him, but correspondence and ephemera related to Gaiman appear in places such as the Robert K. Elder collection at Indiana University, the Charles Vess papers at Virginia Commonwealth University, and the Comic Book collection at Cornell University. The single search box recognizes phrase searching, Boolean operators, wildcards, and nesting. Results are ranked by relevancy, but they can also be sorted by date, title, and archive. Content is drawn from WorldCat, which is described in more detail in chapter 3. Records offer details about the size of the collection, finding aids, contact information, notes, summaries, and relevant subject headings.

Archives Hub is similar to ArchiveGrid, but it focuses on the United Kingdom. It covers 220 institutions and is based at the University of Manchester. Search options include keywords, titles, creators, names, and subjects. Browsing options and a subject finder search box are also provided. A keyword search for Doris Lessing yields forty-two results, such as the Doris Lessing Archive at the University of East Anglia and the Natasha Kroll Archive at the University of Brighton Design Archives, which has a screenplay of *The Grass Is Singing*. Entries for collections have information such as contact, scope and content, administrative/biographical history, conditions governing access, conditions governing use, subject, personal names, and geographical names.

The **British Film Institute (BFI) National Archive** is a good example of an individual archive, with collections of primary and secondary documents related to film and television, including posters, images, publicity material, original scripts, letters, and other artifacts. The BFI is principally concerned with British film and contains nearly a million titles. Their online database is an easy-to-use interface that has information collected since 1933, though it only represents about half of what is available in the collection. Simple searches can be done in film and television works, books, serials, articles, press cuttings, scripts, documents, ephemera, and stills, while advanced searches allow you to search by categories such as series, production company, credits, cast, genre, and synopsis. Results offer reference numbers, titles, dates, production countries, production companies, synopses, category genres, subjects, credits, casts, and collections. The collection information and the reference number lead researchers to locate the item in the physical archives.

The *Dictionary of Literary Biography* and the *Oxford Dictionary of National Biography* are both mainly biographical sources, but they do provide some relevant information for locating archival resources. Both resources are described in more detail in chapter 2. Biographical essays in the ***Dictionary of Literary Biography*** tend to have a section called "Papers," which has a short overview of some of the locations of the author's correspondence and manuscripts, with some descriptions of their holdings. The ***Oxford Dictionary of National Biography*** has a section called "Archives" for some entries (sometimes in the "References" section), which lists archives and libraries that have the author's papers and has a short description of the holdings. For example, the entry for William Golding reveals that some of his correspondence and literary papers can be found at the University of Reading Library.

The ***British Archives: A Guide to Archive Resources in the United Kingdom***, edited by Janet Foster and Julia Sheppard, is a directory of the many archival repositories found throughout the United Kingdom. It is in its fourth edition, has 1,231 entries, and is composed of the collections of 478 institutions. Since it was published in 2002, some of the contact information might not be current, but it can still give the correct name of an archive and show the kinds of collections housed there. The beginning of the book gives guidance on how to use it, descriptions of how entries are arranged, and lists of organizations, publications, and websites. Entries for the individual archives are arranged alphabetically by the town or city's name, and contain the name of the archive, full contact information, hours and days of operation, rules for access, the archive's acquisitions policy, conservation practices, the availability of finding aids either online or in the archive, and information about published guides. There are also brief descriptions of the archives, including the date ranges of holdings, major collections, and the existence of other materials besides manuscripts. Services such as photocopying and microform readers are noted. Three appendixes report archives that have transferred collections, have no collections, or did not respond to the editors' inquiries. The main index has repository titles, parent organizations, significant predecessor organizations, organizations itemized in the appendixes, personal names, and titles of collections. A search for Ted Hughes in this index leads to University of Exeter Library (368), which has a major collection of his papers. Numbers in the index are the individual repository numbers instead of page numbers. There is some subject indexing in the "Guide to Key Subjects." The subject heading for "Literature" in this index is further subdivided by general, plays, poetry, popular, and writers. *British Archives* is especially valuable for locating archives in specific geographic regions.

The **Harry Ransom Humanities Research Center** at the University of Texas (UT) at Austin has one of the biggest collections of archival material related to modern and postmodern literature in the world. This collection contains the papers and materials for such authors as Doris Lessing, Anthony Burgess, and John Osborne. The books and microforms of the research center are part of the regular UT libraries catalog. Searches can be limited to the center's materials by using the locations pull-down menu. Specialized search functions, including date, language, and format are available on the "Advanced Search" page. Since manuscripts and other formats cannot be searched in the catalog, finding aids for "Manuscripts," "Performing Arts," "Photography," "Film," and "Art" can be found on the website. The finding aids can be browsed by collection name, curatorial area, and recent acquisitions, with simple searches and advanced searches possible. Either of these queries will search the finding aid, biographical sketch, container list, indexes, title, creator, or dates. There are also search options for formats such as periodicals, photographs, costumes, personal effects, and maps.

One example of an archive with a significant author collection is the Mc-Farlin Library at the University of Tulsa, which has the **Jean Rhys Archives**. This collection covers the dates 1920–1982 and includes twenty-three boxes, two photo albums, and one oversized folder. These archives are divided into four series: "Writings," "Correspondence," "Photographs," and "Personal Papers." A finding aid for each series can be found online, providing brief descriptions of each item and a code, such as "2:14," that leads to the box, photo album, or folder that would need to be examined to locate that item.

Earlier in the chapter we discussed the British Library. The other major repository in the United Kingdom is the **National Archives**, which is a government institution with a large online presence. The Public Record Office, the Historical Manuscripts Commission, the Office of Public Sector Information, and Her Majesty's Stationery Office are all part of the National Archives. The emphasis of this archive is government papers, so there will be fewer materials related to literary authors. Still, someone researching literature might want to use the resources found here to gain a greater understanding of the social and political issues that influence many writers. For example, if you were researching Salman Rushdie's book *Midnight's Children*, it might be helpful to search for official government documents about the partition of British India. The collection has more than ten million records for materials like manuscripts, photographs, and maps. The website for the National Archives has several major finding aids that will help you locate documents: the Catalogue, DocumentsOnline, ARCHON Directory, and Access to Archives.

One of the most important finding aids for the National Archives is the **National Register of Archives**, which was established in 1945 out of the Reports and Calendars produced since 1869 by the Royal Commission on Historical Manuscripts. This source can be used to find the location of records relating to British history and consists of 44,000 unpublished lists and catalogues that describe archival holdings of 53,000 individuals, 9,000 families, 32,000 businesses, and 116,000 organizations in the United Kingdom and overseas. For example, a search for Iris Murdoch will show that manuscripts and correspondence can be found at Oxford University, Bristol University, London University, Leeds University, and Kingston University. The indexes are available online, but the lists themselves need to be examined in the reading rooms.

The two-volume *Location Register of Twentieth-Century English Literary Manuscripts and Letters: A Union List of Papers of Modern English, Irish, Scottish, and Welsh Authors in the British Isles*, edited by David Sutton, is a union list of manuscripts and letters for deceased or living twentieth-century British literary authors that are located in publicly available archives and collections in Britain. British authors include those from England, Ireland, Scotland, and Wales, along with immigrants and refugees who lived part of their lives in the British Isles. Some postmodern authors in this register are Anthony Burgess, William Golding, Ian McEwan, and John Osborne. The entries are in alphabetical order by author over the two volumes and then by titles. Each entry contains a short description, dates of items or collections, formats, locations, and a statement of provenance with a manuscript number. Notes after each entry mention collections in other countries that also hold items by that author. An appendix at the end of the second volume lists the addresses of institutions mentioned throughout the set, though the information might be out of date since this set was published in 1988.

Fortunately, the Research Projects Team at the University of Reading Library created an online supplement to this set in 2003 called the **Location Register of English Literary Manuscripts and Letters,** which updates works for the 1988 edition and the 2003 supplemental materials. Some new entries in this online version but not in the original are Zadie Smith and Jeanette Winterson. There is a keyword search for author, title, or word or phrase and a browse search for author or title. Once you have results, select details to see the descriptions, notes, and locations for each item. You can mark records to save them and then go to the "Kept" link to sort your records and then print or e-mail them.

In addition to consulting resources that are specifically about British archival material, look for those that focus on archives in the United States because some British materials can be found in American collections, such as Donald DeWitt's two annotated bibliographies. *Articles Describing Archives and Manuscript Collections in the United States: An Annotated Bibliography* contains published articles about manuscript collections, archives, and special collections that were written in 1997 and is organized by broad subject headings. The "Literature" and "Fine Arts" categories are especially valuable. Entries are recorded alphabetically by author's name, and the annotations identify the types of materials listed in collections as well as the people and events that are mentioned in the collections. The index will help uncover where British authors might be included in American collections. For example, using the index will result in discovering that some of Iris Murdoch's manuscripts are in the University of Iowa Library. The *Guides to Archives and Manuscript Collections in the United States: An Annotated Bibliography* was published in 1994 and is a bibliography of published finding aids. Manuscript materials on different topics are organized by broad subject categories with finding aids listed alphabetically under these categories, with the section called "Literary Collections" being the most relevant. Some of the titles described in this section that might be helpful are *English Literary Man-*

uscripts in the Boston Public Library: A Checklist, Guide to Literary Manuscripts in the Huntington Library, British Literary Manuscripts, A Guide to
the Modern Literary Manuscripts Collections in the Special Collections of the
Washington University Libraries*, and more. Each entry has a complete citation and a brief annotation. The index at the end can be employed to locate
specific authors and relevant topics and places.

FINDING DIGITAL ARCHIVES

Europeana. The Hague: National Library of the Netherlands. www.europe
ana.eu.
OAIster. Dublin, OH: OCLC. oaister.worldcat.org.

As mentioned at the beginning of this chapter, archives are starting to be
digitized on a large scale. Though these digital copies will not be acceptable
surrogates in every case for the original archival material, they can help researchers get started and can ensure that rare objects are handled only when
absolutely necessary, thus preserving them for future generations. Though
these digital archives are fairly common, finding them can be difficult. The
same reference sources that once helped navigate physical archives do not
always exist in the digital environment. Luckily, new tools have started to
make research in digital archives more efficient.

One of these tools is **OAIster**, from OCLC, a free union catalog that allows users to search through millions of records for open-access items online. Open-access journals and scholarly resourcs are included, as are open
archives material that has been digitized. Thirty million records are provided from 1,500 international contributors, including the British Library
and the University of London. A simple keyword search is the main entry
point, though an advanced search is available, with fields such as keyword,
title, author, corporate name, conference name, accession number, ISBN,
ISSN, language, keyword, personal name, place of publication, publisher,
series, standard number, and subject. Limiters such as date range, audience,
content, format, and language are also available in the advanced search.
This might be helpful, for example, in finding electronic archival material
for the creator of James Bond, Ian Fleming. Searching for the author and
limiting the results to archival material retrieves several downloadable archive items from around the world.

More focused than OAIster, **Europeana** is a broad search tool that has digital items from archives and museums across Europe. Created by the National
Library of the Netherlands, this is an excellent single search for researchers

looking to use digital documentation related to England, particularly since it contains the British Library's digital collections, in addition to the Louvre and other important institutions on the Continent. A search for Salman Rushdie, for instance, retrieves multiple interviews, documentary clips, and other emphemera that might be relevant for scholars and which are available immediately through the Internet. Of note is the fact that many of these videos document resources created outside of England, including some from France and Spain. This truly international emphasis is particularly valuable, as many other resources overly represent items from the United Kingdom or the United States.

Though these are just two of the search tools available online through museums and archives, it is likely that many more will pop up over the next several years, as digital archives become more prevalent. Though tracking down individual collections online might be difficult, finding these types of tools takes the guesswork out of the process. Rather than hunting for digital collections like a needle in a haystack, they allow researchers to have confidence that they have found the largest part of what is available. These searches also help ensure that the digital content used is reliable since these searches do not simply retrieve any old image available online, but instead retrieve the authorized image from the institutional source.

EXAMPLES OF DIGITAL COLLECTIONS

Documenting Ireland: Parliament, People, and Migration. Southampton, UK: DIPPAM. www.dippam.ac.uk.

Electronic Literature Collection. Cambridge, MA: Electronic Literature Organization. collection.eliterature.org.

Modern English Collection. University of Virginia Library Electronic Text Center. search.lib.virginia.edu/catalog/u2447344.

New World Cinema: Independent Features and Shorts, 1990–Present. Alexandria, VA: Alexander Street Press. alexanderstreet.com/products/new -world-cinema-independent-features-and-shorts-1990-present.

Also mentioned earlier, some primary sources are now available in digital collections, which can take many different forms, including collections that are born digital, commercially available collections, and digital collections created by an archive, a university, or a scholar. The following examples illustrate these different possibilities. More examples of freely available digital collections are covered in chapter 11. As discussed earlier, the easiest way to navigate these collections is to find a good search tool that will allow you to look through multiple collections at once, though this might not always be possible, especially when content is locked behind a subscription login.

One type of resource is a collection of items that are digitized by an educational or governmental institution and are available for free online due to their cultural importance. **Documenting Ireland: Parliament, People, and Migration** (DIPPAM) is one such collection. A virtual archive of sources related to the experience of Irish immigration from the nineteenth century to the late twentieth century, DIPPAM has many archival documents that are fully searchable and available online.

The *Electronic Literature Collection* was one of the first notable international e-literature collections and is an example of a born-digital content. Some authors published these texts in other formats, such as their own author website, but in most cases these primary texts are only available here. Much of the work is very experimental, particularly in terms of investigating the boundaries and possibility of digital literature, which matches one of the main goals of postmodernism. The Electronic Literature Organization published this virtual two-volume collection. Volume 1 was published in October 2006, and volume 2 was published in February 2011. Both volumes were published under Creative Commons licensing, so works can be freely shared, noncommercially, between individuals, libraries, and schools, provided that appropriate attribution is maintained and the works are unmodified. You can browse by keywords, authors, or titles.

The **Modern English Collection** was created as a freely available collection by the University of Virginia Library Electronic Text Center from materials in their physical collections and contains fiction, nonfiction, poetry, drama, letters, newspapers, manuscripts, and illustrations from 1500 to the present. While some parts of the collection are only accessible to members of the University of Virginia because of copyright issues, other parts are publicly accessible. This collection has both American and British authors. Originally, you could browse by author's last name or by category of interest, but they are moving the collection to Virgo, their catalog search. The full-text items in this collection can be searched through the catalog using facets like "Online Texts" and "Online Manuscripts."

Another type of collection is one that is created by a database vendor for a niche group of libraries, containing a specific collection of archival material and usually focusing on a few physical archive collections. This type of resource is generally available by subscription only. **New World Cinema: Independent Features and Shorts, 1990–Present** is a commercially available collection through Alexander Street Press that libraries can either acquire as a one-time purchase or through an annual subscription. This online streaming video collection, which might be considered a primary-source collection since it has the original films, offers approximately two hundred full-length feature films from independent distributors such as Kino Lorber, First Run Features, Film Movement, MK2, and the Global Films Initiative, along with some fifty award-winning shorts. Works from more than sixty countries are included, with seventeen films from the United Kingdom, as well as films from the former colonies. You can browse by videos, directors/producers, actors, genres, country of origin, awards, and clips, or do advanced searches on title, director/producer, actor, awards, subject, language, subtitle language, and year released. Classroom performance rights are provided, along with tools to identify and annotate sections of the films.

CONCLUSION

Archival research today is a mixture of traditional methods involving print resources, where the researcher digs through physical materials, and more modern techniques that involve new digital tools, digital reproduction options, and born-digital primary sources. We recommend making yourself aware of both print and electronic resources when attempting archival research. Remember that researching postmodernism in archives has some unique issues, such as the fact that the manuscripts and ephemera of many living authors will not yet be part of an archive or special collection. Formats are also going to be a new challenge because of changing software and storage capabilities. Finally, remember that copyright can be especially challenging since many postmodern texts are not in the public domain.

Archival research can be both very demanding and rewarding. The documents found in archives often lead to original, and sometimes groundbreaking, research. The resources outlined in this chapter are meant to be starting points. They will help you locate relevant archives, but the actual work of sifting through the materials found in the archive, and then reading and using those materials, will be up to the individual researcher.

NOTES

1. Jamie Andrews, "'Laid Aside'? Collecting Contemporary Literary Archives and Manuscripts," *Archives* 35, no. 2 (2010): 10–12.

2. Matthew Kirschenbaum, *Mechanisms: New Media and the Forensic Imagination* (Cambridge, MA: MIT Press, 2008), 21–22.

Chapter Nine

Multimedia and Performance Art

Film, television, popular music, and live performance play an important role in the study of postmodern literature. The rise of multimedia technology and the blurring of boundaries between different types of artistic output expand the spectrum of topics that literary scholars might explore. Many artists are fluid in the way they produce their work and their mode of self-expression; for example, Ruth Prawer Jhabvala wrote both screenplays and novels during her long career. New types of art are also being let into the literary canon. Beatles lyrics, samurai films, or *Monty Python's Flying Circus* might all be considered literature. As a result, scholars must be willing to research across media.

The *Journal of Popular Culture* is a good place to start for research that takes this wide view of critical scholarship. This peer-reviewed journal has a broad scope and is published by the Popular Culture Association, making it appealing to scholars interested in multiple types of resources. This journal can give the beginning researcher a jumping-off point into media scholarship. Articles are high quality and written by some of the most important individuals in the field. This journal uniquely represents postmodern research because it approaches literature from a contemporary cultural studies viewpoint.

Indexes and bibliographies specific to various types of media help identify scholarship in fields related to literature, which are not covered in *ABELL* or *MLAIB*. Though the search strategies discussed in earlier chapters will work well in these resources, keywords and subject headings might not be familiar. To help combat this problem, learning the vocabulary of media studies is important. Also understand that finding the primary or original recordings is sometimes challenging. The quality of the recordings, restoration, and "features" can set one version of a film or album apart from another. The savvy researcher has to know formats and technologies in ways that are not generally required when researching contemporary literature in print.

Though this chapter is meant to provide a basic overview for the study of film, television, popular music, and other recorded resources, it cannot act as a surrogate for more specialized guides about these topics in specific genres or settings, such as *Media Research Methods* by Barry Gunter, *Media Research* by Ina Bertrand, or *The Ashgate Research Companion to Popular Musicology* by Derek Scott. Scholars are encouraged to use the resources listed here as a place to begin their journey, but not as a final destination.

FILM AND TELEVISION

There are many types of resources important to studying film, including companions, movie streaming services, title directories, academic indexes, and bibliographies. Though this section is by no means comprehensive, it should get you started in your research, while reviewing each type of item you might need when working in this area of study.

General Companions and Directories

Barrow, Sarah, and John White, eds. *Fifty Key British Films*. Routledge Key Guides. New York: Routledge, 2008.
Corrigan, Timothy. *A Short Guide to Writing about Film*. New York: Pearson/Longman, 2014.
Katz, Ephraim. *The Film Encyclopedia: The Complete Guide to Film and the Film Industry*. 7th edition. New York: Collins Reference, 2012.
Miller, Toby, and Robert Stam. *A Companion to Film Theory*. Malden, MA: Blackwell, 1999.
Murphy, Robert, ed. *Directors in British and Irish Cinema: A Reference Companion*. London: British Film Institute Publishing, 2006.
Rockett, Kevin, and John Caughie. *Companion to British and Irish Cinema*. London: Cassell/British Film Institute Publishing, 1996.
Vincendeau, Ginette. *Encyclopedia of European Cinema*. London: Cassell/British Film Institute Publishing, 1995.

Before we discuss choosing the right edition of a film and then finding that edition, we should start with a few companions and guides. Whenever entering a new area of interest, begin with well-respected volumes that can be referenced in a pinch. The British Film Institute (BFI) has many titles like this, and though they are a little older, they are excellent introductions to the topic of postmodern cinema in the UK. For a broad overview of moving images, the **Encyclopedia of European Cinema** is a collection of entries about films, people, movements, and trends across the continent, including in the UK. A more concentrated and updated work based on the encyclopedia is the *Companion to British and Irish Cinema*, which contains articles in alphabetical order about titles, directors, actors, movements, and schools of thought, as well as awards, filmographies, and other helpful reference lists. Though the emphasis is on British cinema, connections to European and American movies are also discussed. Finally, *Directors in British and Irish Cinema: A Reference Companion* has 980 entries focusing on the auteurs of British and Irish moving pictures, including filmographies and descriptions of the career for each individual.

Beyond these BFI titles, there are some other useful resources from various publishers. *A Short Guide to Writing about Film* walks novice scholars through the process of writing film studies research. This guide introduces readers to film theory and terminology, in addition to serving as a primer on composing various types of documents, such as reviews and full research papers. *A Companion to Film Theory* is also an introductory text that presents concepts related to film theory, containing authorship, genre, enunciation, narration, film editing, semiotics, cognitivism, psychoanalytic theory, spectatorship, queer theory, gender, class, culture industries, politics, theory in a digital age, cultural exchange, ethnography, postcolonialism, historical allegory, and others. Well-known theorists wrote many of the essays specifically for this volume. Another introductory text that approaches film from a different perspective is *Fifty Key British Films*. For those who might not have a strong understanding yet of the essential films in the history of British cinema, this volume, one of the Routledge Key Guides, is valuable. Some of the films featured are *The Red Shoes*, *Remains of the Day*, and *The Wicker Man*. These signed entries offer basic information such as production company, producer, and director, in addition to a summary evaluation of the film's importance and a list of further reading. Another basic reference work, *The Film Encyclopedia: The Complete Guide to Film and the Film Industry*, can act as a tool to help scholars navigate the complex concepts and terms associated with film studies. Now in its seventh edition, this encyclopedia has 7,500 brief entries for people, trends, movies, and movements. Entries for people tend to include filmographies. Overall, these guide should provide a reasonable introduction to the field of film theory and give a strong foundation of reference materials to use later.

Genre

Keaney, Michael. *British Film Noir Guide*. Jefferson, NC: McFarland, 2008.
Newman, Kim, ed. *BFI Companion to Horror*. London: Cassell, 1996.

Rosenstone, Robert, and Constantin Parvulesu. *A Companion to the Historical Film*. Malden, MA: Wiley-Blackwell, 2013.

There are also a number of guides that deal with specific genres or topics,
such as horror, film noir, gender in cinema, or gangster movies. Some examples of this type include the *British Film Noir Guide*, the *BFI Companion
to Horror*, and *A Companion to the Historical Film*. The **British Film Noir
Guide** provides entries for 369 titles that the author believes should be included in the film noir canon and is similar to other types of reference books,
like a dictionary. For each movie, there is a quote, basic information about
the producer, length, cast, director, and writer, followed by a summary and
assessment. Entries include titles such as *Act of Murder*, *Yield to the Night*,
and *Beat Girl*. There are several appendixes, including works listed by rating,
year, director, and cinematographer. There is also an appendix for the *Edgar
Wallace Mystery Theatre*. The **BFI Companion to Horror** in the Cassell
Film Studies series encompasses many different types of works within this
genre, such as short stories, folk tales, and television series and is also an
entry-based reference work. The main focus, though, is film. Entries cover
titles, people, trends, movements, and other terminology. *A Companion to
the Historical Film* is a collection of essays split into subjects, rather than a
list of entries. These are all related to history and film. These topics include
"History and the Medium of Film," "Filmmakers as Historians," "Telling
Lives: The Biopic," "Cinema and the Nation," "Wars and Revolutions," "Pre-
modern Times," and "Slavery and the Postcolonial World." An index is also
provided. Though this is not a comprehensive list of genre companions, these
represent three types of companions available to researchers, from those that
are closer to reference works to simple collections of essays.

Film Adaptations

Cartmell, Deborah. *A Companion to Literature, Film, and Adaptation*. Malden, MA: Wiley-Blackwell, 2012.
Cartmell, Deborah, and Imelda Whelehan, eds. *The Cambridge Companion
to Literature on Screen*. New York: Cambridge University Press, 2007.

In addition to genre companions, there are also some reference sources
specific to adaptations of literature in film. Generally, to find articles about
adaptations, the film indexes listed here and the literary indexes in chapter 4
will have research articles. That said, there are some special considerations
with adaptations, and these are explored in *A Companion to Literature, Film
and Adaptation* and *The Cambridge Companion to Literature on Screen*.

A Companion to Literature, Film, and Adaptation, a volume in the Blackwell Companions to Literature and Culture series, includes essays from major scholars on adaptation broken down into parts: "History and Contexts," "Approaches," "Genre," "Authors and Periods," "Beyond Authors and Canonical Texts," and "Case Studies." Essays cover the major themes and trends in scholarship about adaptations. Similarly, *The Cambridge Companion to Literature on Screen*, one of many Cambridge Companions to Literature, is also a group of significant essays from some of the best-known scholars on adaptation, broken into groups based on topic and theme: "Theories of Literature on Screen," "History and Contexts," "Genre, Industry, Taste," and "Beyond the 'Literary.'" Both will address the theory and peculiarities specific to the field of study surrounding literary adaptations.

Films

Amazon Prime. Seattle: Amazon.com. www.amazon.com.
Criterion Collection. New York: Janus Films, 1984–.
Hulu. Los Angeles, CA. www.hulu.com.
Netflix. Los Gatos, CA. www.netflix.com.

Once you have the companions and guides required to grasp the basics of film studies, the next challenge is finding the appropriate version of the film you wish to study. When examining a book, researchers must discover the best edition, and the same thing should be done with a film. This might be simple in some cases because there is only one version easily accessible. In other situations, the process will be complex. When you evaluate a film version, consider the special features available, the quality of the image, the accessibility of the technology required, cost, and any other factors that might impact a project. Choosing the correct version is not as easy as it might appear initially. Special features, such as added commentary, are a primary factor to recommend one edition over another. Quality features can provide information about the making of the film. Special editions, in particular, will often have content not available in the original. Evaluate the usefulness of these add-ons, for some do not benefit scholars and are not worth the added cost. For instance, interviews or special audio tracks with director commentary are quite useful, while gag reels might not be.

The integrity of the film's images and audio can also be important. Keep in mind that some DVDs are simply transfers from an older VHS copy of the film. These editions will retain many of the faults of the original. Lesser-known titles made in the 1950s and 1960s are often brought to new formats in this way. In general, look for versions made from the original. Usually, this will provide better-quality images for the final product.

Similarly, letterboxed editions generally work better for scholars because they ensure that no part of the screen is lost when the images are transferred to Blu-ray, DVD, or VHS. The original widescreen aspect ratio is preserved. Without this technique, the edges are cut off. Most people recognize letterboxing by the black strips at the top and bottom of the screen. Choosing a variant with this feature is important.

Also avoid editions that might have been tampered with in some way. One particularly troublesome trend in the United States that should be guarded against is the creation of copies of films with material cut out that is objectionable to certain religious denominations.[1] These versions cannot be used for serious scholarship. Films that are bootlegged might also be missing important scenes or might have visual deficiencies that make them inappropriate, and those that were originally made in black and white, but have been colorized, are inadvisable in many instances because they do not retain the original style of the movie.[2] The copy used must be fully intact and should be an authorized version to avoid problems, such as missing scenes or quality issues.

Criterion is one company that can be relied on to make particularly high-quality editions of classic and academically significant cinema. The **Criterion Collection** is well known for technical superiority and excellent supplements. Early Criterion movies released on laser disc might require a trip to a specialized library to view the occasional special feature only available in this format. Later editions are available on DVD or Blu-ray. Some British postmodern titles are not easily obtainable anywhere other than from Criterion's Eclipse series—high-quality versions of hard-to-find media. These include rarities important to this period, such as Basil Dearden's underground films, *Sapphire*, *The League of Gentlemen*, *Victim*, and *All Night Long*.

When the ideal edition is found, make sure that the technology to watch it is available. Potential formats include Blu-ray, DVD, streaming, VHS, or on an obsolete technology, such as laser disc or original 8 mm film reel. As a result, though you might be tempted to throw out that VHS player in the attic, it is advisable to keep it for the rare occasion when some media is not available in any other way. Having a player capable of handling both Blu-ray and DVD is also a good idea. Plan on traveling to a regional research library to use novel technology, and research film collections in your area that might be able to provide access to uncommon tools, like laser disc.

Streaming is the newest format and appears to be supplanting DVD and Blu-ray. **Netflix**, **Hulu**, **Amazon Prime**, and other up-and-coming video distributors are dominating the home-viewing market. Hulu Plus, the subscription version of Hulu, offers roughly eight hundred Criterion Collection films to stream instantly. One drawback is that the special commentary and other features available through Blu-ray or DVD are absent from the streamed media. This is true for most streaming services, so they might not be sufficient for everyone. Netflix also offers a mail-order video delivery service for those titles unavailable for instant viewing or for instances where the special features are essential. In addition to lacking special content, users should be aware that Netflix might stream a version of a movie that has been cropped to fit a smaller screen size or that is censored—for instance, a version of the film originally made for television instead of the theater release. Though many Netflix offerings are reliable, scholars are urged to be wary of potential problems.

British Film Directories

British Universities Film and Video Council: Moving Image and Sound, Knowledge and Access. London: BUFCV. bufvc.ac.uk.

Burrows, Elaine, et al., eds. *The British Cinema Source Book: BFI Archive Viewing Copies and Library Materials*. London: British Film Institute, 1996.

European Film Gateway. Frankfurt: Association des Cinémathèques Européennes and the Europeana Foundation. www.europeanfilmgateway.eu.

Film Index International. Ann Arbor, MI: Chadwyck-Healey. collections .chadwyck.co.uk.

Gifford, Dennis. *The British Film Catalogue, 1895–1994*. 3rd edition. 2 volumes. Chicago: Fitzroy Dearborn, 2001.

Goble, Alan. *Complete Index to British Sound Film since 1928*. New Providence, NJ: Bowker Saur, 1999.

———. Complete Index to World Film. www.citwf.com/indexx.asp.

Internet Movie Database. Seattle: Amazon.com. www.imdb.com.

Scottish Screen Archive. Glasgow: National Library of Scottland. ssa.nls.uk.

Screenonline. London: British Film Institute. www.screenonline.org.uk.

Search Collections. London: British Film Institute. www.bfi.org.uk/education -research/bfi-reuben-library/searching-collections.

Directories and catalogs to British films can help you discover resources with which you might not already be familiar. These list all of the films produced in a specific location, during a time period, or dealing with a subject. Because they are often exhaustive collections of even rare titles, these directories are important for those without a strong understanding of the media available related to a particular study. Consulting a directory early on can broaden your research significantly.

To identify British cinema during the early part of the postmodern period, start with *The British Film Catalogue, 1895–1994*. Containing entries for nearly every British movie from the covered dates, this is one of the most important early reference guides to the subject and the closest resource to a national filmography. Denis Gifford meticulously compiled this list over twenty years. Each entry includes major credits, actors, actresses, role names, and run times. Split into two volumes, the first part represents feature films and the second documentaries.

Another British film catalogue worth noting, the *Complete Index to British Sound Film since 1928* (*CIBSF*), covers most British actors, directors, cinematographers, movies, and other topics related to British cinema during the sound period. Because *CIBSF* is a sister resource to the **Complete Index to World Film** (CITWF), CITWF contains many of the same entries. CITWF is an online movie database available for free and includes cinema from 1888 to 2012. Using the advanced "online-movie database" search, researchers are able to build complex queries with different categories, such as origin, which can be set to the United Kingdom. In order to search for titles using "origin," you must combine it with another search field. Researchers should remember that the international nature of postmodern art results in some British filmmakers who are better associated with films originating in U.S. movements, such as James Nares's work during the New York No Wave cinema movement. As a result, origin might not always be an ideal search option. Title, person, year, genre, production company, and series are also searchable. The subscription version of CITWF includes roughly seven hundred thousand references to journal articles and books but is only available to libraries and other organizations.

Another scholarly resource for identifying British movies is **Film Index International**, which allows queries based on famous personalities as well as titles and other information. ProQuest offers this resource online, though the British Film Institute has had a major influence on its creation. About 125,000 films are listed, as well as 80,000 cinema personalities. Plot summaries and prize lists make this especially assistive. Awards, people, or titles can be searched as subject fields using the advanced options, and date ranges can be set. The default sort for retrieved resources is by date, though it can be reset to alphabetical order. Records for individuals involved in the entertainment industry are especially useful because they have filmographies and biographies.

In addition to these scholarly indexes, the popular **Internet Movie Database** (IMDB) can also serve as a powerful tool for finding information about films according to national origin. This database is generally reliable and contains information about millions of people and titles. Advanced search options through IMDB are especially useful and allow you to focus on various aspects of movie trivia that are not always easy to find in other ways, for instance, the heights of actors or the gross of a production. The "Collaborators and Overlaps" feature enables retrieving information about individuals who worked on multiple movies together, or to find films on which various artists collaborated. There is also a browse function that includes country of origin, featuring the United Kingdom. One caution with IMDB: users generate content, though salaried staff have some editorial control. As a result, a resource like CITWF remains an essential authoritative tool against which IMDB should be checked whenever possible.

Beyond these indexes, researchers should also look for sources in the British Film Institute's **Search Collections**. Recordings, books, articles, and reviews are all a part of the institute's massive collections. This catalog search can be used as another entry point to both the movies and the secondary documentation about them. The catalog allows searching by category (e.g., films, articles, books, scripts, or other ephemera). There is a simple keyword search by category, or an advanced search with extensive options for fields, such as production company, series title, genre, synopsis, date, subject, or cast. Several sort options, including date, genre, production company, or country are also useful to help rank results. BFI's collections are some of the most robust in the world, and the sheer volume of resources represented is worth noting. When searching, be sure to click from the introduction tab to the "search" at the top of the page—this might be confusing the first time. The ***British Cinema Source Book: BFI Archive Viewing Copies and Library Materials*** is a print index based on the institute's holdings and catalog. Though most of the items enumerated here are represented in the online catalog, some materials are only itemized in print, particularly scripts and press books. BFI's **Screenonline** website is also a handy reference to British film with lengthy articles on various topics. Screenonline complements the catalog itself by providing basic background information that informs the study of film.

In addition to these resources from BFI, other open-access tools might also be of use. For British films in the postmodern period, these include the **British Universities Film and Video Council: Moving Image and Sound, Knowledge and Access** (BUFVC), Scottish Screen Archive, and the European Film Gateway. BUFVC is actually a suite of tools from the British Universities Film and Video Council that can assist with all types of media research related to the United Kingdom. News on Screen, discussed in chapter 7, is one of these resources, as well as indexes that relate to television, radio, moving images, DVDs, and Shakespeare in film. The television resources include a database of press packs from Channel 4 between 1982 and 2002, an index of television and radio broadcasts stretching back to 1995, and *TV Times* listings between 1955 and 1985. A gateway to websites about moving images, a catalog search of film and sound archives across the United Kingdom, and a directory of in-print and out-of-print DVDs appropriate to academic audiences are provided to aid researchers. Most of these products are available to all users, but some might be limited to BUFVC members, such as the *TV Times* index and the index of TV and radio broadcast information. Together, these resources create a powerful suite of tools for those interested in British film.

Created by the National Library of Scotland, the **Scottish Screen Archive** is primarily an index, though it also includes 1,500 selected clips and even some full-length reproductions of videos. As the name suggests, the focus of this archive is Scottish film, though documentaries, newsreels, educational material, home movies, and advertising make up the bulk of the thirty-two thousand records. As a result, an important Scottish movie like Bill Forsyth's *Gregory's Girl* is not likely to be located in the index, whereas an education film of Maya Angelou talking about Robert Burns's poetry is present. There is a keyword search on the homepage, which can be limited to all titles, titles with video clips, or titles with full-length films. When the search is performed, limiters are present on the left-hand side of the screen to help narrow down the results. These include video, decade, place, subject, genre, series, biography, sound, fiction, color, and copyright status. A slide-bar that allows you to limit by year is also present at the top of the results pages.

A broader gateway to film documentation and other resources is the **European Film Gateway**, a portal to resources from across the continent, listing a few institutions in Britain. Though some of the other tools mentioned in the section focus more on the United Kingdom, other archives across Europe are likely to hold items that are related. Notably, this gateway does not merely link users to collections of digitized films, for posters and other ephemera related to cinema are also presented. As with some of the other collections, newsreels, documentaries, and informative productions are fairly prevalent in the archive, though you will also find results related to cinematic history. One example would be a search for *Laurence Olivier*, which retrieves twenty-five video clips related to the actor, in addition to images and censorship documents. There are filters on the left side of the results screen to aid researchers in focusing the query. These have year, language, and media. As with BFI's collection of scripts and other ephemera, the bonus material available through these archives can be quite useful and difficult to track down.

Full-Text and Bibliographic Sources

Entertainment Industry Magazine Archives. Ann Arbor, MI: ProQuest. www .proquest.com.

FIAF International Index to Film Periodicals. Ann Arbor, MI: Chadwyck-Healey. collections.chadwyck.co.uk/.

Film and Television Literature Index. Ipswich, MA: EBSCO. www.ebsco.com.

Film Literature Index. Bloomington, IN: Indiana University, 1976–2001. webapp1.dlib.indiana.edu/fli/index.jsp.

In addition to primary recordings, popular and industry articles from the time period can be helpful to place films in historical context or to study the movies as an industry. **Entertainment Industry Magazine Archives** offers articles from popular magazines across various types of media. This ProQuest product covers content from the early twentieth century until 2000 and is particularly advantageous because it contains trade publications and mass-market periodicals for consumers, making the study of popular media as it was received and produced much easier. Advanced search options are available, which include date limiters and options to query the entire content of articles.

In addition to primary documents and objects, there are many resources that focus on secondary literature for film research. The **Film Literature Index** (FLI) from Indiana University is the most important of these. This index allows advanced searching through film scholarship by titles, person names, and company names. Indexes by subject heading, person name, production title, or corporate name are easy to use and are not common in other, similar resources. The scope of the FLI is somewhat limited, from 1976 to 2001, though with citations for nearly seven hundred thousand articles, this is far more comprehensive than similar databases for these date ranges. There is also a print version, though the digital version is far more convenient because it allows for keyword searching.

The International Federation of Film Archives produces the **FIAF International Index to Film Periodicals**, important for finding secondary resources related to film, like *Sight and Sound* and *Positif*. FIAF indexes half a million articles from across many countries, with a full-text version that has many of the most famous movie journals. FIAF covers articles from 1972 forward in three hundred and forty-five periodicals. Fields available through the advanced search query film or television title, author, publication date range, country of publication, article title, subjects, language, or article type. Each of these also features a link to a browsable thesaurus. Results can be limited to TV- or film-related articles to narrow the search. There is also a FIAF Document Collections index that allows searching through items held in library and archive collections related to film.

The **Film and Television Literature Index** is published by EBSCO and includes a variety of journals and books, as well as film images, from 1914 to the present. These cover topics such as cinematography, film theory, preservation, screenwriting, and restoration. The full-text version has a robust collection of resources. Abstracts and indexing are presented for every article.

British Television

Baskin, Ellen. *Serials on British Television, 1950–1994.* Burlington, VT: Ashgate, 1996.

Many of the resources mentioned for film also apply to television, including the journal indexes, Netflix, Hulu, and the other streaming sources. Even BFI's holdings are quite extensive with regard to television and feature 750,000 off-air recordings and production archives. That said, there are references particular to British TV. As mentioned in chapter 7, the BBC has an alphabetical index of the shows aired over its long history, with links to information and related streamed videos. This browsable tool only represents part of the archive, which also houses digitized content from various BBC productions.

A print resource for British TV, *Serials on British Television, 1950–1994*, tracks over nine hundred serials that have aired in Britain from 1950 to 1994. Entries for different shows give insight into actors and actresses, series subjects, run times and dates, episodic information, and other reference data that is important to researchers of television. Indexes are also present.

MUSIC

Though an entire research guide could be written just on popular music, we will attempt to provide a cursory overview sufficient to get scholars of postmodern culture started. British popular music was extremely influential in the latter half of the twentieth century and is a thriving area of concern within musicological and sociological circles. Lyrics are often considered contemporary works of poetry and are studied by literary scholars. As a result, becoming familiar with how to find recordings and literature about this music can be significant.

Recordings

iTunes. Cupertino, CA: Apple Inc. www.apple.com/itunes/.
Spotify. London. spotify.com.
Pandora Radio. Oakland, CA: Pandora Media Inc. pandora.com.

Researchers of music will find the same roadblocks in accessing copies of media as those working with moving images. Sound recordings can be on anything from early wax cylinders to records, eight tracks, cassette tapes, CDs, MP3s, and a multitude of other file types and physical formats that are even less well known. You are encouraged to be mindful of constraints related to format and should plan accordingly.

The quality of recordings will vary. Critical editions are common for traditional or classical music, though not for popular. To find copies of albums, take advantage of the many new media services, including **iTunes** and online radio stations. **Spotify** and **Pandora Radio** are just two services that can make finding older, out-of-print, or hard-to-discover records much easier. The quality of streamed recordings will not be as good as CD, though this might change over time. Liner notes and other related ephemera might also be important so that the CD is preferable when the supplemental material is significant, for instance, definitive track listings or lyrics. The Beatles' *Sgt. Pepper's Lonely Hearts Club Band* is famous for the album's cover art by Peter Blake and Jann Haworth, and also for several songs with confusing lyrics, such as "Lucy in the Sky with Diamonds." Luckily, this album was one of the first to contain printed lyrics, helping to clarify these misheard words conclusively.[3] This is just one example of a cover that might be of value to researchers, for both its cultural and practical importance.

Companions and Encyclopedias

Frith, Simon, Will Straw, and John Street, eds. *The Cambridge Companion to Rock and Pop.* New York: Cambridge University Press, 2001.

Gammond, Peter. *The Oxford Companion to Popular Music.* New York: Oxford University Press, 1991.

Larkin, Colin, ed. *The Encyclopedia of Popular Music.* New York: Oxford University Press, 2009. www.oxfordmusiconline.com.

If you are unfamiliar with music research, start with a few companions or guides to ensure that you have a good handle on the concepts. Examples of companions that might help with research in postmodern popular music are *The Oxford Companion to Popular Music* and *The Cambridge Companion to Rock and Pop.* **The Oxford Companion to Popular Music** is more an encyclopedia or dictionary than it is a companion. With entries related to songs, people, companies, trends, and movements, and covering musical styles as varied as reggae, jazz, blues, Broadway musicals, country western, and rock and roll, this companion is a valuable desk reference for those just getting started. In contrast to the *Oxford Companion*, **The Cambridge Companion** *to Rock and Pop* is a collection of essays by well-known scholars of popular music, broken into subject groupings. These subjects are loosely defined as "Context," "Texts, Genres, Styles," and "Debates." Indexes and a reference list are also valuable. Though these guides differ in the type of introductory material they provide, they are both well worth perusing.

A reference guide to the people, bands, production companies, and other information discussed in the literature is also handy. *The Encyclopedia of Popular Music* is offered in either a searchable online version through Oxford Music Online or in print. This is a guide to movements and artists. Covering 1900 to the present, over twenty-seven thousand entries provide information about labels, venues, trends, styles, festivals, and people related to the development of popular music. Artist entries have full discographies in addition to biographies. This ten-volume set is considered a standard reference work in the field.

Catalogs and Directories

British Library Sound and Moving Image Catalog. London: British Library Board. cadensa.bl.uk.
British Library Sounds. London: British Library Board. sounds.bl.uk.
CECILIA: Find Music Collections in UK and Ireland. United Kingdom and Ireland Branch of the International Association of Music Libraries, Archives, and Documentation Centers. www.cecilia-uk.org.
Library and Archives Catalog. Cleveland, OH: Rock and Roll Hall of Fame, 2013. catalog.rockhall.com.

Once companions and encyclopedias have provided a sound foundation, the next place to go for research is the British Library catalogues, since the library has one of the best collections for national music, which contains all recordings published commercially in the United Kingdom as well as documentary copies of some radio broadcasts, privately made audio, and international publications. The archive of commercially published recordings will be of particular interest to scholars researching British postmodernism since it offers difficult-to-find music that represents a time of significant cultural change, often exemplified in the United Kingdom by the rise of rock and roll. The **British Library Sound and Moving Image Catalog** allows advanced searching through archival recordings. Of these advanced options, the limiter for broad classification categories is particularly convenient because it enables searches to be narrowed to a type or era of music. Date, format, classification, and collection limiters are also valuable to help focus a search. A listening service is available at the library's St. Pancras and Boston Spa locations. The holdings are notable for primary recordings and also for a large body of popular publications representing local music and culture. Online, **British Library Sounds** presents some of these audio collections. Though the music is often not available, many related audio compilations of interest to British postmodern scholars are presented, such as "Observing the 1980s," "Disability Voices," and the "Oral History of Sound Recording." Browsing options are based on the type of recording, beyond a basic search. Featured audio proffers oral histories and dialect studies in addition to musical selections. Because of copyright, popular music and jazz recordings are relatively scarce, though other types of material, like interviews, are still quite useful.

Another catalog that can identify collections is **CECILIA: Find Music Collections in UK and Ireland**. Rather than a catalog for a single institution, CECILIA searches the music collections of museums, archives, and libraries across the UK and Ireland to help researchers identify useful items. A single keyword search box is available on the home page, or there is an advanced option, though this inquiry is tailored to UK library patrons looking for music near them, rather than researchers. There are few fields or limiters. The results are listed according to the facility holding the materials. As a sample query, *Beatles* retrieves two music collections, one at the Museum of Liverpool Life, which is likely to have strong holdings. Approximately seventy-seven thousand records are searched through this interface.

The Rock and Roll Hall of Fame **Library and Archives Catalog** also has substantial collections that are worth exploring to help identify resources related to popular music. Their catalog is the primary access point to the library holdings. Though there are no options for searching country of origin, the catalog uses Library of Congress subject headings, discussed in chapter 3, which can limit results to England, Ireland, Scotland, or Wales. In addition to audio recordings and a wealth of archival material, a substantial number of scholarly periodicals and books are represented in the collection. Because the Hall and Fame has an exhaustive collection of resources, employ it to identify what is available about a given artist. For instance, if you search for the Irish singer Van Morrison, you get academic works like *Celtic Crossroads: The Art of Van Morrison* by Brian Hinton mixed with records for albums such as *Inarticulate Speech of the Heart* and archival resources, including a press kit from 1970. Options to limit by format from the results screen makes navigating this list of resources easy for scholars who are more interested in secondary resources rather than the actual archive collections.

Music Charts

Academic Charts Online (ACO). London: Academic Rights Press. ipm.academiccharts.com.

Another tool for identifying Britain's bands, songs, or musical movements is Music Industry Data (Music ID). Primarily a search of music charts by keyword, date, or country, this is a powerful way to find key albums, bands, and songs during the postmodern period, or to analyze the importance of an album in Britain as compared to other geographic areas. As an example, The Cure's 1992 single "High" did much better in Britain and Australia than in the United States, peaking at 8 and 5 on the charts, respectively. This information is valuable to a scholar interested in The Cure's cultural legacy outside the United States. Another way that Music ID can be helpful is by identifying the culturally significant music during a given event or period in British history. One case might be a scholar studying how the Falklands War influenced British culture. This individual might find it beneficial to know the hit single for May 15, 1982, was "A Little Peace" performed by Nicole Hohloch. Music ID also plays small portions of the identified album or song.

This database supersedes in many ways the print indexes that were previously used for the same purposes: *British Hit Singles and Albums*, the *Complete Book of British Charts*, *Collins Complete British Hit Albums*, and *British and American Hit Singles*. Scholars without access to Music ID will still find these convenient. In their latest editions, most provide charts into the late 1990s or 2000s.

Digital Archives

British Music Archive: Preserving Britain's Lost Musical Heritage. Leicester, UK: British Music Archive, 2011. www.britishmusicarchive.com.
Contemporary World Music. Alexandria, VA: Alexander Street Press. womu .alexanderstreet.com.
Smithsonian Global Sound for Libraries. Alexandria, VA: Alexander Street Press. glmu.alexanderstreet.com.

For lesser-known songs, the **British Music Archive: Preserving Britain's Lost Musical Heritage** allows users to listen to unreleased recordings from historically significant artists. Primarily focused on the 1960s, this collection has annotations that discuss the record and tracks available, as well as MP3 recordings of some songs listed in each entry. Featured bands include The Mandrakes, Coconut Mushroom, and Wellington's Boot. The archive allows a keyword search with limiters such as genre and format. This can be a good resource for finding more underground music from the era, as compared to the mainstream hits covered in other venues.

For music from across the Commonwealth, two Alexander Street databases identify and make available contemporary tunes. **Smithsonian Global**

Sound for Libraries and its companion, **Contemporary World Music**, are robust collections of different types of music from international artists, including both traditional and popular titles. Contemporary World Music is especially useful for postmodern researchers since it contains diverse recordings from the latter half of the twentieth century and is searchable or can be browsed by genre, ensemble, instrument, cultural group, place, and language. Contemporary World Music contains a particularly important release for scholars of the United Kingdom, *The Voice of the People*, which is a twenty-volume recording of English, Irish, Scottish, and Welsh traditional music from the 1970s and 1980s.

Indexes and Bibliographies

International Index to Music Periodicals. Ann Arbor, MI: Chadwyck-Healey. iimp.chadwyck.com.
Music Index. Ipswich, MA: EBSCO. www.ebsco.com.
RILM Abstracts of Music Literature. Ipswich, MA: EBSCO. www.ebsco.com.
Rock's Backpages. London: Backpages Limited. www.rocksbackpages.com.
Wagstaff, John, ed. *The British Union Catalogue of Music Periodicals*. Burlington, VT: Ashgate, 1998.

Literary scholars will also find contemporary writing about the rise and development of rock and roll in Britain to be culturally significant, and this genre could stand alone as a category of its own within literary history. In addition to the previously mentioned Entertainment Industry Magazine Archives, **Rock's Backpages** has popular and industry articles about the development of the music scene. Interviews, feature stories, and reviews from important critics are pulled from U.S. and UK magazines such as *Rolling Stone*, *NME*, *Melody Maker*, and *Sounds*. The database covers twenty-three thousand articles from 1960s to the present and has an advanced search with date, genre, and artist fields. MP3s for some interviews are also available and searchable using the interface.

As a supplement to Rock's Backpages, ***The British Union Catalogue of Music Periodicals*** contains entries for 270 less well-known publications particular to Britain, and especially regional publications that might not get mentioned elsewhere. The location of music periodicals, bibliographic information, and a short history of the genre of writing are provided in this print resource.

Major indexes related to the subject include Music Index and RILM Abstracts of Music Literature, both available as EBSCO databases. **RILM Abstracts of Music Literature** contains conference proceedings, articles in journals that are not specifically related to music, monographs, dissertations, and critical editions of music, making it a broad resource. Coverage extends back to 1967 in most cases. **Music Index** starts in 1970 and offers indexing and abstracting for several hundred journals related to both classical and popular music.

The **International Index to Music Periodicals** (IIMP) has music journals and magazines back to 1874, a far greater span of years than other music indexes. IIMP includes popular music, classical music, music education, and performance. The database is current, and abstracts are present for most articles written in the last fifteen years. The advanced search options include date limiters and other fields to help researchers pinpoint articles.

PERFORMANCE ART

Farrago Poetry. Kent, UK: Farrago Poetry and E-Poets Network. london.e-poets.net.

Indiefeed: Performance Poetry. www.indiefeedpp.libsyn.com.

International Bibliography of Theatre and Dance. Ipswich, MA: EBSCO. www.ebsco.com.

Poetry Slam, Inc. Chicago. www.poetryslam.com.

Theatre in Video. Alexandria, VA: Alexander Street Press. alexanderstreet.com.

Though finding secondary literature about performance, including book readings and slam poetry, is covered in other places, we have mentioned this type of media here because recordings of live events are difficult to locate. Luckily, there are a few resources to help you.

One reason that this period is so unique is that many postmodern authors have interviews, readings, and other media recorded for popular dissemination. The BBC Archives, British Library Sound, and Poetry International all provide access to author audio. The British Library also holds sound recordings of live stage performances, most notably from the Royal National Theatre, the Royal Shakespeare Company, and the Royal Court Theatre. The collection goes back to the 1960s and also contains several theater festivals, including the Edinburgh Festival and Fringe and the London International Festival of Theatre. The West End, touring companies, and provincial theaters are additionally represented. Video recordings are also available for some performances, particularly more contemporary theater. This valuable collection is searchable through the library's sound catalog.

Some of these recordings might be available through Alexander Street Press's **Theatre in Video**. With videos of 250 performances and 100 documentaries, this subscription collection is one of the largest of its type to include contemporary British theater, for instance, John Osborne's *Luther*. Containing presentations from theaters across the world, including the London stage with institutions such as the Greenwich Theatre, it is hard to find a streaming resource presenting the same unique mix of media. There is an advanced search that will query various fields, with the most valuable being transcripts, playwright, performer, and subject. Databases with recordings of dance performances, opera, and music are also accessible by subscription. International newsreels are additionally available, though this content is less important to postmodern scholars since it only goes up to 1966.

For theater performances, also consult the **International Bibliography of Theatre and Dance**, which contains theater reviews and trade publications in addition to scholarly literature. Published by the Theatre Research Data Center at Brooklyn College since 1984, indexing is provided for sixty-thousand resources, including books, journal articles, and dissertations. *International Bibliography of Theatre and Dance* is also available as a twelve-volume print set.

Slam poetry is one of the more important movements in postmodernism in the UK. Though books of printed slam poetry are available, scholars are much better able to understand it when they can hear and experience it. Few printed sources have companion audio recordings. Some slam competitions and other events are available on CD or DVD for purchase, and these are ubiquitous online. Start with a list of specific slam poets and then search on YouTube and other social media to see if the poet has posted videos. The drawback of this method is that social media must be vetted for appropriate copyright considerations. **Farrago Poetry**, a slam community specific to Britain, and **Poetry Slam, Inc.**, an international nonprofit, might assist with this. While there are some recorded collections of slam poetry online, these are usually small and often focus on American poets. The blog *Indiefeed: Performance Poetry* publishes a new slam poem every week, including international authors. These are just a few microcosmic resources in the larger and more complex universe of spoken word. Hopefully, as this form of literature develops, more and better recordings will be available that capture some of slam's ethereal power.

CONCLUSION

This chapter will only get you started. Ultimately, as a scholar, you will need to decide the importance of diverse media to your work. Many researchers are taking advantage of the new possibilities that cross-media scholarship provide. The cultural revolution within postmodernism complicates the research landscape, but also expands the horizons. Fresh connections between various forms of expression require novel perspectives and innovative research skills. To master them, you must embrace the diversity of sources and cultivate your understanding of indexes and search strategies.

NOTES

1. Christine McCarroll, "Morals, Movies and the Law: Can Today's Copyright Protect a Director's Masterpiece from Bowdlerization?" *Journal of High Technology Law* 331, no. 5 (2005): 331–55.

2. Michael Schudson, "Colorization and Authenticity," *Society* 24, no. 4 (May 1987): 18–19.

3. Mark Lewisohn, *The Complete Beatles Chronicle: The Definitive Day-by-Day Guide to the Beatles' Entire Career* (Chicago: Chicago Review Press, 1992), 236.

Chapter Ten

Critical Theory

In order to research postmodern literature, scholars must have a working understanding of critical theory and the role it plays in contemporary literary criticism. As a central set of philosophical principles that inform postmodernism and current scholarship in the humanities, the importance of theory cannot be overstated. Critical theory is defined by Max Horkheimer as philosophy that seeks "to liberate human beings from the circumstances that enslave them."[1] These forces are social, cultural, and economic constructions that define collective norms and hierarchies. In the lens of critical theory, these structures are viewed as determining the role people play in their larger culture, based on gender, race, class, or other factors. Critical theory seeks to deconstruct these social edifices to show how they impact people and, ultimately, to free individuals.

Generally, critical theory is dated as beginning in 1929 with the Frankfurt School and, most notably, with theorists Horkheimer and Theodor Adorno.[2] Over the past fifty years, it has grown to encompass thinking concerned with a wide variety of issues, such as race, class, sexuality, and gender. Common themes include critical analysis of socially constructed and normative forces, an interest in discourse, a preoccupation with the nature of truth, and a focus on democratic change within societies.[3]

In its loosest sense, critical theory provides a framework for approaching literary texts as cultural artifacts that reify social norms. This perspective allows critics to find socially significant textual examples of common, restrictive hierarchies in their society. By identifying these forces in important works of literature, the critic is able to name, examine, and explore their meaning to the society at large.

For instance, using gender theory to examine *I Shall Wear Black* by Terry Pratchett might show how the story takes traditional concepts of femininity and reworks them by making the hero a teenage girl. This strong female character is perhaps a conscious attempt to create a new female role model for young women, empowering them to examine more critically their social realities. Articles written using a critical framework are common, so it is important to be prepared for them. The imperative to understand theory, even if you do not use it, cannot be overstated because theory is central to current literary scholarship.

Theory is also central to postmodern thought and so influences the literature. Born out of the liberal movements of the 1960s, literary theory helps contemporary writers undermine, rewrite, critique, and question social hierarchies, cultural trends, and restrictive constructs. Without an understanding of critical theory, researchers lack the bigger context of the critical tradition that has sprung up around deeply democratic notions common in late twentieth-century writing.

Think of theory as a lens through which contemporary literary scholars view the traditional makeup of society and culture. This lens has become increasingly important because it provides a theoretical underpinning to understand why these constructions exist, why they continue, and how they can be changed. One job of a literary critic is to describe these forces, and critical theory is one of the best tools to do it.

USING THEORY IN YOUR RESEARCH

Bertens, Hans. *Literary Theory: The Basics*. 3rd edition. New York: Routledge, 2013.

Bronner, Stephen. *Critical Theory: A Very Short Introduction*. Oxford: Oxford University Press, 2011.

Culler, Jonathan. *Literary Theory: A Very Short Introduction*. 2nd edition. Oxford: Oxford University Press, 2011.

Eagleton, Terry. *Literary Theory: An Introduction*. 2nd edition. Minneapolis: University of Minnesota Press, 2008.

Klages, Mary. *Literary Theory: A Guide for the Perplexed*. New York: Bloombury Academic, 2007.

Nealon, Jeffrey, and Susan Giroux. *The Theory Toolbox: Critical Concepts for the Humanities, Arts, and Social Sciences*. 2nd edition. Lanham, MD: Rowman & Littlefield, 2011.

Tyson, Louis. *Critical Theory Today: A User-Friendly Guide*. 2nd edition. New York: Routledge, 2006.

Though using critical theory is often imperative, finding the right theories, understanding them, and making them work in an argument will take time for even advanced students. Critical treatises are often difficult to read. Without a thorough understanding of these texts, applying them is nearly impossible. Because of this, literary critics should start with a thorough introduction to theory, its use, and its limitations.

Two excellent texts to start with are *Literary Theory: A Very Short Introduction* and *Critical Theory: A Very Short Introduction* by Jonathon Culler and Stephen Bronner, respectively. Both of these are in the Oxford Very Short Introduction series, well known for giving basic primers to complex topics. This series employs specialists who have a documented ability to explain the concepts in their field in a clear and concise way. **Literary Theory: A Very Short Introduction** has eight chapters that define theory and literature as well as discuss cultural studies, language, rhetoric, narrative, performativity, and identification. There is also an appendix that looks at theoretical schools and movements. **Critical Theory: A Very Short Introduction** has eight chapters defining and discussing theory, the Frankfurt School, the early history and methodology of theory, key terms, figures, and treatises up to the new millennium. Ordered in a loose chronology, the work is narrative and accessible. Both of these books are easy to read and offer a solid foundation for further exploration. They also include indexes and further reading lists to point you toward more advanced titles.

Another well-known introduction to the topic is **Literary Theory: An Introduction** by famed critic Terry Eagleton. Eagleton is a British literary scholar and has the ability to make complex concepts easy to understand for those new to the field. As a result, this volume is especially valuable for novices struggling to comprehend poststructuralism or deconstruction. Often considered the first survey of theory covering the 1960s to the present, this volume is indispensable. Now in a second edition with an anniversary preface by the author, the book is broken up into chapters focused on varying critical schools, including phenomenology, hermeneutics, reception theory, structuralism, semiotics, poststructuralism, and psychoanalysis. An extensive bibliography and robust index make this work particularly beneficial.

Critical Theory Today: A User-Friendly Guide is another classic guide to literary theory. Written by Lois Tyson, this works as either a survey or a reference source. Each chapter discusses a new type of theory and is broken down into subheadings to make navigation easy. Topics like psychoanalysis, Marxism, feminism, new criticism, reader-response theory, structuralism, deconstruction, new historicism, queer theory, race theory, and postcolonialism are included. Unlike the other texts, *Critical Theory Today* also provides examples that demonstrate the applications of each theory with well-known literary texts. Often used as a textbook in classes focused on this topic, the work includes study questions to ensure that readers understand and can apply the ideas. Each chapter also gives a further reading list and suggestions for those who are more advanced. An index makes this work accessible as a reference tool.

Written as a textbook, *The Theory Toolbox: Critical Concepts for the Humanities, Arts, and Social Sciences* provides a history of ideas, historical movements, and concepts. Readers are asked to theorize for themselves, allowing them to understand the methods behind the creation of philosophical thought. With nine chapters broken into broad categories, represented as authority, reading, subjectivity, culture, ideology, history, space/time, posts, differences, and agency, this work is able to draw conclusions from the similarities of frameworks linked by these general concepts. In addition to indexing, a bibliography and a further reading list are added to help the reader explore these concepts.

Literary Theory: A Guide for the Perplexed is similarly written for students, but the well-known series of guides is a good basic entry point for how scholars work. Considered one of the most accessible introductions, Mary Klage's book covers topics including structuralism, queer theory, deconstruction, feminism, discourse theory, race, postcolonialism, and postmodernism.

A nuanced and advanced introduction is in Hans Berten's *Literary Theory: The Basics*. This volume goes in depth into the history of theory and its development and use over the past fifty years. The first several chapters focus on theory into the 1980s, with a strong emphasis on structuralism, and the second grouping discusses specific schools of contemporary thought, including poststructuralism, new historicism, cultural materialism, postcolonialism, sexuality, gender, and ecocriticms. A bibliography and index are also provided. Scholars with some previous understanding will discover that this text is a good next step to expand on cursory knowledge of how literary theory is shaping the field today and how it developed.

REFERENCE WORKS

Burgett, Bruce, and Glen Hendler, eds. *Keywords for American Cultural Studies*. New York: New York University Press, 2007.

Cuddon, John, and M. A. R. Habib. *Penguin Dictionary of Literary Terms and Literary Theory*. Edited by Matthew Birchwood. 5th edition. Penguin Reference Books. New York: Penguin Books, 2014.

Lentricchia, Frank, and Thomas McLaughlin, eds. *Critical Terms for Literary Study*. 2nd edition. Chicago: University of Chicago Press, 1995.

Macey, David. *Penguin Dictionary of Critical Theory*. New edition. Penguin Reference Books. New York: Penguin Books, 2002.

Merriam-Webster Online Dictionary and Thesaurus. Springfield, MA: Merriam-Webster, 2014. www.merriam-webster.com.

Murfin, Ross, and Supryia Ray. *The Bedford Glossary of Critical and Literary Terms.* 3rd edition. New York: Bedford/St. Martin's, 2009.

Wake, Paul, and Simon Malpas, eds. *Routledge Companion to Critical and Cultural Theory.* 2nd edition. New York: Routledge, 2013.

For reference works related to literary theory, scholars have plenty of dictionaries, glossaries, companions, and handbooks from which to choose. Keeping an excellent dictionary of terms nearby to help you wade through language specific to critical theory might be important, even for advanced scholars. In addition to the reference resources listed here, having a more basic dictionary accessible for unfamiliar vocabulary is also essential, such as the **Merriam-Webster Online Dictionary and Thesaurus**.

The **Penguin Dictionary of Literary Terms and Literary Theory** and the **Penguin Dictionary of Critical Theory** by John Cuddon and David Macey, respectively, are good companion resources to have on your shelf if you are working with critical theory. Now in its fifth edition, the *Dictionary of Literary Terms and Literary Theory* delivers an overview of literary terms, movements, and key figures, while the *Dictionary of Critical Theory*, also in a new edition, has a reference to crucial critical concepts, philosophers, and frameworks. Both include prefaces and are arranged alphabetically. Together they are a powerful tool for navigating literary scholarship across various viewpoints.

The third edition of **The Bedford Glossary of Critical and Literary Terms** also contains a reference to critical and literary words, in addition to giving examples to help further explicate their role in literary scholarship. The descriptions are thorough without burdening the reader with unnecessary information. A bibliographic reference and index are also included.

A combination of both a dictionary and an introduction to concepts, the **Routledge Companion to Critical and Cultural Theory** first presents critical theories in survey essays, then supports researchers by presenting a dictionary of key terms and ideas. The introductory essays in the first part include topics such as structuralism, semiotics, narratology, Marxism, poststructuralism, historicism, psychoanalysis, deconstruction, feminism, gender, queer theory, postmodernism, race, and postcoloniality. These essays survey the theoretical landscape for each topic, while the second part of the companion defines terms, concepts, and people. A bibliography concludes the work. This is an efficient combination suitable for scholars who might not need a more detailed introduction but want a reference guide to theories that are unfamiliar—for instance, trauma theory or Marxist theory.

Though conceived as an introductory text for courses about culture, ***Keywords for American Cultural Studies*** might be of interest for advanced scholars who want to explore further the language used in critical inquiry. In sixty-four essays, each chosen word is explored, theories about that term are explained, and arguments central to critical debates are described. This can be extremely important as an introduction to the discourse of theory, which is sometimes difficult to master. For instance, the terms *diaspora* and *secularism* are thoroughly covered with an explanation of their historical meaning, their current use in context, and ongoing related debates. ***Critical Terms for Literary Study*** is similarly conceived and useful for the same reasons. This volume includes terms like *popular culture* and *imperialism/nationalism*. For each one, historical context is explored, debates surrounding the term are investigated, and then strategies for using the word in critical studies are listed.

APPLYING THEORY TO RESEARCH

Graff, Gerald, and Kathy Birkenstein. *They Say, I Say: The Moves That Matter in Academic Writing*. 2nd edition. New York: W. W. Norton, 2012.

Thomas, Calvin. *Ten Lessons in Theory: An Introduction to Theoretical Writing*. New York: Bloomsbury, 2013.

Tyson, Lois. *Using Critical Theory: How to Read and Write about Literature*. 2nd edition. New York: Routledge, 2011.

Once you understand critical theory, the next task will be to use it in the service of literary criticism. A few different books might aid in this process, though some are targeted at undergraduate students rather than those who are more advanced.

Using Critical Theory: How to Read and Write about Literature by Lois Tyson and ***They Say, I Say: The Moves That Matter in Academic Writing*** by Gerald Graff and Kathy Birkenstein are both directed to an undergraduate audience but still hold value for those who do not have a working knowledge of how to use theory in writing. *Using Critical Theory* is broken into chapters that each focus on how a particular theoretical framework facilitates an argument about literature. Chapters discuss reader response, new criticism, psychoanalysis, Marxism, feminism, queer theory, African-American theory, and postcolonialism. The last chapter explores how to remember what has been learned about applying theory, and multiple appendixes deliver examples of different types of theory with real, well-known literary texts. *They Say, I Say* also offers examples throughout about how to make specific rhetorical moves in academic writing, while providing basic explanations of necessary skills, such as simple ways of using, quoting, and summarizing what other people have said. These examples become more advanced as the book continues—for instance, writing metacommentary, refuting potential detractors, and distinguishing what you say from the ideas in the works you are quoting. Though some concepts will be too basic for experienced scholars, as introductory texts, these are both a fine place to start.

For more advanced researchers, ***Ten Lessons in Theory: An Introduction to Theoretical Writing*** is an excellent, thoughtful, and sophisticated introduction to the use of theory in critical work. Calvin Thomas encourages readers to have a better understanding of foundational theoretical texts on a fundamental level. He evaluates the quality of these texts and ultimately considers theoretical writing as a genre. The book is broken into two parts, each with five lessons, and includes an introductory section that endeavors to explore the nature of theory. The lessons discuss specific theoretical texts and approaches, as well as topics like interpreting literature and the meaning of theoretical terms. This introduction is nuanced and holds something for everyone.

Though these resources might help guide the use of theory, practice is the best method to learn the skill of writing with it. The goal should be to use theory naturally to create meaning. One trick is to make sure that you can put the concepts described into your own words. If someone who is not affiliated with literary criticism reviews what is written, and they can follow its logic, then there is a good chance it will convey meaning using this theory to those who already know something about it.

Never try to use concepts that you do not fully understand. Though this might seem like an obvious warning, more advanced scholars sometimes fall into the trap of thinking they cannot admit when they are stumped by something that is new to them. The best approach is to maintain the time and the space to explore new critical theory and to understand it fully. Read about each theorist, and pick apart the pieces of their arguments. If guidance is required, do not hesitate to seek out someone who can help shape your thinking. Remember that when you push yourself and your discipline to look at new concepts, mistakes will happen. Allow the space to make these mistakes. That is how you know it is challenging work.

FINDING THE RIGHT THEORY

Buchanan, Ian. *A Dictionary of Critical Theory*. Oxford: Oxford University Press, 2010.

Cashmore, Ellis, and Chris Rojek, eds. *Dictionary of Cultural Theorists*. Arnold Student Reference. Milton Park, UK: Hodder Educational Publishers, 1999.

Fieser, James, and Bradley Dowden, eds. *The Internet Encyclopedia of Philosophy*. www.iep.utm.edu.

Groden, Michael, Martin Kreiswirth, and Imre Szeman, eds. *The Johns Hopkins Guide to Literary Theory and Criticism*. 2nd edition. Baltimore, MD: Johns Hopkins University Press, 2004.

Lechte, John. *Fifty Key Contemporary Thinkers: From Structuralism to Post-Humanism*. Routledge Key Guides. 2nd edition. New York: Routledge, 2008.

Magill, Frank, ed. *Critical Survey of Literary Theory*. 4 volumes. Ipswich, MA: Salem Press, 1987.

Makaryk, Irena, ed. *Encyclopedia of Contemporary Literary Theory: Approaches, Scholars, Terms*. Toronto: University of Toronto Press, 1993.

Payne, Michael, and Jessica Rae Barbera, eds. *Dictionary of Cultural and Critical Theory*. 2nd edition. Hoboken, NJ: Wiley-Blackwell, 2010.

Simons, Jon, ed. *Contemporary Critical Theorists: Lacan to Said*. Edinburgh: Edinburgh University Press, 2004.

Zalta, Edward, ed. *Stanford Encyclopedia of Philosophy*. Stanford, CA: Stanford University, 2014. plato.stanford.edu.

To identify texts or get started in a new area of theory, refer to a host of dictionaries, encyclopedias, and other resources related to critical theory. Though some of these are reference works, they are more valuable for identifying which theory to use and so are included in this section. When choosing a theory, make sure to pay attention to the reasoning behind employing that particular text. Spend some time reading other papers with this critical perspective, and be sure that the scholarly paradigms within the field are understood. Remember that being able to work from one theoretical perspective does not make a researcher capable of jumping fluidly into another. Let these encyclopedias and other reference resources guide pivotal choices.

Of the resources listed in this section, the ***Encyclopedia of Contemporary Literary Theory: Approaches, Scholars, Terms*** is the most significant. With 170 contributing authors, this encyclopedia is split into three parts. Part 1 focuses on theories, schools of thought, and their historical development. Part 2 is about theorists. Part 3 covers key language in literary theory. Each part contains mini-essays that feature long lists of primary and secondary sources for further reading, and extensive cross-referencing. This is an important tool for identifying and understanding new ideas and perspectives on literature.

Oxford University Press's *A Dictionary of Critical Theory* has 750 entries about different schools and approaches to critical theory. Defining and identifying perspectives across the field of literary interpretation is the main focus. The recommended resources that accompany each entry are especially useful for researchers, and the interdisciplinary nature of the entries helps broaden the scope of information available. A list of recommended web resources is also included in the back matter.

The Johns Hopkins Guide to Literary Theory and Criticism, also discussed in chapter 2, has 240 entries that cover theorists and movements but also looks at regional contributions, historical developments, and movements in other disciplines that might be of use. This guide is in its second edition and is important for novices and advanced scholars alike. Entries include primary and secondary bibliographies, are cross-referenced, and are indexed by topic and by names.

With an extensive bibliography and a broad scope, the *Dictionary of Cultural and Critical Theory* is an excellent resource with many renowned contributors from across the field of literary study. This dictionary provides a comprehensive, challenging entry point into literary criticism. Cross-referencing is substantial, with terms like "binary oppositions" and "narratology" displayed in capital letters in the text of entries to indicate that they are defined elsewhere in the same volume. Magill also has a series of volumes dedicated to this topic called *Critical Survey of Literary Theory*. This series is a little older than the others and does not have the same sophistication, but it covers a broad range of topics more thoroughly compared to the other resources.

An important companion for many of the other references here, the *Dictionary of Cultural Theorists* focuses on the people that create theory and the ideas for which they are responsible. Of special use to researchers is the list of primary works attributed to each. Theorists are also linked to other thinkers whom they were influenced by or whom they influenced. This is an invaluable resource that captures a specific set of connections not evident in other reference works. Two newer, but less comprehensive and less cross-referenced resources with similar content are *Contemporary Critical Theorists: Lacan to Said* and *Fifty Key Contemporary Thinkers: From Structuralism to Post-Humanism*.

Online, the *Internet Encyclopedia of Philosophy* and the *Stanford Encyclopedia of Philosophy* can both be helpful for finding lengthy entries about theorists. The *Internet Encyclopedia of Philosophy* is peer-reviewed and provides browsing by keyword and by topic. Articles are essay length and feature extensive lists of resources for further reading. Author entries have

biographies in addition to information about the author's ideas and the philosophical communities with which they were associated. Though browsing is
effective, there is no advanced search to allow for more complex subjects.
The **Stanford Encyclopedia of Philosophy** does have field searching by title
and author. Entries are organized alphabetically and can be browsed from
the main page. Extensive cross-referencing makes this alphabetical interface
particularly valuable. Entries contain lengthy bibliographies, as well as links
to other Internet resources and suggestions for other related essays. Biographical entries are available, in addition to concepts, movements, works,
and other types of information.

Though you might not be especially familiar with what theories apply to
the primary works you are studying before the start of the research process,
each of these reference sources is designed to assist in finding the right ideas.
Use them carefully and really think about what school of thought is the best
fit for the message you are trying to convey to the reader. Remember that
applying a new theory to a work is one way to explore aspects that might
not have been looked at previously. Having a robust understanding of what
theories might be appropriate is key to successful research in the humanities.

BIBLIOGRAPHIES

A Year's Work in Critical and Cultural Theory. Oxford: Blackwell, 1994–.
     ywcct.oxfordjournals.org.
Baker, William, and Kenneth Womack, eds. *Recent Work in Critical Theory,
     1989–1995: An Annotated Bibliography*. Westport, CT: Greenwood Pub-
     lishing, 1996.
Lineback, Richard. Philosopher's Index. Ipswich, MA: EBSCO. www.ebsco
     host.com.
Marshall, Donald. *Contemporary Critical Theory: A Selective Bibliography*.
     New York: Modern Language Association of America, 1993.
Nordquist, Joan, ed. *Feminist Literary Theory: A Bibliography*. Santa Cruz,
     CA: Reference and Research Services, 1998.
Orr, Leonard, ed. *Research in Critical Theory since 1965: A Classified Bib-
     liography*. Westport, CT: Greenwood Publishing, 1989.

You can use many of the bibliographies mentioned earlier to research critical
theory, including *MLAIB* and *ABELL*. Additionally, the **Philosopher's Index**
might be of use to critics looking for articles about the philosophical development of theories that are often applied to literature. Created by the Philosopher's Information Center, the Philosopher's Index contains over five hun-

dred thousand records for articles back to 1940. Available in print or through EBSCO, Ovid, or ProQuest, this resource is extensive. Each online version has different advanced searching options common to the database publisher.

As noted earlier, many of the reference resources listed additionally contain primary or secondary bibliographies that can guide research in critical theory. Bibliographies dedicated to literary theory or to related topics are also handy. The most important serial bibliography in this area is *A Year's Work in Critical and Cultural Theory*. Mentioned in chapter 4, this is an annual narrative bibliography that describes the important contributions to humanities and social sciences related to critical theory over the past year. This is a close companion to *A Year's Work in English Studies* and carries the same mark of quality and rigor often ascribed to its better-known companion.

A bibliography of value from the Modern Language Association is *Contemporary Critical Theory: A Selective Bibliography*, which contains essays as well as a lengthy list of resources with two thousand annotated entries. Though published in 1992, and therefore somewhat out of date, this resource is convenient for those wishing to identify foundational scholarship written during the 1980s, a period when critical theory was flourishing. Note that foreign research is excluded.

Recent Work in Critical Theory, 1989–1995: An Annotated Bibliography is another work that is a little older, though it can help scholars pinpoint foundational literature. This bibliography is focused on books across a wide array of disciplines. Author and subject indexes are included. Each chapter presents a list of resources under a broad topic heading. Also broken up by theoretical approaches, *Research in Critical Theory Since 1965: A Classified Bibliography* is another resource that covers a vast array of literature and includes an index, though it is again somewhat outdated.

In addition to bibliographies that broadly discuss critical studies, many concentrate on specific points of view, for instance, *Feminist Literary Theory: A Bibliography*. There are too many of these to list here, but scholars are encouraged to explore the resources available to them in their subfield. Many academic journals also regularly publish bibliographies.

CONCLUSION

Learning a theoretical framework can take an entire career for some critics. The complexity of theories and the skill required to effectively apply them to the interpretation of literature takes practice and a deep understanding of the subject. Familiarizing yourself with the development of critical theory is essential. The better understanding gained of how individual movements and schools of thought have developed, and how they fit together, the easier it will be to make connections in scholarly works. Taking time to really learn theory is imperative to success as a contemporary literary scholar. Though we have listed many resources to get started, there is no substitute for doing the work and learning through trial and error. Eventually, writing about theory should come naturally and with confidence provided that the requisite time is taken to be successful.

NOTES

1. Max Horkheimer, *Critical Theory* (New York: Seabury Press, 1982), 244.
2. James Bonham, "Critical Theory," *Stanford Encyclopedia of Philosophy*, last modified March 8, 2005, plato.stanford.edu/entries/critical-theory.
3. Ibid.

Chapter Eleven

Other Web Resources

Though many, if not most, of the resources that we have looked at have been accessible online, there are also those that defy definition, since they are the novel products of a new media environment. A general discussion of how to evaluate what is found on the web is important, as new resources become available every day. Though this guide cannot list all of these new websites, we can provide the tools to decide if they are worthwhile.

For many years, the basic rule was that online resources accessed through a library and vetted by publishers were the only trustworthy scholarly websites. This rule is changing rapidly. Since the number of resources is expanding, the task of deciding which are trustworthy is complex.

Online digital humanities projects are becoming increasingly important. They often take the form of an archival database, though sometimes they include visual representations of data, text manipulation tools, or other new ways to look at the written word. Along with these projects, scholarly organizations, like NINES: Nineteenth-Century Scholarship Online (www. nines.org), dedicated to peer-reviewing archives, have sprung up to ensure their quality. A twentieth-century equivalent has yet to develop, but there is no doubt that this type of organization is important to the future of the online humanities.

Though one could argue that digital archives are a new form of postmodern scholarship, collections dedicated to postmodern literature are rare due to copyright laws. That said, what postmodern scholars might lack in viewable, traditional archival content outside of subscription databases, they gain in the sheer volume of literary artifacts online. Outlets for creating new forms of literature in digital spaces have exploded, and this rich collection of multimedia content is available for analysis in ways that have not existed in the past.

One particular strength of the postmodern period is that it allows authors willing to explore new forms of expression a robust set of tools for this endeavor. Much like writers at the dawn of the print age, those working today are not always creating pieces that look exactly like a novel of the past. This is also an opportunity for postmodern scholars, if they choose to take advantage of the tapestry of new research being done. As work coming out of places like the MIT Hyperstudio and other programs focused on revolutionary research in the humanities shows, the future is open for critics who think about research differently.

With all these resources, one important factor remains. The information we rely on to anchor our scholarship must be of high quality. This has always been central to academic work and will likely remain at the core of our research methods. In order to ensure that resources meet these standards, consider the following factors.

Authority: Who created the content? Who maintains it? Do they have professional or academic qualifications that make this resource reliable enough for scholarly research? At times, this can be difficult to unearth online. If the author is not immediately clear, a visit to an "about" or "contact" page to reveal this information might be required. Though the old rule of thumb is to look for a .edu or .gov, because these denote that it is an educational or governmental webpage, remaining critical in your assessment of pages that are personal in nature under these domains is appropriate, particularly those created by students. Also remember that corporate entities sometimes offer useful information—for instance, Penguin posting a press release about an author's newest work. The important thing is that you know who wrote it and whether the author is reliable.

Accuracy: Are there factual errors evident on this website? Are there grammatical or spelling errors? Do the links work and seem maintained? Does the author cite his or her resources properly? All of these questions will assist in identifying if a website is accurate. Websites where the answer is no to even one of these questions should give reason to pause and think. Independently verifying the information on a web page is a good idea if there are doubts about whether or not it can be trusted. Even if the answer is yes to all these questions, you still need to be aware of hoaxes and other intentionally misleading resources. For whatever reason, if something does not seem right, trust your own instinct and try to find a better source. With the plethora of resources available, there is no reason to use anything that is questionable.

Objectivity: What did the author hope to achieve with this website? Were there any secondary motives? What did the author stand to gain from convincing people of this point of view? Though the persuasive nature of many online resources makes total objectivity unlikely, understanding the potential motive of the writer can help vet the information. If someone stands to gain financially or socially from convincing people of a particular point of view, then the website should be questioned. Even an indirect suggestion that this person might benefit should be considered—for instance, a page critically evaluating an author's literary success with ads for the writer's next book prominently displayed. Watch out for clear indications that someone is not objectively producing the information. Another example would be a literary executor posting information online that promotes an author or someone with a disputed manuscript creating a web page about why it is authentic. Also be wary of pages that are either severely critical or exceptionally laudatory since the author might have a notable bias.

Coverage or Scope: Who is the audience for this website? How in-depth is the information? Is there academic merit evident? Many websites will be geared toward enthusiasts, the public, or school children. Though they might still have quality information, they might not be appropriate for the level of research being conducted. Also look at what the website does, and does not, contain. A website might not have relevant material pertinent to a specific inquiry.

Currency: When was this written? How frequently is it updated? Though currency is not often as important to literary scholars compared to other fields, it has more bearing for some postmodern authors. A blog post written ten years ago about Zadie Smith might no longer accurately reflect her writing or biographical details about her life. Ensuring that you have up-to-date information about living authors is quite important. Currency is also vital because newer blog posts will often deal with topics that are more interesting to scholars right now, since they do not have to go through the same timely, albeit rigorous, evaluation process as articles and books. This allows posts about new books, upcoming events, and breaking news to flourish long before a scholarly publication can be disseminated. This process can help ensure that researchers stay at the cutting edge of the field.

What follows is a list of resources with an explanation of each category. Though this list cannot be exhaustive, if you understand how each type can help retrieve reliable information, you will be able to work with new materials as they come along. The ephemeral nature of Internet sources generally means some of these might be obsolete eventually, but understanding the nature of the tools will remain useful long after they are gone.

SCHOLARLY GATEWAYS

Internet Public Library. www.ipl.org.
Liu, Alan. Voice of the Shuttle. vos.ucsb.edu.
Lynch, Jack. Literary Resources on the Net. andromeda.rutgers.edu/~jlynch/ Lit.

Scholarly gateways can be essential places to start when looking for relevant material online. Because the links listed in gateways are vetted by academics, they are more reliable entry points to web resources than a simple Google search. The gateways listed in this section have been around for several years, but others might eventually supersede them. The ephemeral nature of the web means that the best resources are constantly changing and evolving. If you find gateway sites beyond those listed here, consider who created them and how often they are updated. Sometimes, broken links can indicate that a site is no longer maintained.

One of the best-known gateways for literary research is Alan Liu's **Voice of the Shuttle** (VOS). This was one of the earliest digital humanities projects, beginning in 1994 and opening to a global audience in 1995. Voice of the Shuttle is maintained by a development team out of the University of California at Santa Barbara and is now on its second incarnation. The easiest way to navigate this resource is by browsing categories from the homepage. The most relevant classification for postmodern literature is "Contemporary (British and American)," under "Literature (in English)." This provides links to authoritative web pages related to the postmodern period in British literature, and there is a subcategory for "Contemporary British Authors." Other subcategories include "Criticism," "Journals," "Listservs," and "Conferences." This website is continuously being updated, but the sheer volume of links makes broken ones more likely. With the advent of link checkers, this problem will likely become less and less prominent.

Until then, tracking down the new address for a web page might be possible in a few different ways. One technique is to find the root web address before any forward slash; for instance, in the address *vos.ucsb.edu/browse. asp?id=3*, the root would be *vos.ucsb.edu*. This root address should take you to the main page for that website, and links might be present that match the desired content. Another option is to search for the title of the web page on Google. Though both of these methods can be helpful, neither is guaranteed, and sometimes a link will simply remain inoperative.

The **Internet Public Library** is a resource run primarily by information science students and hosted by Drexel University. Striving to deliver a public site to find reliable information on the web, the library offers an online chat and a curated collection of links to free data about many subjects, including British literature. Because of its broad scope and public-service philosophy, this is a good way to get started. The site can be browsed by category from the front page, or searched by keyword. Listed items have summaries accompanying them and are cataloged with Library of Congress subject classifications. Since these are continuously maintained by library students, they grow as the materials available multiply.

Jack Lynch's **Literary Resources on the Net**, hosted by Rutgers University, is another general guide that has a category devoted to twentieth-century British, Irish, and Commonwealth literature. Within this category, entries are in alphabetical order and focus on authors. Though most authors listed are modern, some prominent contemporary writers are represented, such as Julian Barnes, Jeanette Winterson, Salman Rushdie, and T. C. Boyle. The last update on this page was in 2006, calling into question its continuing usefulness.

Because keyword searching is the primary method of navigating the Internet, websites like Literary Resources on the Net are increasingly less prominent. Curated sites like the Internet Public Library are likely to be more in line with the future expectations of researchers since the importance of curated entry points to the web remains. The proliferation of information results and the expansion of easy-to-find, but unreliable, materials ensures this. The savvy researcher must be aware of the short cuts to trustworthy material.

ELECTRONIC TEXT ARCHIVES

Internet Archives. archive.org.
Open Library. openlibrary.org.
UK Web Archive. www.webarchive.org.uk/ukwa/.
Wayback Machine. archive.org/web/.

As we discussed in chapter 8, working in a recent literary period has benefits and drawbacks for finding archives of material online. Free archives on the web are not as common as in other literary periods since copyright limits what can be made available. Some material has not yet made it to archives because authors are still living. Many resources for finding digital copies of books exist, but most of them require payment per book or a subscription. Those archives that are available are generally web based, capturing the historical state of sites online.

One such page is the **UK Web Archive**, created by the British Library to ensure that important UK websites are preserved. Since its start in 2004, the archive has collected sites that represent the "rich diversity of lives and interests" throughout the UK. This archive can be searched, browsed by subject category, or navigated through an alphabetical list by title. Special collections are also presented, dealing with topics such as blogs, the London terrorist attacks, and the Queen's Diamond Jubilee. Web pages for literary magazines like *Granta*, author pages for writers such as Jeanette Winterson, and pages related to various types of writing, for instance, poetry slams or novels, are all represented. Entries are archived at set intervals, and individual groups for specific ones can be searched. A rich source for text that can be mined and interpreted in ways that scholars could never consider before, web archives can also generate visualizations based on terms as they appear in the archived data. Though literary scholars are just starting to work with this type of research, the potential for drawing meaning is great.

The **Wayback Machine** and its parent site, the Internet Archive, are other resources for contemporary writing and media online. The Wayback Machine is a database of 240 billion web pages going back to 1996. This is the biggest collection representing the history of the web, and for postmodern scholars, it serves as a major source of information. Scholars can, for instance, track the development of an author's blog over many years, or the expansion of a page related to a specific school, movement, or trend. As online writing becomes more important, this page will offer an entry point into the variant editions of a piece of writing as it appeared in different online venues. User comments, reposts, and other information that can help critics determine the reader response to an event or piece can also be found. Because this archive is so diverse, the full potential for integrating it into research has yet to be understood, offering postmodern scholars an exciting opportunity to break new ground in literary criticism.

The Wayback Machine can be navigated with a chosen URL. You can also use a basic or advanced keyword search. The advanced options might be limited to the Wayback Machine or expanded to the entire Internet Archive. Different fields are available, including title, creator, description, collection, media type, date, or date range. Three custom search fields are also provided that give the option to be more specific with greater or lesser values. The ability to search only specialized formats such as JSON or XML is also present with the advanced option. Scholars are encouraged to experiment with searching to get the most from these choices.

In addition to the Wayback Machine, the **Internet Archive** offers many other resources that are freely available on the web. Copyright might limit what is accessible from the postmodern era, though some video and audio media will be beneficial. Audio and video collections contain recordings of music as well as poetry readings, book talks, and other ephemera that would have been difficult to find before the advent of the Internet. A TV news search is also available to find broadcasts from the past few years, such as some from the BBC. This content might be queried with the same simple and advanced options described above.

The Open Library, another part of the Internet Archive, is also valuable. Register for a free account and borrow books online, just like from a local library. For instance, Jeanette Winterson's *Sexing the Cherry* or Julian

Barnes's *Metroland* are available. Some encyclopedias and other types of academic resources are also viewable. This is a valuable tool for finding and using items. WorldCat records are often linked to items in the Open Library catalog, which endeavors to have one page for every book ever written, though not all of these are available to borrow. WorldCat links will find print books located at libraries close to the user if they cannot check them out digitally, which is further discussed in chapter 3. Your academic library should also have access to many ebook collections through Overdrive, ebrary, EBSCO eBook, or other platforms. These can be searched in much the same way as the other databases described in earlier chapters, and they are often reached through a library's catalog.

In the future, there might be sites like Netflix that offer unlimited access to ebooks or audiobooks for a monthly fee. Oyster is an up-and-coming website that already does this for iPhone users, though with only one hundred thousand titles, it does not yet rival the electronic collections of many academic libraries. Audible offers audio books, but only a few each month for subscribers. As these technologies develop, the ease of finding resources online through a local library or through other services is likely to grow. Researchers are encouraged to follow these exciting developments as they unfold.

AUTHOR, PROMOTIONAL, SOCIETY, AND FAN SITES

Author websites, promotional pages, fan sites, and other types of resources are widely available through the Internet. There are so many that it would take a whole new volume to list them comprehensively. Instead, we highlight a few different types of pages that you might find on the web. Each of these are important for different reasons but can offer significant benefits to researchers.

Author Sites

Akers, Sean. Colum McCann. colummccann.com.
Gray, Alasdair. Alasdair Gray. www.alasdairgray.info.
Official Roald Dahl Website. www.roalddahl.com.
Roberts, Ryan. Ian McEwan Website. www.ianmcewan.com.

Most authors writing today, or in the past twenty years, have official websites sponsored by either the author or the author's publisher. Ian McEwan, for instance, has an official website maintained by Ryan Roberts called the **Ian McEwan Website** (Roberts also maintains websites for Julian Barnes, James

Fenton, Hermione Lee, and Ian Hamilton). This site includes a bibliography of criticism, as well as an authoritative list of the author's publications. Contact and publicity information, interviews, and appearances are enumerated. Because it is the official website, the information is more authoritative, though there might still be a bias, since the author often controls the content. Any scholar doing research on McEwan would do well to start here. The website is just one example of a well-maintained author page.

Another example worth noting is **Colum McCann**, an official website containing interviews, tour dates, photos, excerpts, a bibliography, and media. This website belongs to the author, though it is maintained by a third party, and it acts as an advertising tool. In contrast, the **Official Roald Dahl Website** is maintained by a literary estate, associated museum, and not-for-profit organization, all dedicated to the author. For characters and stories created by the author, the website provides lesson plans, media, news, and other information intended to facilitate the study of Dahl's work across grade levels. There are also links to a timeline and digitized archival materials, in addition to information about the charity, the museum, and an online shop. Some authors who are not as commercially popular might have more personal websites, such as **Alasdair Gray**, which showcases the work of this Scottish writer. Featuring information about the author's work and some full text for poetry, interviews, and other information, this is a creative outlet that gets updated regularly. All three of these websites were created for different reasons, which are easily identifiable by thinking critically about their content.

Promotional Sites

Bridget Jones: Mad about the Boy. New York: Random House. www.ran
   domhouse.com/book/228035/bridget-jones-mad-about-the-boy-by-helen
   -fielding.
The Day Aberystwyth Stood Still. London: Bloomsbury Publishing. www
   .bloomsbury.com/uk/the-day-aberystwyth-stood-still-9781408810255.
NW. New York: Penguin Books. www.penguin.com/book/nw-by-zadie-smith/
   9781594203978.

Promotional sites for new novels or other works are also common. For instance, Penguin's promotional website for Zadie Smith's *NW* has a summary, preview chapter, interview with Smith, list of quotes from reviews, and other data that might be important to a study of this novel. Though you will not get as much detail as you might from an official author website, relevant resources to get started with will be identified. Other examples of this type of website are the publisher information for ***The Day Aberystwyth Stood Still*** and ***Bridget Jones: Mad about the Boy***. Each book has different audiences, and the information provided appeals to these demographics.

Author and Academic Society Sites

Association for Scottish Literary Studies: Scottish Literature's International Voice. asls.arts.gla.ac.uk.
British Council: Literature. literature.britishcouncil.org.
Cfp.english.upenn.edu: A Service Provided by Penn English. call-for-papers .sas.upenn.edu.
CFP List: An Academic Call for Papers Database. www.cfplist.com.
Doris Lessing Society. dorislessingsociety.wordpress.com.
International Anthony Burgess Foundation. www.anthonyburgess.org.
Salman Rushdie Society. salmanrushdie21stcentury.wordpress.com/salman -rushdie-society.
Royal Society of Literature. rslit.org.

Well-established authors could also have a website for a scholarly group or society, for instance, the **Doris Lessing Society**. These websites are likely to contain bibliographies of sources, lists of conferences, information about author-centered scholarly journals, and other types of resources that might assist those studying the writer. As an example, the Doris Lessing Society maintains a bibliography of Lessing's work, books about Lessing, recent articles, and other information. Panels about Lessing at conferences are also highlighted. The organization hosts a student essay contest and publishes *Doris Lessing Studies*, a digital journal. These societies are central to the scholarship about any major author, and researchers are encouraged to use them as a starting place. Join societies for authors who you will study extensively.

The Salman Rushdie Society and the International Anthony Burgess Foundation also have websites that are relevant here. Where the **Salman Rushdie Society** site is similar to the one for the Doris Lessing Society, featuring multimedia, conferences, contact information, and other relevant resources, the **International Anthony Burgess Foundation** is a bit more advanced, housing articles, information about events, timelines, a call for submissions to the Observer/Anthony Burgess Prize for Arts Journalism, and current news about the author's writing. The quality of resources available and the level of activity from these societies depend on how strong of a contemporary critical following is enjoyed by the author.

To explore the development of postmodern British literature more broadly, check websites for literary societies and organizations around Britain. These websites often contain information about many current authors and ways of studying them. The **Royal Society of Literature** is one such organization that holds events and awards funding to support British literature. A library of items related to these endeavors is available and searchable, either by author name or keyword. This collection of audio files is particularly helpful since a search for an author like Hilary Mantel will retrieve interviews she has given related to aspects of her writing, such as darkness or the art of historical fiction. The literature team for the British Council Arts Group is another organization with a broad mission to support festivals, programs, and other opportunities for writers in England and around the globe. Their websites, **British Council: Literature**, is particularly beneficial because it contains a writers directory, where an author such as Peter Ackroyd can be searched. When Ackroyd's entry is opened, there is a biography, critical assessment, bibliography, list of awards, and other information. There is also a writers map that can help you identify authors based on a region.

Finding the websites for scholarly organizations that represent a subject is also important. For instance, the **Association for Scottish Literary Studies: Scottish Literature's International Voice** is the central hub for literary study related to this topic. Articles, essays, conference announcements, association publications, and other beneficial material can be downloaded here. The information is especially worthwhile because, like author societies, scholarly associations related to a type of literary output can help researchers stay up to date on developments in the field. Also, larger associations often publish important works related to their specialty area. If an author society does not exist, these types of organizations are the next best thing.

Beyond the individual websites that contain calls for papers for a single conference or association, there are websites that serve as clearinghouses for submission information. Two of these that are important for literary studies are Cfp.english.upenn.edu and the CFP List. Though the name is odd, **Cfp.english.upenn.edu** is one of the oldest and best-established websites to disseminate information about requests for submissions in literary studies. The archive can be searched, or browsed by category, containing topics like "popular culture," "postcolonial," and "twentieth century and beyond." The query is a specialized Google search, and results are ordered according to relevance, though they can be limited to a time range, such as "past month," or re-sorted by date with the search tools button at the top of the screen. Records might list contact information, organizers, conference information, keynote speakers, and a summary of potential submission topics. In addition to conference papers, book submissions and journal requests are also represented. Similarly, the **CFP List** is a bigger resource that collects calls for submissions from a larger variety of humanities disciplines. A more advanced website than Penn State's, the CFP List has both map and calendar interfaces that allow researchers to limit to a specific conference location, date range, or submission due date. A browse function is also present, with classifications such as "British" or "literary theory." A list of upcoming deadlines is convenient. The database can be searched by a simple keyword inquiry, and records present the event date, location, abstract due dates, summary of the request, and contact information. Both of these websites are handy to identify potential places to send research when it is completed.

Fan Sites

Discworld and Terry Pratchett Wiki. wiki.lspace.org/mediawiki/index.php/ Main_Page.

Harry Potter Wiki. harrypotter.wikia.com/wiki/Main_Page.

Rowling, J. K. Pottermore. www.pottermore.com/en-us.

Shields, Niamh. *Eat Like a Girl*. eatlikeagirl.com.

Tardis Data Core: The *Doctor Who* Wiki. tardis.wikia.com/wiki/Doctor_ Who_Wiki.

With popular writing, informative fan sites might exist to navigate the fictional universe of the books. Though these sites are not scholarly, and should not be consulted as though they are academic, they might be sufficient as reference aids while trying to first navigate a new author's works. Wikis, or collaborative websites with user-generated content, are particularly common in this category of resource. Some of the largest are the **Discworld and Terry Pratchett Wiki**, **Tardis Data Core: The *Doctor Who* Wiki**, and the **Harry Potter Wiki**. Each of these contains an extensive network of entries written by fans that aid readers in keeping track of characters, objects, locations, and other relevant information in these well-developed fantasy universes.

Another new type of website are those that continue or complement the story told in a work of fiction, for instance, additional short stories with the same characters that take place after the end of a novel. When a story moves between media, it is called *transmediation*. One famous example of transmediation is J. K. Rowling's Harry Potter website, **Pottermore**. This is not simply a website about Harry Potter; it extends the story by adding new narratives related to the fictional universe written by the author. Websites that complement and extend the original narrative are likely to become more common as writers explore boundaries using the Internet. Fanfictions are derivative works that reuse established fictional worlds, premises, or characters, but that are not written by the original author or creative entity. These stories are available on many websites and are a less authoritative version of the same principle cast of characters and themes, which might be particularly important to those interested in reader-response theory. Worth noting is the fact that some authors are quite hostile to fanfiction, while others embrace it. Whether authoritative or not, the transmediation of postmodern fiction in new online permutations is an exciting and growing area of study.

Author blogs are another interesting example of writer websites and in some ways might work in reverse as compared to Pottermore. For instance, the British travel and food blog *Eat Like a Girl*, written by Niamh Shields, preceded Shields's book *Comfort and Spice*. As a result, the book is actually the work derived from the born-digital content in her blog. Sheilds's blog, then, is an important resource to study the development of contemporary food and travel writing, a genre that has received a great deal of attention in academic settings.

Ultimately, all these types of author web pages play a role in researching postmodern British literature. They are all significant because they reflect the complex relationship between contemporary authors and the Internet. Contemporary authors often have a host of web resources surrounding their writing, all of which create the culture of the work. Researchers must find and consider these Internet sources whenever they are doing a serious study of a postmodern writer.

CULTURAL AND HISTORICAL WEB RESOURCES

British Cartoon Archive. www.cartoons.ac.uk.
British Museum. www.britishmuseum.org.
Exploring 20th Century London. www.20thcenturylondon.org.uk.
Hacken, Richard. Eurodocs. eudocs.lib.byu.edu/index.php/Main_Page.
History Online. www.history.ac.uk/history-online.
Internet Modern History Sourcebook. www.fordham.edu/Halsall/mod/modsbook.asp.
National Archives. www.nationalarchives.gov.uk.
Tate. www.tate.org.uk.

Like author websites, those that reflect the culture and history of the United Kingdom are too many to list. Instead, we cover a few representatives that hold value for postmodern researchers. Knowing that these types of resources are available, we encourage you to find others similar to them.

One particularly useful type of historical resource is government documents related to the UK during the identified period of time. The best place to start any search for these documents is the **National Archives** of Britain, briefly described in chapter 8. The archives's catalog, as well as the growing online collection of archival documents, make this website the best entry point to British history. The catalog has basic search options that can be refined in the results screen. There are also many research guides that give samples to pinpoint the information needed, including a guide to what is and is not available online. Only about 5 percent of the archives are digitized, though they have endeavored to ensure that the most popular records are online. A copy of items that are not electronically accessible can be ordered. Many cabinet records and other popular government materials are digitized.

Another website, **Eurodocs**, maintained by Richard Hacken at Brigham Young University, containing a section for twentieth- and twenty-first-century resources about the United Kingdom. These are available in the section titled "Britain 1919 to the Present," and with links to documents like the "Cabinet Papers" from the British National Archives, "Cold War Origins" from the Wilson Center's Digital Archive of the Cold War, and speeches, interviews, and other documents from the Margaret Thatcher Foundation. As these examples suggest, this website gives links to archives of British primary documents from one central location.

Online history gateways and source books might be important for studying the historical and cultural milieu in Britain during the postmodern period. For British history, the biggest online gateway is **History Online**, maintained by the Institute of Historical Research at the University of London. Browse by type of resource, such as books, grants, historians, journals, libraries, projects, teachers, theses, and tools, or do a keyword or person search. There is category browsing with options like "20th Century," "21st Century," and "Humanities."

The **Internet Modern History Sourcebook** from Fordham University is also useful as a gateway to web resources. Categories cover topics like "Pop Culture," "21st Century History," "Social Movements," and "Europe Since 1945." Each category includes links to helpful entries that explore many difference aspects of the topic. The sourcebook can also be searched with keywords. These sourcebooks and gateways will often point to specialized archives, such as Exploring 20th Century London or the British Cartoon Archive. There are too many of these to list here, though both are strong examples of the type of web content that is proliferating as the field of digital humanities grows.

Exploring 20th Century London is a large collection of articles and digitized archival items related to the history of London from 1900 to 2000. Accessible using a timeline, themes for browsing, places, or a keyword search with advanced limiters on the retrieval screen, this database contains a wealth of information about London—for instance, objects and articles related to the

Brixton Riots of 1981 and 1985. The **British Cartoon Archive** is another collection of archival content related to the late twentieth century. With biographies of cartoonists, a keyword search, an advanced search, and browsing categories, navigation of the archive is fairly smooth. Advanced options include artist, publication, date, title or caption, format, embedded text, notes, implied text, subjects, collections, copyright, location of the artwork, and other options. Largely made up of political cartoons, one particularly valuable search in this database might be for *Iraq*, which retrieves thousands of comics related to this topic, from 1917 to the present. Again, though there are too many of these archives to list comprehensively, these are just two examples of the archival sources available.

Often, museums that are important to history or a cultural period have online components. The most important of these is the Tate's online component and the British Museum's page. The blogs, media, online collections, digital features, and other resources found at these websites can help explore the art of the postmodern period. **Tate**'s online gallery has images of artwork, blogs, media channels, articles about specific artists, research, and other education links. The website can be searched by keyword, such as *postmodern*, and results contain individual artworks and full subject categories. Similarly, the **British Museum**'s website has links to digital images, research, educational links, and current exhibits. The website can also be searched. Though *postmodern* does not retrieve many results, the broader *contemporary* retrieves a subject category and multiple subcategories. There are many other galleries and museums in Britain that also have interesting online presences that are worth checking for their value to your research. Remember that often museum websites now offer full catalogs and extensive online collection guides, which can be especially assistive.

The number of cultural and historical sources for this period are infinite. Exploring what is out there for an area of interest is valuable. As you do, remember the rules for evaluating web resources discussed earlier in this chapter to ensure that these sources are reliable.

BLOGS AND OTHER SOCIAL MEDIA

Google Blog Search. www.google.com/blogsearch.
Meltwater IceRocket. www.icerocket.com.

In addition to more traditional academic websites, blogs and other forms of social media are becoming increasingly significant. Because social media is generally creator driven, looking for blogs written by entities or individuals that are already trusted as experts is generally the best approach. Be extra sensitive to reliability with any form of social media. Generally, even blogs written by specialists cannot be cited in serious research. That said, blogs by renowned scholars or writers can be used to keep abreast of new trends, forthcoming publications, fresh ideas, and vital research contributions. They are a far more immediate form of publishing academic thought than journals and books, and this immediacy can allow researchers to stay current.

To find blogs in a subject area, you can search broadly in any engine, though this might not retrieve the best results. There are specialized search engines such as **Google Blog Search** and **Meltwater IceRocket** that are far more accurate. Searching for a specific creator by name or organization is probably the easiest way to find a blog. For instance, if you wanted to find a blog about digital humanities, you might search for Dan Cohen, who is a well-known scholar who writes a respected digital humanities blog. Be wary of blogs by those who are not clearly associated with a research organization, such as a university, library, or think tank.

Twitter is another useful social media outlet that can be searched with Meltwater IceRocket. Many authors have accounts on Twitter, and sometimes they have conversations with other artists that could be significant to research. Neil Gaiman, for instance, has an active Twitter account that can tell researchers a good deal about his writing and personality.

CONCLUSION

Scholarship has changed quickly and has evolved to the point where many research sources are available digitally. In order to remain on top as a scholar, you need to be familiar with both well-established and up-and-coming digital research tools. This section endeavors to cover some of those up-and-coming tools, though there is the potential that humanities scholarship could change even more as our traditional notions of the book grow. The best scholars will remain aware of the trends and will change with them. Visualizations, new media, and other currently revolutionary types of humanities investigation might eventually become central to the endeavor of understanding and interpreting literature. Be prepared to continue to alter your course with the times in order to ensure success.

Chapter Twelve

A Thorny Problem

Our final chapter presents a research problem common to scholars of postmodern British literature and uses this scenario to provide a step-by-step overview of how to navigate a similarly difficult situation. We have decided to focus on researching a new novel by an established author because, for those interested in contemporary writers, one of the most fruitful lines of inquiry is criticism about a recent publication. By being one of the first scholars to publish about a new title, there is the opportunity to become established as a significant early critic. One of the most celebrated and well-known contemporary authors is Neil Gaiman, author of postmodern classics such as *American Gods* and *Anansi Boys*. In June 2013, Gaiman published *The Ocean at the End of the Lane*, his first novel for adults since *Anansi Boys* and a recent National Book Award winner. For a scholar wishing to start an original line of inquiry, this book is an excellent opportunity to explore Gaiman's work.

As mentioned throughout this volume, researching a postmodern author presents many unique challenges, which are particularly evident when exploring a fresh title. Because scholarly publications that deal with contemporary authors are scarce, and especially those that deliberate about recently published books, broadening search strategies to find relevant criticism is necessary. By casting a wider net through expanded search terms, a larger number of resources, and a nontraditional set of potential materials, researchers can find items that might otherwise be overlooked. Similarly, work by postmodern authors has a tendency to move from one medium to another, complicating the steps to find all versions. This is particularly true if a book is being made into a film, as is the case with *The Ocean at the End of the Lane*. Multimedia sources are also essential because authors often create podcasts, taped interviews, blog posts, and tweets to promote releases. We will walk through the research process for *The Ocean at the End of the Lane* to explore how a scholar might cope with these common issues.

ABOUT GAIMAN

Before researching a particular novel, it is important to get some basic knowledge about an author's life and the works he or she has published. This can be helpful later on when identifying locations of relevant resources. *Contemporary Authors Online* and *British Fantasy and Science Fiction Writers since 1960*, one volume in the *Dictionary of Literary Biography*, both from Gale, are two of the best reference sources for biographical and critical overviews of an author who is still publishing. In addition to biographical essays that focus on the author's writing career, these resources also give bibliographies of primary and secondary works.

For those unfamiliar with Gaiman, he is a fantasy and science fiction writer who was born in 1960 in Portchester, England, but since 1992 has lived in the United States. As a child he was an avid reader who spent a good deal of time at the library and was influenced by many classic science fiction and fantasy writers, such as J. R. R. Tolkein, Ursula LeGuin, and G. K. Chesterton, each of whom has a great deal of scholarship related to their work that could be used as a jumping off place for inquiry into Gaiman's writing. He began his career as a journalist, and his first books were biographies of Duran Duran and Douglas Adams.

Eventually, he started publishing short stories and comics, and especially the graphic novels *Violent Cases* and *Black Orchid*. His Sandman series was considered groundbreaking and helped usher in the new modern age of graphic novels. Gaiman also began to garner a following for his fantasy and science fiction books, the first of which was *Good Omens*, a collaboration with Terry Pratchett. Other early titles include *Neverwhere* and *Stardust*, which introduced distant relatives of the Hempstock family, who are central to *The Ocean at the End of the Lane*. In 2001 he published the bestselling *American Gods*, followed by *Coraline* in 2002, *Anansi Boys* in 2005, and *The Graveyard Book* in 2008, which also features a Hempstock. Gaiman has additionally written episodes for television shows such as *Babylon 5*, *Neverwhere*, and *Doctor Who*, and screenplays for the films *MirrorMask* and *Beowulf*. His marriage in 2011 to musician Amanda Palmer has resulted in a lot of creative inspiration for both artists. A Newberry, a Carnegie Medal, Hugos, Nebulas, a World Fantasy Award, Bram Stoker Awards, Locus Awards, British SF Awards, a British Fantasy Award, Geffens, an International Horror Guild, and Mythopoeic Awards number among his honors. *The Ocean at the End of the Lane* is his most recent novel.

LOOKING FOR GAIMAN

Once the basic biographical sources have been consulted, brainstorming search terms is the next step in researching a new novel. Because few resources are created right after a book appears, finding a wide variety of articles published about the writer across his or her career will provide an entry point into this most recent work. As a result, searches should be constructed to find information across a spectrum of topics, using many different words. These terms can be used in the databases and catalogs discussed in the next section. Choosing the keywords first can ensure that the most is made of the resources available.

To find resources about Gaiman, remember that the simplest searches are often the best place to start. Using *Neil Gaiman*, or simply *Gaiman*, will likely retrieve a good amount of information, since his surname is not especially common. The titles of works that are related to the one being studied can also be fruitful, for instance, other works that mention the Hempstock family, *Stardust* and *The Graveyard Book*. Library of Congress subject searches for "Gaiman, Neil--Criticism and interpretation," "Gaiman, Neil--Interviews," and "Gaiman, Neil—Bibliography" should also retrieve some of the major critical collections, such as *Feminism in the Worlds of Neil Gaiman*, *The Neil Gaiman Reader*, *Neil Gaiman and Philosophy*, and *Neil Gaiman's* The Sandman *and Joseph Campbell*.

Though *Neil Gaiman* is the most obvious keyword phrase, be aware that searching other names might also retrieve relevant articles or books. Though he does not use pen names anymore, in his early years Gaiman wrote under them for certain kinds of publications, and particularly for reviews. He assumed names such as Richard Grey and Gerry Musgrave. He has also worked with other authors and artists throughout his career, including Alice Cooper, Dave McKean, Gene Wolfe, and Michael Reaves. Finding information about each of these collaborative projects will require different search strategies, so know enough about Gaiman's canon to identify which of his co-creators is of special importance. Chapter 3 explains in more detail some of the challenges of searching for multiple names.

The issue of collaborative authors is even more significant when dealing with graphic novels, which were particularly prominent in Gaiman's early career. Because these works deal with themes similar to those in *The Ocean at the End of the Lane*, such as the endurance of mythological creatures and the power of memory, both explored in the Sandman series among others, articles about these works could be beneficial. Often, graphic novels have many individuals attributed as creators; a writer, an illustrator, a letterer, an inker, and a cover artist might all be given credit. The best approach is to be aware of all possibilities and to search for different variable terms and creators.

For graphic novels, also consider the type of index being used. A database focused in literature might be more likely to have articles about Gaiman as the writer, whereas an art index might have more resources discussing the illustrator, inker, or cover artist.

Gaiman is a philosophical author who integrates contemporary thought to deepen his exploration of topics like feminism and folklore, a technique that is common to many postmodern authors, so you might also need to search for theories or concepts that underpin some of his writing. To get to resources that might cover this aspect, you could, for instance, pair Gaiman's name with the keyword *myth**, which is broad, or with a theorist, like *Joseph Campbell*. These searches narrow results to writing that discusses Gaiman's work from a particular framework or perspective. Simply searching for a broad category without Gaiman's name, like using the subject heading "Myth in Literature," will also be valuable to retrieve more general writing about topics that have an impact on Gaiman's work but which are not yet linked to him directly by criticism. These resources could assist researchers in thinking of new arguments to pursue that will contribute to the conversation taking place about Gaiman.

Exploring Gaiman's many allusions is also imperative, such as those to the threefold goddess in *The Ocean at the End of the Lane*. Like many postmodern writers, Gaiman often uses allusions to folkloric and mythological figures to examine contemporary cultural trends and patterns. The original context and significance of these references is vital to discern the meaning of his works. To research them, reference sources such as the *Oxford Dictionary of Classical Myth and Religion* or the *Dictionary of British Folk Customs* could be advantageous, or articles might be discovered that investigate how topics like the triple goddess are integrated into literature. Databases such as Credo Reference, ebrary, and *MLAIB* are excellent places to start with simple keyword searches, such as *triple goddess* or *the water of life*, or turn to LC subjects, such as "Mythology, Norse," "Anansie (Legendary characters) legend," or "Folklore—Great Britain" to find material that will explicate embedded references. These resources are key because they contextualize a work like *The Ocean at the End of the Lane*. With newer novels, tracing cultural influences and finding related literature can expand possible avenues for research.

Beyond searching for author names, theories, and allusions, consider looking for famous characters, places, quotes, or symbols. The other mother in *Coraline*, who is similar to Ursula in *The Ocean at the End of the Lane*, or the Faerie Market in *Stardust*, a recurring phenomenon in the town that first introduced the Hempstock family, are both well known and might be discussed in articles. Each of these could give insight into characters and themes in *The Ocean at the End of the Lane*. With contemporary authors who have particularly strong followings behind specific characters, places, or series, searching these as keywords can be especially fruitful.

WHERE TO LOOK

After choosing search terms, the next step is to discover academic sources related to the topic. In this case, identifying scholarship might be challenging because Gaiman is a relatively new author and *The Ocean at the End of the Lane* has only been out since 2013. For instance, a recent search in *MLAIB* resulted in only 59 academic articles about Gaiman. Some mention his writing but do not focus exclusively on him. In contrast, a search for *Aldous Huxley* netted 467 academic journal articles. A subject search in WorldCat for *Gaiman Neil* yielded 105 books, few of which are published by university presses and most of which would not be considered scholarly works of criticism.

The resources that do exist about Gaiman tend to be biographies (sometimes juvenile biographies) and popular books, such as the 2008 *Prince of Stories: The Many Worlds of Neil Gaiman* from St. Martin's Press. These books will be useful, but they might not provide the analysis a researcher needs to fully elaborate on Gaiman's most recent novel. In addition to monographs about Gaiman, he is discussed in some essay collections about topics such as British fantasy writers, but the numbers are limited. There are no reference materials that focus primarily on Gaiman, though some composite volumes contain entries about him, such as *Contemporary Literary Criticism*.

Furthermore, finding primary sources, such as letters and manuscripts, will be a struggle. As discussed in chapter 8, many contemporary authors have not yet donated their papers to an archive, and Gaiman is no exception. Someday, his archival material will likely be found at institutions in both the United States and Britain, but not yet. Though archival materials are not available, newspaper articles, reviews, blog posts, and other kinds of popular media can aid in research, many of which are available through Gaiman's websites, NeilGaiman.com and MouseCircus.com. Book reviews are particularly worthwhile because they are the first pieces written about a novel, and they give insight into the immediate critical reception. In this case, one such review by Benjamin Percy in the *New York Times* is quite illustrative, "It All Floods Back In: Neil Gaiman's 'Ocean at the End of the Lane.'"[1] The writer-in-residence at St. Olaf College and a former faculty member at the University of Wisconsin–Stevens Point, Marquette University, and Iowa State University, Percy's estimation of the novel is an important contribution, despite the fact that it was not published in an academic journal. Blog posts or interviews from the author can also clarify the context in which he or she wrote the novel, in the same way a letter or manuscript might. For instance, Gaiman created a blog post on January 13, 2011, called "I Took My Love to Hobart in the Rain," which gives readers an idea of the provenance for the character of Lettie in *The Ocean at the End of the Lane*.[2]

To find scholarly works about Gaiman, search broadly in a host of indexes, databases, and other resources covered throughout this book. Start with *ABELL* and *MLAIB*, though these do not retrieve as many articles as one would hope. Branch out to places like JSTOR and Project Muse, which have high rates of humanities articles. Another option that might retrieve a large number of resources is Google Scholar. Through Google Scholar, you should find several thousand primary and secondary sources, though some are peer-reviewed and others are not. One benefit to using Google Scholar is that it retrieves results that mention Gaiman anywhere in the full text of an article, making it easier to identify articles that are not primarily about him but that contain paragraphs or small sections discussing him. With authors who are as new as Gaiman, even essays outside the traditional peer-reviewed journals might be consulted, though you will need to consider whether or not they are appropriate for your purposes. Similarly, searching in the Dissertations and Theses database from ProQuest to see if any other graduate-level work has been done on the topic is an excellent idea.

Because of the scarcity of materials published about the author, starting with a search in WorldCat rather than in your library's local catalog could save time. The likelihood that resources located at multiple libraries will be necessary is quite high since there are not many monographs about Gaiman. Searching in WorldCat first shows which resources your library owns, but also gives a better idea of what else is available. Also, by looking in World-Cat, researchers can identify academic book-length studies with bibliographies, such as *The Neil Gaiman Reader*. These will list other resources, which is of great assistance early in the research process. Although no book-length bibliographies exist that describe primary or secondary sources written by or about Gaiman, mining the reference in these bibliographic lists, as well as those included in dissertations, can work in the same way. This is one particularly useful trick that can save a lot of time and broaden a literature review.

Another strategy is to examine general bibliographies related to science fiction writing or graphic novels. These are mostly article length, though you will be able to find some books, such as *Fantasy Authors: A Research Guide* and *Graphic Novels: A Bibliographic Guide to Book-Length Comics*. Article-length bibliographies should be searchable in notable humanities indexes and databases, such as *MLAIB* and *ABELL*, alongside other critical articles and monographs.

Discovering general research about the genres in which Gaiman works is another way to expand your research. For instance, an article about trends in fantasy writing over the past thirty years might allow you to show how *The Ocean at the End of the Lane* fits within these trends or is at the forefront of them. Another example might be an article about the role of classical myth and folklore in contemporary culture, which you could use to extrapolate the significance of the water of life in *The Ocean at the End of the Lane*. In both these cases, though there is unlikely to be an article already written about these subjects as they appear in *The Ocean at the End of the Lane*, broad scholarship about larger trends and themes can be used to ground a study of one novel. Another strategy is to find research about older stories with similar themes, like Hans Christian Anderson's *The Snow Queen*, which also features a brave young girl, a young boy who has been the unknowing host of evil, a cold, calculating female villain, and a lake of eternity. By finding articles about this famous fairytale, researchers can draw comparisons and conclusions about the provenance of *The Ocean at the End of the Lane* and its relationship to tropes in traditional fairy tales. This related scholarship can expand your thinking about a novel and take you in new directions.

Though scholarly resources might be difficult to locate for Gaiman's work, a myriad of media sources related to him are available. Audio and video readings exist widely and can be obtained from various platforms. The best collection online for these resources is Gaiman's self-titled website. The content is unique and interesting because past writers have not been able to make resources of this nature available, but it is also daunting due to the fact that audio and video are only as searchable as the data attached to them. Looking on media websites like YouTube can be a great help, but resources should be vetted to make sure they are authentic and authoritative. Other types of media related to Gaiman are movies or television series made from his books since his work tends to move fluidly across platforms. For instance, *Coraline* the book became *Coraline* the movie, and *The Graveyard Book* became the *Graveyard Book Sudoku*. As these stories move through media, they gain new meanings. Uncovering every instance of a work becomes more difficult, though the content itself is rewarding.

The type of media required will determine where it is likely available. Movies and television shows are often accessible through online streaming services such as Netflix or Hulu, or as DVDs with special features. Interviews or book readings are often online, for free, at websites like YouTube or the Internet Archive and might also be unearthed at websites for organizations that hold these events, such as scholarly associations. Podcasts or recordings can also be uncovered on websites for organizations, or on media streaming platforms like iTunes. Author websites also often document obtainable media as a means of promoting new works, such as *The Ocean at the End of the Lane*, and related events.

There are also indexes devoted to films and television, such as the Film Literature Index, FIAF International Index to Film Periodicals, and Film and Television Literature Index, which are discussed further in chapter 9. These resources might give you information about Gaiman as a film or television writer, or they might retrieve articles about Gaiman's novels that have been turned into films, such as *Coraline* or *Stardust*, or films in production, like *The Ocean at the End of the Lane*. Sometimes, film journals also publish articles that compare the movie to the source text based on some theme or aspect of the story. Searching in resources like Rock's Backpages or Music Index might also retrieve information about Gaiman's collaborations outside of print, television, or film, with, for instance, his wife, Amanda Palmer, or close friend Tori Amos, both popular musicians. Remember that you might need to turn to articles from more popular magazines or reviews to broaden research and to get a better idea of the place Gaiman inhabits in contemporary culture, which might be found using indexes like BHI: British Humanities Index and the American *Reader's Guide to Periodical Literature*. For a scholarly resource that expounds on popular culture, try the *Journal of Popular Culture*. Sources about graphic novels should also be searched, for instance, the *Comic Journal* and the *Journal of Graphic Novels and Comics*, as well as electronic indexes, such as the Graphic Novel Archive.

Above all, avoid inflexibility. When researching a newer novel like *The Ocean at the End of the Lane*, remain open to a variety of methods and sources. Since Gaiman's work tends to cross genres and media, do not make the mistake of assuming that you will not unearth constructive sources in disciplines outside of literature. Resources that are freely available online are worthwhile for research, but be careful about the quality of these sources. Evaluate them cautiously to make sure they contain reliable information. False rumors and extremely biased articles exist online when searching for someone as famous as Gaiman.

TIPS AND TRICKS

In addition to the steps just outlined, there are several tips and tricks to be aware of when researching a newer author like Gaiman. First, take advantage of Internet sources. A lot of beneficial content will be missed if you do not search online. Gaiman has an active personal website and Twitter account, and he also has a lively online fan base. If you truly want to understand an author like Gaiman, researching his online persona is required, especially related to a novel, like *The Ocean at the End of the Lane*, written since he established this persona. There is a strong possibility he documented the writing process for this work in various online forums, such as the blog post "I Took My Love to Hobart in the Rain," mentioned earlier. Also, do not limit searching to literature sources. Mentioned several times already, this is worth repeating because it is important for the genre crossing that often occurs with postmodernism. You will find resources about graphic novels, folklore, television, and film advantageous.

Also, make an effort to keep up with the new information that comes to light about Gaiman and the additional research that is being done. We recommend that you consider setting up search alerts on Google and in databases because scholarship and other materials are being published about him on an almost daily basis. If alerts are set up to come to your e-mail or an RSS feed, you will know right away when items become available.

Additionally, think about alternative methods of research. Instead of the usual literary criticism, a research project that interviews his fans might be a revealing avenue to understand better why his works inspire such loyalty among readers. Taking advantage of digital tools, for example, visualization such as word clouds, and data mining that can be used to interpret large collections of novels could lead to a breakthrough. For instance, these technologies might lead to articles about the language used in *The Ocean at the End of the Lane* by allowing an analysis of the most frequently used words and how they are related to the themes of the novel.

CONCLUSION

Research is an ongoing process that often takes you in directions unimagined when you began. Though we have made many recommendations in this chapter and throughout this volume, there will be times when, for instance, starting with basic reference sources will not be especially fruitful and you will need to change course. Research, like writing, is recursive. Moving back and forth between sources, finding new items, performing steps out of order, and returning to indexes with novel search terms are all a part of the process. Though many people think of this as a means to an end, it might be more accurate to view the development of research through the methods we have outlined in these chapters as a transformative act that shapes the way we think.

Though the goal for most academics is to learn one area of study so well that the research becomes second nature, keeping your skills up to date remains essential if only to ensure that your work never becomes obsolete. Cutting-edge scholars are exploring new opportunities for data analysis, archival research, media, and other postmodern innovations with an eye toward what is now possible that might not have been previously. The breakthrough scholarship of tomorrow is likely to be from scholars who understand the evolving nature of research and who use novel methods of inquiry in ways not yet imagined.

To ensure that you are one of these scholars, remain flexible and informed. We have endeavored to explain the types of sources commonly encountered, in addition to making recommendations for those materials that are currently at the center of scholarship in the postmodern period. The ever-evolving nature of electronic resources means that any resource might be superseded at any time, but with a strong research foundation, the type of information needed should be easily identifiable, as well as the category of work that will contain it, whether an index, bibliography, dictionary, handbook, or archive. Be aware of how scholarship is changing, but remember that many of the fundamental concepts related to research are likely to stay the same.

Hopefully, after reading this volume, you will not shrink from even the toughest research challenge. With the right set of tools, any problem can be tackled. Do not let the extraordinary number of resources currently available overwhelm you. Using the resources listed here, and those that have yet to be written, we are confident that you will find the required answers. If you do not, your local reference librarians are always available to assist.

NOTES

1. Benjamin Percy, "It All Floods Back: Neil Gaiman's 'Ocean at the End of the Lane," *New York Times*, June 27, 2013, www.nytimes.com/2013/06/30/books/review/neil-gaimans-ocean-at-the-end-of-the-lane.html?pagewanted=all.

2. Neil Gaiman, "I Took My Love to Hobart in the Rain," *Neil Gaiman: Journal*, January 13, 2011, journal.neilgaiman.com/2011/01/i-took-my-love-to-hobart-in-rain.html.

Appendix

Though we have endeavored to represent a wide variety of resources related to postmodern British literature, the very nature of this subject lends itself to interdisciplinary inquiry. We could not fully explore the many topics that your research might touch on, but we have created this appendix as a supplement to guide you. Each of the disciplines listed here has the same basic types of sources as literary inquiry. These include guides, reference materials, bibliographies, and indexes. The tips given throughout the preceding chapters should also apply in other fields of interest. Additionally, we have tried to list specialized items that might have a unique and significant role for a particular area of study. To find items in this appendix, consult your local library. Searching in the catalog, talking with a librarian, and browsing through available digital resources should get you started. Interlibrary loan might be required for sources that are hard to find or not collected by your library. Keep in mind that some of these titles are similar to this research guide and will serve as an excellent introduction to research in a new field.

GENERAL REFERENCE

Guides

Blazek, Ron, and Elizabeth Aversa. *The Humanities: A Selective Guide to Information Resources.* 5th edition. Englewood, CO: Libraries Unlimited, 2000.

A standard textbook used in library science courses to introduce humanities research, this work covers topics such as philosophy, visual arts, religion, performing arts, literature, and language. Discussing roughly 1,400 items that are central to the study of the humanities, sections cover both standard sources and the patterns that underpin the way we use research. The volume still has value for humanities researchers, despite the fact that it is badly in need of an update. This is most useful when paired with a more recent item, such as Dubnjakocvic and Tomlin's *A Practical Guide to Electronic Resources in the Humanities*, listed below.

Dubnjakovic, Ana, and Patrick Tomlin. *A Practical Guide to Electronic Resources in the Humanities*. Oxford: Chandos, 2010.

Encompassing items related to the performing arts, visual arts, architecture, language, literature, philosophy, and religion, this annotated guide is broken up by genre, such as scholarly articles, indexes, and archives. With a focus on high-quality, up-to-date electronic resources, this relatively recent volume fills some of the gaps apparent in *The Humanities* by providing information about the best new materials available in the past decade.

Kieft, Robert, ed. Guide to Reference. Chicago: American Library Association, 2008–. www.guidetoreference.org.

Kieft's Guide to Reference is an online database that supersedes ALA's *Guide to Reference Books*, which was the standard resource for information about different research publications across disciplines for many years. Including entries about print and electronic materials, the online version updates the print volume with new entries and more evaluative information about the many works published after 1996, when the *Guide to Reference Books* was last updated. With over sixteen thousand entries, this database makes finding and comparing items easier than ever and is the American equivalent of the *Walford* guide listed below.

Lester, Ray, ed. *The New Walford: Guide to Reference Resources*. 3 volumes. London: Facet, 2005–.

Under a new publisher, *The New Walford: Guide to Reference Resources* is essentially the ninth edition of the standard reference work *Walford's Guide to Reference Material. The Arts: Visual Arts, Music, Language, and Literature* is the third volume, edited by Peter Chapman and Helen Edwards. Published in 2010, this volume is revised and updated to reflect the rapid developments in reference resources. The new release contains print and electronic materials indexed by topic and classified by categories describing their subject and format. Two other volumes are also available, covering technology, science, and medical sources, and the social sciences.

Indexes and Bibliographies

Academic OneFile. Farmington Hills, MI: Gale Cengage. www.gale.cen gage.com.

This index features fourteen thousand indexed journal titles, with six thousand full-text resources, making it nearly as comprehensive as Academic Search Complete. Academic OneFile indexes scholarly publications from major bibliographies such as ERIC, RILM, and PsycInfo, as well as more popular titles from contemporary media, such as NPR, CNN, and the *New York Times*. Reference works from Gale's well-known catalog of titles are also provided.

Academic Search Complete. Ipswich, MA: EBSCO. www.ebscohost.com.

With 13,690 indexed and abstracted journals, and 9,100 that are full text, Academic Search Complete is the most comprehensive interdisciplinary database of scholarly publications and general interest magazines. Topics such as science, technology, social sciences, and the humanities are incorporated.

BHI: British Humanities Index. Ann Arbor, MI: ProQuest. www.csa.com.

This index for humanities research covers architecture, archeology, art, antiques, cinema, current affairs, education, economics, environment, foreign affairs, gender studies, history, language, law, linguistics, literature, music, painting, philosophy, poetry, political science, religion, and theater. With roughly eight hundred thousand records that feature abstracts, this is a large database that has 370 scholarly and popular titles published primarily in the UK. Available online via subscription with records from 1962 to the present.

Essay and General Literature Index. Ipswich, MA: EBSCO. www.ebscohost .com.

Indexing primarily multi-author essay collections, as well as annuals and serials, this resource covers writing in the humanities and social sciences back to 1985. Nearly eighty-six thousand items are indexed in about seven thousand printed anthologies.

Humanities International Index. Ipswich, MA: EBSCO. www.ebscohost.com.

Journals, books, and reference sources are indexed from subjects across the humanities. Over 3.2 million records from multiple sources are available. Published in print until 2004. Some records go back as far as 1950s, though most do not go back further than the 1990s.

Omnifile Full Text Mega. Ipswich, MA: EBSCO. www.ebscohost.com.

Full text for 3,100 journals back to 1994 and indexing and abstracting for 5,100 publications is provided. This product has content across many subjects, such as the sciences, social sciences, humanities, and arts.

ProQuest Central. Ann Arbor, MI: ProQuest. www.proquest.com.

Though not a single index, ProQuest Central is an aggregated database that collects twenty-seven smaller resources in one package, including about one thousand titles in the arts and humanities. Many popular newspapers are also available, such as the *New York Times*, *Washington Post*, and *Wall Street Journal*. As a combination of the most-used ProQuest databases, ProQuest Central provides interdisciplinary content through one unified database of nearly nineteen thousand publications, most of them full text.

Web of Science. New York: Thomson Reuters. webofknowledge.com.

One of the largest citation indexes available, Web of Science has the sciences, social sciences, and humanities. Because Web of Science enables citation searching, scholars can trace who is citing whom. For humanities researchers, the Arts and Humanities Citation Index is the most relevant, with 1,700 humanities journals indexed. Special features are available, such as citation mapping, which allows you to see a web of articles connected by citations. Though citation indexes are not as important to humanities research as they are in the social sciences or hard sciences, they can be quite useful for finding new or related publications.

ART

Reference

Chilvers, Ian, ed. *The Oxford Dictionary of Art and Artists*. 4th edition. New York: Oxford University Press, 2009.

Formerly the *Concise Oxford Dictionary of Art and Artists*, this resource is small enough to keep on the shelf as a handy reference to art galleries, concepts, movements, artists, styles, techniques, and museums. With 2,500 entries in its fourth edition, and spanning ancient Greece to the present, this compact dictionary covers a lot for such a small package.

Oxford Art Online. New York: Oxford University Press. www.oxfordarton line.com.

With Grove Art Online (the digital version of *The Grove Dictionary of Art*, listed below), the *Benezit Dictionary of Artists*, and other Oxford art titles, this is the preeminent art reference tool. Oxford Art Online allows one easy-to-navigate entry point to content, including articles and bibliographies from many well-known reference sources, as well as some items commissioned specifically for this database. Most of these works are also available in print.

Turner, Jane, ed. *The Grove Dictionary of Art*. 34 volumes. New York: Grove, 2003. Also available online at Oxford Art Online, www.oxfordart online.com.

The major dictionary dealing with the study of art, *The Grove Dictionary of Art* has forty-five thousand entries in thirty-four volumes. Topics touch on all the visual arts, including photography, sculpture, painting, architecture, drawing, printmaking, and decorative arts. The scope is unparalleled, and entries concern many Western and non-Western countries, as well as diverse historical periods. The international nature of this resource is also demonstrated in the six thousand contributors from twelve different countries. The dictionary is available in print or online through Oxford Art Online.

Guides

Arntzen, Etta, and Robert Rainwater. *Guide to the Literature of Art History*. Chicago: American Library Association, 1980.

Though this resource needs a significant update, there are still some useful titles about painting, drawing, decorative arts, printmaking, applied arts, sculpture, and architecture. Resources are organized into four sections, "General Reference Sources," "General Primary and Secondary Sources," "Particular Arts," and "Serials." Entries with annotations are provided for bibliographies, dictionaries, encyclopedias, directories, sales records, handbooks, primary documents, visual resources, and secondary sources. Subject and author indexes are also present. The more recent *Guide to the Literature of Art History 2* (listed below) updates and supplements some of this information, though it is not a revised or second edition.

Marmor, Max, and Alex Ross. *Guide to the Literature of Art History 2*. Chicago: American Library Association, 2005.

A supplement to the *Guide to the Literature of Art History* (listed above), Marmor and Ross's volume provides information about newer resources that have become available following the publication of the original guide. The work is similarly organized and covers the same type of research, including bibliographies, sales records, handbooks, primary documents, visual resources, secondary sources, and other important materials.

Pollard, Elizabeth B. *Visual Arts Research: A Handbook*. New York: Greenwood Press, 1986.

Though some sections of this work are out of date, especially "Computerized Reference Services," the approach taken to art research gives it value that endures. Chapters emphasize concepts, techniques, and the types of resources one might use to complete research in art history, with titles like "Introduction: Research Strategy," "Searching the Library for Information," "Biographical Information," "Art History Sources," "The Art Work as a Starting Point," "Techniques and Materials," and "Visual Art Periodicals." The strength of this resource is that it walks through studying an artist or piece of artwork and provides some foundation in how to analyze the object as well as the process used to create it.

Sacca, Elizabeth J., and Loren R. Singer. *Visual Arts Reference and Research Guide, for Artists, Educators, Curators, Historians, and Therapists*. Montreal: Perspecto Press, 1983.

Much like *Visual Arts Research*, *Visual Arts Reference and Research Guide* is not up to date, though it has enduring value that should be recognized. Because art is one area where classic reference works remain important to historical researchers, resources like this retain their significance. *Visual Arts Reference and Research Guide* highlights topics such as how to use and how to find various reference tools for the study of art, including library catalogs, dissertations and theses, government documents, children's books, and photographs.

Indexes and Bibliographies

Art Abstracts. Ipswich, MA: EBSCO. www.ebscohost.com.
Art Index. Ipswich, MA: EBSCO. www.ebscohost.com.

Art Abstracts and Art Index cover roughly the same content, with subjects such as art history, criticism, architecture, archeology, antiques, museums, graphic arts, industrial design, landscape architecture, interior design, folk art, painting, photography, pottery, sculpture, decorative arts, costume design, film, television, textiles, advertisement, and non-Western art. Both provide indexing for six hundred periodicals (280 peer-reviewed), thirteen thousand dissertations and theses, and over two hundred thousand art reproductions. As the name suggests, Art Abstracts also has abstracts for this content. Retrospective coverage is available through the Art Index Retrospective.

Art and Architecture Complete. Ipswich, MA: EBSCO. www.ebscohost.com.

An index that covers about 780 journals and 230 books, with full text for about 370 journals and 220 books, Art and Architecture Complete also includes sixty thousand images from various sources. Full-text coverage goes back to 1937 for some titles. Subjects such as architecture, costume design, antiques, conservation, archeology, decorative arts, graphic arts, interior design, landscape design, painting, photography, printmaking, and sculpture are represented.

Art Source. Ipswich, MA: EBSCO. www.ebscohost.com.

Art Source combines Art Index and Art Abstracts with the EBSCO database Art and Architecture Complete (all listed above).

ARTBibliographies Modern (ABM). Ann Arbor, MI: ProQuest. www.proquest.com.

With modern and contemporary art back to the mid-nineteenth century, ABM is the premier index for publications in this area, containing articles, books, dissertations, exhibition catalogs, reviews, and artist's books. Materials in the collections of the Tate Library are represented, making this of particular interest to scholars of British culture and history. Publications go back to 1974, and some extend as far as the 1960s. Most subjects in art are available, notably, art history, conservation, restoration, photography, folk arts, illustration, philosophy, symbolism, and woodwork.

Bibliography of the History of Art (BHA) and Répertoire International de la Littérature de l'Art (RILA). Los Angeles: J. Paul Getty Trust, 1975–2007. www.getty.edu/research/conducting_research/bha.

BHA and RILA are both freely available online through the Getty Research Institute. RILA was the precursor to BHA, covering 1975–1990. BHA was created in 1990 by combining RILA and Répertoire d'Art et d'Archéologie. BHA and RILA index articles, dissertations, conference proceedings, books, exhibition catalogs, dealer catalogs, and other materials related to European and American art (after Columbus) from late antiquity and after. BHA has titles published before 2007. After 2007, BHA was superseded by the International Bibliography of Art (listed below).

DAAI: Design and Applied Arts Index. Ann Arbor, MI: ProQuest. www .proquest.com.

Indexing and abstracts are provided for articles, news items, and reviews featured in design and applied arts bibliographies starting in 1973. Topics include computer-generated graphics, typography, web design, architecture, animation, industrial design, and other fields related to applied arts.

International Bibliography of Art (IBA). Ann Arbor, MI: ProQuest. www .proquest.com.

Primarily focused on Western art from antiquity to present, this is the preeminent index of scholarly publications about this topic. IBA superseded BHA (listed above) in 2008. Indexing is available for six hundred core journals from 2008 to the present. All types of art and art created globally since 1945 are represented. In addition to journal articles, essay collections, monographs, conference proceedings, and exhibition catalogs are also indexed.

Images

AP Images. New York: Associated Press. www.apimages.com.

AP Images contains millions of images reaching as far back as 1826 from the Associated Press and its partners. Photographs are freely searchable or browseable and are generally from newspaper stories. Most feature prominent historical events, people, or daily life. Information about the photograph and descriptions make it easier to search this collection.

ARTstor. New York: ARTstor. www.artstor.org/index.shtml.

ARTstor is a collection of 1.6 million digital images of art objects from around the world. You can search pictures by keyword or by advanced options, such as collection, date, classification, or geography. Browsing the content by collection, classification, or geography is another option. Highly developed descriptions and information about the images help make searching more accurate. Images can be "zoomed in" for better viewing.

Getty Images. Seattle: Getty. www.gettyimages.com.

Getty, a stock photo supplier, has an extensive selection of photographs very similar to AP Images that can be viewed for free online. Some video and music clips are also available. Images are searchable through highly developed advanced options. Often, these visuals are advertising or news related.

GEOGRAPHY

Atlases

Cunliffe, Barry, Robert Bartlett, John Morrill, Asa Briggs, and Joanna Bourke, eds. *The Penguin Atlas of British and Irish History: From Earliest Times to the Present Day*. New York: Penguin, 2002.

Providing maps, photographs, and other graphics that demonstrate information about Britain and Ireland from the Neolithic period to the present, this is an excellent source for geographic information about the cultural, social, and economic development of the British Isles. Maps and color images were commissioned for this resource, and postmodern scholars will be happy to see some that cover Britain into the late twentieth century.

Gilbert, Martin. *The Routledge Atlas of British History*. 5th edition. New York: Routledge, 2012.

Now in its fifth edition, this is an excellent atlas of British history that presents maps focused on the Middle Ages until the present. With information about the wars in Afghanistan and Iraq, as well as the coalition government and the European Union, these maps and the essays that accompany them are presented chronologically and touch on economics, military movements, social issues, population trends, and other topics.

Overy, Richard. *Collins Atlas of 20th Century History*. New York: Collins, 2006.

Of use to postmodern scholars, this atlas focuses on the twentieth century and features many places internationally, though there are more locations from the West. Contents contain maps, graphs, images, and other illustrations of historical data. The second half of the atlas will be of greater interest to postmodern researchers, as it deals with the period following World War II.

Reference

Cohen, Saul B., ed. *The Columbia Gazetteer of the World*. New York: Columbia University Press, 1952–. www.columbiagazetteer.org.

The significant print resource of this same title has been superseded by the online revised and expanded edition. With 170,000 entries about many international locations, the scope of *the Columbia Gazetteer* is unique and valuable. Entries discuss demography, trade, physical geography, political boundaries, culture, history, agriculture, place-names, and other information. The online format makes this information more accessible through browsing and search options.

Mills, A. D. *A Dictionary of British Place-Names*. Revised edition. New York: Oxford University Press, 2011.

The revised edition contains seventeen thousand entries that detail the origin and development of place-names, in addition to maps and a general essay about these names throughout the British Isles. This concludes with a helpful bibliography and appendix of websites.

Room, Adrian. *Nicknames of Places*. Jefferson, NC: McFarland, 2006.

Arranged alphabetically by "secondary names," or nicknames, slogans, and alternative names for places, entries give the real name of the place and the location. Appendixes have secondary names for streets, regions, and countries.

Room, Adrian. *Placenames of the World*. 2nd revised ed. Jefferson, NC: McFarland, 2013.

With over six thousand entries describing the history of place-names for natural features, such as mountains and rivers, as well as manmade entities like cities and countries, this reference is international in scope and exhaustive. For each place, a history of the name, description of the location, and etymology of the place-name is given. Appendixes describe common elements of place names in English and in other languages.

HISTORY

Chronologies

Mellersh, H. E. L., and Neville Williams, eds. *Chronology of World History*. 4 volumes. Santa Barbara, CA: ABC-CLIO, 1999.

The *Chronology of World History* is a four-volume set with over seventy thousand entries chronicling international historical events from 3000 BC to 1998. Works of literature, art, music, and dance are indexed by title in the back of each volume, in addition to subjects, places, events, and names. The fourth volume, *The Modern World: 1901–1998*, will be most useful to postmodern scholars.

Williams, Hywel. *Cassell's Chronology of World History: Dates, Events and Ideas That Made History*. London: Weidenfeld & Nicolson, 2005.

Organized with entries for individual years, the breadth and depth of this resource is impressive. Essays discuss trends at the beginning of each section, and spotlight essays are provided for particularly important people and events. This chronology does not simply give information about historical events, it also analyzes these occurrences, comparing regions and patterns. The last few sections, "The Modern World, 1900–2004," "A Continent Divided: Europe from Armageddon to Reconstruction, 1914–89," "Old Empires and New Beginnings: Decolonization and the Fall of Europe," and "Towards One World" will be of special interest to postmodern scholars.

Williams, Neville, and Philip Waller. *Chronology of the Modern World, 1763 to 1992*. 2nd edition. New York: Simon & Schuster, 1994.

Waller, P. J., Neville Williams, John Rowett, and Robert Dallek. *Chronology of the 20th Century: Based on Chronology of the Modern World*. Oxford, UK: Helicon, 1996.

These chronologies list not only significant historical events but also important headlines, music, artwork, and publications, useful for helping to analyze what events were occurring at the same time, and for comparing international movements and trends from year to year.

Reference

Arnold-Baker, Charles. *The Companion to British History*. 2nd edition. New York: Routledge, 2001.

With content until the year 2000, this companion will benefit most scholars of British postmodernism. In 1,400 pages, short encyclopedia entries detail many different aspects of British history, and especially current events. This is an updated version of a reference work that originally took the author thirty years to compile, and the great detail this process afforded is evident in the text.

Biletz, Frank. *Historical Dictionary of Ireland*. Lanham, MD: Scarecrow Press, 2013.

A fully revised edition, this historical dictionary has over six hundred entries for people, places, and events, as well as articles about literature, culture, and the arts in various periods. Some interesting topics related to postmodernism are author Roddy Doyle, Irish cinema, and the critical work of Seamus Deane. Beginning with a chronology and ending with appendixes providing names, such as those for presidents, prime ministers, and other political figures, this work has a wealth of information about Irish history.

Cannon, John. *The Oxford Companion to British History*. New York: Oxford University Press, 1997.

Though this resource only discusses events up to its year of publication, it remains an invaluable source for information about British history. With four thousand entries alphabetically arranged, a wide variety of topics are covered, such as legal history, events, people, places, cultural movements, and military excursions. Entries range from the short, at only a few sentences, to articles of more than 1,500 words, some of which are cited or cross-referenced. Maps and an index contribute to the work's usefulness. Coverage ends before the new millennium but does have some more recent events in the 1990s, such as the election of Tony Blair.

Cannon, John. *The Oxford Dictionary of British History*. 2nd edition. New York: Oxford University Press, 2009.

This well-respected dictionary has been revised and updated to contain historical information into the twenty-first century. Around 3,800 short entries represent contemporary people and events, such as Gordon Brown and David Cameron. A chronology and a section with useful websites are featured at the end.

Connolly, S. J., ed. *The Oxford Companion to Irish History*. 2nd edition. New York: Oxford University Press, 2007.

Now in a second edition, this volume has 1,800 short entries that discuss Irish history from ancient times to the new millennium. Some examples of articles are "Adoption," "Board of Works," and "Home Rule." A subject appendix at the end helps readers identify categories, for instance, "political movements and parties" or "literature." A map appendix is also provided. This reference is particularly helpful because it has been revised with subjects into the twenty-first century.

Dabydeen, David, John Gilmore, and Cecily Jones. *The Oxford Companion to Black British History*. New York: Oxford University Press, 2007.

This companion focuses on black history in Britain, a topic often overlooked but vital to the study of postmodernism. The thematic contents listed at the beginning make it particularly easy to navigate, and entries cover subjects such as dub music, Southall Black Sisters, Ronald Moody, *To Sir, With Love*, and the Caribbean Artists Movement. This book is supplemented by a chronology, selected bibliography, and index.

Davies, John, Nigel Jenkins, Menna Baines, and Peredur Lynch, eds. *The Welsh Academy Encyclopaedia of Wales*. Cardiff: University of Wales Press, 2008.

A wide-ranging look at Welsh history, culture, and geography, this extensive resource has over three thousand entries, reviewing people, places, and events, as well as in-depth explorations of broad topics related to cultural movements and historical periods. Maps and other visuals help demonstrate the concepts explored in the volume.

Lynch, Michael, ed. *The Oxford Companion to Scottish History*. New York: Oxford University Press, 2001.

With entries to the present time, this companion has eight hundred pages of content related to Scottish history. Articles about more important subjects, such as "Culture," are longer, more comprehensive, and broken down into multiple sections, for instance, "Modern Times (1914–): Literature." Shorter entries examine people and places. Appendixes contain a glossary, chronology, maps, genealogies, and a guide to further reading.

Panton, James, and Keith Cowlard. *Historical Dictionary of the United Kingdom*. 2 volumes. Lanham, MD: Scarecrow Press, 1998.
Panton, James, and Keith Cowlard. *Historical Dictionary of the Contemporary United Kingdom*. Lanham, MD: Scarecrow Press, 2008.

The *Historical Dictionary of the United Kingdom* is a two-volume resource with information about the history of and conflict within the United Kingdom. The first volume focuses on England proper, providing concise entries for people, places, and events, as well as more in-depth articles for broader topics. The second volume looks at Scotland, Wales, and Northern Ireland, exploring each area's culture, politics, and history and considering how regionalism influences the way they interact with one another and with England. Chronologies and maps might be particularly useful to some scholars. The *Historical Dictionary of the Contemporary United Kingdom* starts in 1979, making it most relevant to postmodern scholars, covering the 1980s, 1990s, and the twenty-first century. Topics include Margaret Thatcher, the War in Iraq, and the death of Diana, Princess of Wales. An appendix listing members of Parliament is present. All three volumes contain extensive bibliographies for further study.

Panton, Kenneth J. *Historical Dictionary of London*. Lanham, MD: Scarecrow Press, 2001.
Panton, Kenneth J. *London: A Historical Companion*. 2nd edition. Oxford: Tempus Publishing, 2005.

Panton's treatment of the history of London begins with the Roman period and traces people, places, and events to contemporary, metropolitan London. Entries in the *Historical Dictionary of London* are topical, with subjects important to postmodern scholars such as immigration, housing, and health care. A chronology, a list of mayors and other administrators, and a population growth table provide further historical information about the city. Appendixes have a list of websites for further research. *London: A Historical Companion* is an expanded version of the *Historical Dictionary of London* that eliminates some of the appendixes, such as the one containing web resources, but adds maps, images, and more entries.

Plowright, John. *Routledge Dictionary of Modern British History*. New York: Routledge, 2006.

Discussing people, places, historical events, laws, and military conflicts from the Romantic period to the twenty-first century, this volume has brief entries about British history, with a particular emphasis on British politics and legal history. Articles describe topics such as the Gulf War, the political rivalry between Ted Heath and Harold Wilson, and the famous anti-union white paper *In Place of Strife* by Barbara Castle. A list of entries at the beginning helps to make this volume particularly useful.

Stearns, Peter N., ed. *Oxford Encyclopedia of the Modern World*. 8 volumes. New York: Oxford University Press, 2008.

This extensive eight-volume set considers broad historical topics since 1750. Entries are thematically concentrated, dealing with subjects like food, migration, blue jeans, brain drain, and borders, as well as regionally focused themes, such as British literature. Though these overviews are broad, they can be used as entry points to complicated motifs explored in postmodern literature, providing historical context related to creative works. An index in volume 8 aids navigation.

Guides

Butler, L. J., and Anthony Gorst, eds. *Modern British History: A Guide to Study and Research*. London: I. B. Tauris, 1997.

This guide to historical research is similar to the volume you are currently reading. Containing chapters about archives, library research, funding for historical research, theory and practice of history, and thematic chapters dealing with major areas of British history, it can be used by researchers to review this information or get started on historical research projects, though the chapter on "Computing Techniques" is quite out of date.

Cook, Chris, and John Stevenson. *Longman Handbook of Modern British History, 1714–2001*. 4th edition. London: Longman, 2001.

With a revised bibliography and historical entries updated to reflect British history into the new millennium, this well-known research guide gives an overview of the modern period, with a glossary, bibliography, and index to aid researchers. Thematic additions new to this edition include discussions of the Scottish Parliament, the Welsh Assembly, and the European Union.

Flemming, Nicholas, and Alan O'Day. *Longman Handbook of Modern Irish History since 1800*. London: Longman, 2005.

With major sections exploring the political, social and religious, economic, and foreign relations history of Ireland, this is an excellent handbook to guide the reader through events that took place in the modern period. Subsections highlight many subjects, such as women, property, education, and broadcasting. Chronologies appear throughout the volume. There is also a section for biographies of important people and a glossary to define uncommon concepts, such as the Alliance Party, the Campaign for Democracy in Ulster, or the Hunt Commission.

Fritze, Ronald H., Brian E. Coutts, and Louis A. Vyhnanek. *Reference Sources in History: An Introductory Guide*. 2nd edition. Santa Barbara, CA: ABC-CLIO, 2004.

This is a general guide to reference works published about history, organized by topic, country, and format. Contained are 930 reference works, with the most useful being significant journals and websites.

Loades, David, ed. *Reader's Guide to British History*. 2 volumes. New York: Fitzroy Dearborn, 2003.

Recommended readings about British history are listed in this general guide, exploring various turning points, controversies, and themes across a wide time frame. In two volumes, entries are arranged alphabetically, and each starts with a bibliography of the readings discussed in the essay.

Indexes and Bibliographies

Bibliography of British and Irish History. Turnhout, Belgium: Brepols, 2010. www.brepols.net.

The largest index to focus solely on British and Irish history with a range of topics, including monographs, articles, and chapters in edited collections, this bibliography covers 55 BC and to the present. Supplanting the *Royal Historical Society Bibliography of British and Irish History*, this resource was enriched by websites like Irish History Online and London's Past Online, though some of these are now defunct, making this element of the volume less important.

Historical Abstracts. Ipswich, MA: EBSCO, 1955. www.ebscohost.com.

Indexing 2,600 journals going back to 1450 and supporting forty different languages, Historical Abstracts covers topics such as the history of women, education, military conflicts, and foreign relations. The United States and Canada are excluded from this resource because those countries are in America: History and Life. Content extends back to 1955. This is one of the most noteworthy resources for the study of British history.

LANGUAGE AND LINGUISTICS

Encyclopedias, Dictionaries, and Handbooks

Brown, Keith, and Anne Anderson, eds. *Encyclopedia of Language & Linguistics*. 2nd edition. 14 volumes. Boston: Elsevier, 2006. www.science direct.com.

This fourteen-volume encyclopedia, available in print and online, covers the foundations of linguistics, semiotics, morphology, semantics, text analysis and stylistics, religious language, translation, languages of the world, language maps, lexicography, and linguistic anthropology. The last volume contains a glossary, a list of languages, and appendixes for maps.

Crystal, David. *A Dictionary of Linguistics and Phonetics*. 6th edition. Oxford: Blackwell, 2008.

This dictionary is part of the Language Library series and covers terms from fields like semantics, phonetics, phonology, psycholinguistics, syntax, and sociolinguistics. Five thousand terms are defined, making this a standard in the field. The International Phonetic Alphabet, as well as a table of symbols and one with abbreviations, are added for additional utility.

Fawley, William J., ed. *International Encyclopedia of Linguistics*. 2nd edition. 4 volumes. New York: Oxford University Press, 2003.

Over 950 entries cover comparative, descriptive, formalist, functionalist, historical, and typological linguistics. A special focus of this encyclopedia is the interrelations within these branches of the field, as well as the relationship of linguistics to other disciplines.

Kay, Christian, Jane Roberts, Michael Samuels, and Irene Wotherspoon. *Historical Thesaurus of the Oxford English Dictionary*. 2 volumes. New York: Oxford University Press, 2009. Also available online as part of the *Oxford English Dictionary*, public.oed.com/historical-thesaurus-of-the-oed.

This historical thesaurus analyzes words from the *Oxford English Dictionary* and a *Thesaurus of Old English* (Jane Roberts, Christian Kay, and Lynne Grundy, 2nd edition, 2 volumes [Atlanta, GA: Rodopi, 2000]). "The External World," "The Mental World," and "The Social World" are the three main parts of this set.

Momma, Haruko, and Michael Matto, eds. *A Companion to the History of the English Language*. Malden, MA: Wiley-Blackwell, 2008.

This companion has fifty-nine essays that address the linguistic, cultural, social, and literary approaches to language study. The essays are divided into nine categories: "Introduction," "Linguistic Survey," "English Semantics and Lexicography," "Pre-history of English," "English in History: England and America," "English in History: English outside England and America," "Literary Languages," "Issues with Present-Day English," and "Further Approaches to Language Study."

Partridge, Eric, Tom Dalzell, Terry Victor, and Eric Partridge. *The New Partridge Dictionary of Slang and Unconventional English*. London: Routledge, 2013.

This dictionary covers the entire English-speaking world and highlights slang and unconventional English used or created since 1945. Slang and cant, colloquialisms, solecisms and catachreses, catchphrases, nicknames, and vulgarisms are defined. Entries contain the word, part of speech, definition, register, and dating.

Simpson, J. A., and E. S. C. Weiner. *The Oxford English Dictionary* (*OED*). 2nd edition. 20 volumes. New York: Oxford University Press, 1989. Also available online at www.oed.com.

The *OED* is an essential resource that helps researchers understand how the meaning and usage of words have changed over time. The dictionary is available as a twenty-volume work with 291,500 entries. The online edition has more than six hundred thousand entries. Each one contains pronunciation, spellings, etymology, and quotations.

Guides

DeMiller, Anna A. *Linguistics: A Guide to the Reference Literature*. 2nd edition. Englewood, CO: Libraries Unlimited, 2000.

This guide is part of the Reference Sources in the Humanities series and is an annotated bibliography. Around 1,040 sources for linguistics, languages, and related research areas are included. Content begins in 1957 and ends in 1998.

Indexes and Bibliographies

Linguistics and Language Behavior Abstracts. Bethesda, MD: CSA. www .csa.com.

This important source abstracts and indexes the international literature in linguistics and related disciplines in the language sciences with coverage starting in 1973. The database encompasses all aspects of the study of language, touching on subjects such as phonetics, phonology, morphology, syntax, and semantics. Various fields of linguistics, such as descriptive, historical, comparative, theoretical, and geographical linguistics, are highlighted, with 1,500 serial publications, books, book chapters, and dissertations represented.

PHILOSOPHY

Encyclopedias, Dictionaries, and Handbooks

Blackburn, Simon. *Oxford Dictionary of Philosophy*. 2nd revised edition. New York: Oxford University Press, 2008. Also available online at Oxford Reference, www.oxfordreference.com.

With an international scope, the *Oxford Dictionary of Philosophy* contains thousands of entries on all areas of philosophy, as well as some related areas, such as religion, science, and logic. Five hundred biographies are also included.

Borchert, Donald M., ed. *Encyclopedia of Philosophy*. 2nd edition. 10 volumes. Detroit: Macmillan Reference USA, 2006.

This encyclopedia, now in its second edition, describes philosophers and philosophical schools of thought. The two thousand entries explore ancient, medieval, and modern philosophy and philosophers, as well as subfields like epistemology, metaphysics, philosophy of language, feminist philosophy, ethics, philosophy of religion, and more. The last volume has an appendix of additional articles, a thematic outline, bibliographies, and an index.

Craig, Edward, ed. *Routledge Encyclopedia of Philosophy*. 10 volumes. London: Routledge, 1998.

Two thousand entries address all branches of philosophy, such as ethics, aesthetics, political philosophy, metaphysics, and logic. Entries are written by experts in the field, arranged alphabetically, and include a topic overview, thematic essays, or biographical information.

Honderich, Ted, ed. *The Oxford Companion to Philosophy*. 2nd edition. New York: Oxford University Press, 2005.

With more than two thousand brief and in-depth entries, *The Oxford Companion to Philosophy* highlights philosophers, arguments, doctrines, ideas, movements, schools, theories, traditions, and worldviews. The end of the companion has maps that trace philosophical ideas, a chronological table, and an index.

Horowitz, Maryanne Cline, ed. *New Dictionary of the History of Ideas*. 6 volumes. New York: Charles Scribner's Sons, 2005.

This reputable dictionary examines the history of ideas from around the world, from antiquity to the present. Topics such as agnosticism, autonomy, postmodernism, textuality, and virtual reality are discussed. A detailed essay on "Historiography," a reader's guide, and an index conclude this item.

Stanford Encyclopedia of Philosophy. Stanford, CA: Stanford University. plato.stanford.edu.

Stanford University sponsors this open-access peer-reviewed website. A team of experts frequently adds to and updates the content provided. While there is a browseable table of contents, searches can also be performed. Each entry has a detailed bibliography, links to other Internet sources, and cross-references.

Guides

Bynagle, Hans E. *Philosophy: A Guide to the Reference Literature*. 3rd edition. Englewood, CO: Libraries Unlimited, 2006.

Bibliographies, dictionaries, encyclopedias, and indexes are described in this guide. Resources from the ancient world to the present are represented. Annotated entries are provided for general philosophy research, history of philosophy, and branches of philosophy. Though the main focus is Western philosophy, some non-Western ideas are also addressed.

Indexes and Bibliographies

Philosopher's Index: An International Index to Philosophical Periodicals and Books. Bowling Green, OH: Philosopher's Information Center. Available online via various vendors.

Journal articles, books, book chapters, and book reviews are indexed and abstracted beginning in 1940. Subjects include ethics, aesthetics, social philosophy, political philosophy, epistemology, metaphysics, and logic. Both print and online formats are available.

RELIGION

Encyclopedias, Dictionaries, and Handbooks

Bowker, John, ed. *The Oxford Dictionary of World Religions*. New York: Oxford University Press, 1997.

Short entries for people, places, practices, and relevant terminology are listed in the dictionary. In addition to information about individual religions, there are entries on common topics like prayer, ethics, asceticism, confession, cosmology, art, architecture, and music. Most entries provide a bibliography with more sources. The dictionary ends with a topic index and an index of Chinese headwords.

Jones, Lindsay, ed. *Encyclopedia of Religion*. 2nd edition. 15 volumes. Detroit: Macmillan Reference USA, 2005.

The *Encyclopedia of Religion* has more than three thousand entries on religions from all over the world. The second edition completely revises or at
least adds information. With fifteen volumes, this encyclopedia has the space
to address many subjects across a wide scope of religious discourse, including those that deal with the intersection of religion and modern life, such as
"Bioethics and Genetics and Religion," "UFO Religions," and "Ecology and
Religion." In addition to these thematic entries, there are also those focusing
on individual religions, such as Islam, Wicca, and Buddhism.

Von Stuckrad, Kocku, ed. *Brill Dictionary of Religion*. Revised edition. 4
volumes. Boston: Brill, 2007.

This dictionary is the revised edition of Metzler's *Lexikon Religion* and is
translated from the German by Robert R. Barr. Topics are thematic, so specific
religions are discussed within the context of entries on a continent or a type of
practice or belief. Critical issues, biographies, eras, and basic religious practices
are covered. The dictionary contains useful chronologies for various topics.

Guides

Dillon, Martin, and Shannon Graff Hysell, eds. *ARBA In-Depth: Philosophy
and Religion*. Westport, CT: Libraries Unlimited, 2004.

Putting a stronger emphasis on religion compared to philosophy, this guide
has three hundred critical reviews of reference titles. The first part of the book
is organized by resource type and is about philosophy. The second part deals
with religion. General works, the Baha'i Faith, Bible studies, Buddhism,
Christianity, Hinduism, Islam, Judaism, Native American religions, occult-
ism and witchcraft, Shinti, Sikhism, and Taoism are discussed.

Indexes and Bibliographies

ATLA Religion Database. Chicago: American Theological Library Association. Available online via various vendors.

ATLA is a comprehensive reference database designed to support religious
and theological scholarship. More than one million citations from 1,400 international journals and 14,000 multi-author works are present. The database

also has full-text access for more than 238,000 articles, book reviews, and essays from major journals. The scope is international, representing all major religions and denominations.

SCIENCE AND MEDICINE

Encyclopedias, Dictionaries, and Handbooks

Daintith, John, and Elizabeth Martin, eds. *A Dictionary of Science*. 5th edition. New York: Oxford University Press, 2005.

Aspects of science such as biology, human biology, chemistry, physics, earth sciences, and astronomy are addressed. There are also ten chronologies, 160 biographical entries, and eight appendixes that target subjects such as units of measurement, the solar system, the periodic table, and relevant websites.

Gossin, Pamela, ed. *Encyclopedia of Literature and Science*. Westport, CT: Greenwood Press, 2002.

This interdisciplinary dictionary has more than 650 entries about literature and science. An introductory essay explains the history of the field, its growing reputation, and the current state of research. Methodologies, scientists, themes, theories, and writers are represented.

Heilbron, J. L., ed. *The Oxford Companion to the History of Modern Science*. New York: Oxford University Press, 2003.

This companion examines the development of modern science from 1550 to the present. Major scientific disciplines such as chemistry, physics, biology, ethnology, and zoology are explored. Most entries have cross-references and bibliographies. A guide to further reading, Nobel Science Prize winners, and an index complete the companion.

Krige, John, and Dominique Pestre, eds. *Companion to Science in the Twentieth Century*. London: Routledge, 2003.

Longer illustrated essays on topics related to science in the twentieth century are present. Examples of topics include the relationship between science and industry, the importance of instrumentation, and the cultural influence of scientific modes of thought. There is a section on science in many countries, such as the United Kingdom, as well as a general index.

McGraw-Hill Encyclopedia of Science and Technology. 10th edition. 20
  volumes. New York: McGraw-Hill, 2007. Also available online through
  Access Science at www.accessscience.com.

Around 7,100 articles about almost one hundred scientific fields are housed in
this foundational encyclopedia. Signed articles are written by experts, including a notable twenty-five Nobel Prize winners. There are several indexes and
many useful study guides.

Guides

Hurt, Charlie Deuel. *Information Sources in Science and Technology.* Englewood, CO: Libraries Unlimited, 1998.

This guide helps researchers discover resources for the history and development of science and technology. The annotated bibliography includes
multidisciplinary sources from the biological sciences, physical sciences,
mathematics, engineering, and health and veterinary sciences. Dictionaries,
encyclopedias, government documents, biographical directories, indexes,
abstracts, and bibliographies are listed.

Indexes and Bibliographies

Web of Science. New York: Thomas Reuters. webofknowledge.com.

Web of Science has current and retrospective multidisciplinary information
from approximately 8,700 journals. It is the interface for three ISI Citation
databases: Arts and Humanities Citation Index, Social Science Citation Index, and Science Citation Index Expanded. The Science Citation Index Expanded covers more than 150 disciplines. One of the unique features of Web
of Science is the cited reference search, where you can look up an article and
see how many times it has been cited.

SOCIAL SCIENCES

Reference

Darity, William A., ed. *International Encyclopedia of the Social Sciences.*
  2nd edition. 9 volumes. Detroit: MacMillan Reference USA, 2008. Also
  available online at www.gale.cengage.com.

The second edition of a standard social sciences reference work, the *International Encyclopedia of the Social Sciences* is completely updated from the first edition. Economics, sociology, psychology, and education are all represented, and their influence as they have developed during the twentieth century is discussed. Articles explore subjects as diverse as "Baby Boomers," "Cambridge Capitol Controversy," "Curriculum," and "Groupthink." Thousands of scholars contributed nearly three thousand articles for this collection, all of which contain bibliographies.

Kuper, Adam, and Jessica Kuper, eds. *The Social Science Encyclopedia*. 3rd edition. 2 volumes. London: Routledge, 2004.

All six hundred brief entries have been revised for the third edition, and a large portion are new or substantially different. A standard reference work in the social sciences, this encyclopedia provides concise articles that give easy-to-understand descriptions of social science concepts and topics, for instance, feminism, postmodernism, or cultural studies. This is a strong work to keep on the shelf for easy access to basic concepts, terms, and ideas.

Outhwaite, William, ed. *Blackwell Dictionary of Modern Social Thought*. 2nd edition. Malden, MA: Blackwell, 2003.

With two hundred entries addressing many different subjects related to social thought, including political theories, cultural movements, and social philosophies, this dictionary covers a range of topics that might be important to researchers. Of special interest is the entry about "Modernism and Postmodernism." Articles contain recommended reading lists, and the volume has an extensive bibliography.

Smelser, Neil J., and Paul B. Baltes, eds. *International Encyclopedia of the Social and Behavioral Sciences*. 26 volumes. Amsterdam: Elsevier, 2001. Also available online at Science Direct, www.sciencedirect.com/science/referenceworks/9780080430768.

In twenty-six volumes, this is one of the preeminent reference sources in the social sciences. In addition to highlighting a diverse array of subjects, such as psychology, education, sociology, linguistics, and anthropology, this resource also reviews related fields like neuroscience and religious studies. Methodology and application are also represented.

Guides

Aby, Stephen H., James Nalen, and Lori Fielding. *Sociology: A Guide to Reference Information Sources*. 3rd edition. Westport, CT: Libraries Unlimited, 2005.

With 610 entries for reference works in the field of sociology, this is an excellent guide to the available literature. The third edition is substantially revised with new resources and with a particular focus on print and electronic materials published between 1997 and 2004. The work is divided into three parts, "General Social Science Reference Sources," "Sociology," and "Sociological Fields."

Herron, Nancy L., ed. *The Social Sciences: A Cross-Disciplinary Guide to Selected Sources*. 3rd edition. Englewood, CO: Libraries Unlimited, 2002.

Exploring the social sciences, political sciences, economics, business, history, law, anthropology, sociology, education, psychology, geography, and communication, the third edition of this standard guide and textbook includes 1,500 annotated citations for print and electronic resources. Entries are arranged by discipline.

Jacoby, Joann, and Josephine Z. Kibbee. *Cultural Anthropology: A Guide to Reference and Information Sources*. 2nd edition. Westport, CT: Libraries Unlimited, 2007.

Of particular interest to postmodern scholars who might be pursuing cultural studies, *Cultural Anthropology* includes annotated entries organized by topics such as general sources, subfields, methodologies, humanities-related resources, ethnic studies materials, and supplemental items.

Li, Tze-chung. *Social Science Reference Sources: A Practical Guide*. 3rd edition. Westport, CT: Greenwood Press, 2000.

With a broad view of the social sciences, this guide has entries for roughly 1,600 resources that come from a wide variety of fields, such as business, economics, education, geography, history, law, political science, psychology, sociology, and anthropology. The volume is split up into two parts: general social science resources and disciplinary materials. Most materials published before 1980 are excluded unless they have enduring value.

O'Brien, Nancy P. *Education: A Guide to Reference and Information Sources*. 2nd edition. Englewood, CO: Libraries Unlimited, 2000.

About five hundred entries for standard reference sources in education are included. More general social science publications that cover education are also represented. Both print and electronic resources are listed, most published between 1990 and 2000.

Indexes and Bibliographies

PsycINFO. American Psychological Association. www.apa.org/psycinfo.

With 3.5 million records for psychology research going back to the mid-seventeenth century, PsycINFO is one of the largest collections of indexed research about psychology. Of particular interest for literary scholars is its coverage of linguistics. PsycINFO provides access to high-quality records for peer-reviewed resources, primarily from 1920 forward.

SocIndex. Ipswich, MA: EBSCO. www.ebscohost.com.

SocIndex has 1,300 journals going back to 1894, as well as books, conference proceedings, and other resources. Around 2.1 million records provide information about a variety of subjects, including psychology, social structure, sociological theory, sociological history, anthropology, addiction, religion, gender studies, cultural studies, marriage and family, social work, and racial studies.

Sociological Abstracts. Ann Arbor, MI: ProQuest. www.proquest.com.

Indexing content for roughly two thousand sociological journals, Sociological Abstracts also includes conference papers, dissertations, books, and book reviews. The backfile for this resource begins in 1952, making it quite extensive. Content is international, with a large subsection of the literature indexed from scholars outside of North America. Cited reference linking is available online.

Web of Science. New York: Thomas Reuters. webofknowledge.com.

Web of Science has current and retrospective multidisciplinary information from approximately 8,700 journals. It is the interface for three ISI Citation databases: Arts and Humanities Citation Index, Social Science Citation Index, and Science Citation Index Expanded. The Science Citation Index Expanded covers more than 150 disciplines. One of the unique features of Web of Science is the cited reference search, where you can look up an article and see how many times it has been cited.

THEATER

Encyclopedias, Dictionaries, and Handbooks

Chambers, Colin, ed. *Continuum Companion to Twentieth Century Theatre.* New York: Continuum, 2002.

Topics such as performers, playwrights, directors, designers, choreographers, theater companies, countries, trends, and genres are addressed in brief entries. Longer essays on general subjects like "Dramaturgy" are also provided. All total, there are over 2,500 entries written by 280 experts and professionals in the field.

Cody, Gabrielle H., and Evert Sprinchorn, eds. *Columbia Encyclopedia of Modern Drama.* 2 volumes. New York: Columbia University Press, 2007.

This encyclopedia provides cultural context for major figures and plays from 1860 to the early twenty-first century. There are about 1,400 articles signed by 450 scholars. Because it is one of the few resources in this area to present information after 2000, it is particularly helpful for postmodern scholars.

Pavis, Patrice. *Dictionary of the Theatre: Terms, Concepts, and Analysis.* Translated by Christine Shantz. Toronto: University of Toronto Press, 1998.

This dictionary is translated from French by Christine Shantz. Theoretical, technical, and semiotic terms and concepts are given. Definitions are supported by examples drawn from international plays and playwrights from a range of time periods. Entries have cross-references and further reading lists. There is also a thematic index and a bibliography.

Trussler, Simon. *Cambridge Illustrated History of British Theatre.* Cambridge: Cambridge University Press, 1994.

British theater from first-century Roman times to 1990 is represented. There are twenty-two chapters that each address a specific time period. The history and development of British theater, along with important plays and figures, is emphasized. Of special interest are the illustrations of theater layouts and photographs of performances. There is a reference guide, a chronology of events, a glossary of theater terms, a "who's who" of significant people, a select bibliography, and an index.

Guides

Simons, Linda Keir. *The Performing Arts: A Guide to the Reference Literature*. Englewood, CO: Libraries Unlimited, 1994.

Annotations for resources in the performing arts are presented, with an emphasis on theater and dance. Sample topics are costuming, lighting, makeup, stage design, puppetry, magic, mime, and the circus. Resources such as bibliographies, catalogs, indexes, dictionaries, encyclopedias, companions, biographical sources, review materials, and professional organizations are covered.

Indexes and Bibliographies

International Bibliography of Theatre and Dance. Ipswich, MA: EBSCO. www.ebscohost.com.

The International Bibliography of Theatre and Dance (IBTD) lists books and articles about theater and the performing arts. IBTD has resources published around the world and in several languages from 1864 to the present. Topics such as the entertainment industry, circus arts, dance, festivals, film, musical theater, and opera are represented. There is an emphasis on theater-as-performance, in contrast to the literary criticism in the *MLAIB* and other humanities indexes.

Index

Index

About the Authors

Arianne A. Hartsell-Gundy is the head of the Humanities Section and librarian for literature and theater studies at Duke University. She has a master of arts degree in comparative literature and a master of library science from Indiana University. Her research interests include information literacy, graduate student pedagogy, collection analysis, and digital humanities.

Bridgit McCafferty is the director of the University Library at Texas A&M University–Central Texas, where she formerly acted as the liaison for the English and film studies programs. She has a master of library science degree from Indiana University, in addition to a master of arts in literature. Research interests include library administration and digital libraries.